National Housing Models

National Housing Models

Application of Econometric Techniques to Problems of Housing Research

Proceedings of a conference sponsored
by the Federal Home Loan Bank System

Edited by
R. Bruce Ricks
Federal Home Loan Bank Board

Lexington Books
D.C. Heath and Company
Lexington, Massachusetts
Toronto London

Library of Congress Cataloging in Publication Data
Main entry under title:

National housing models.

"Proceedings of a conference sponsored by the Federal Home Loan Bank System."
Includes bibliographies.
1. Housing- United States- Mathematical models.
I. Ricks, R. Bruce, ed. II. Federal Home Loan Bank System.
HD7293.N367 301.5′4′0973 78-39031
ISBN 0-669-82958-7

Published simultaneously in Canada.

Printed in the United States of America.

International Standard Book Number: 0-669-82958-7

Library of Congress Catalog Card Number: 78-39031

Table of Contents

List of Tables vii

List of Figures ix

Preface xi

Chapter 1
An Econometric Analysis of the U.S. Residential Housing Market,
Eugene A. Brady 1

The Model 2
The Sectoral Breakdown of the Housing Model 16
An Interdependent Intersectoral Model 30
Forecasting Housing Starts with the Model 32
Policy Making with the Model 32
Discussion 42
Appendix 1A: Alphabetical Listing of Variables 45
References 46

Chapter 2
Housing Starts in 1966 and 1969: A Comparison Using an
Econometric Model, *James B. Burnham* 49

Discussion 58
Appendix 2A: Listing of Variables 67

Chapter 3
Monthly Housing Starts, *Ray C. Fair* 69

A Model of the Housing and Mortgage Market 69
The Estimation Technique 76
The Data 79
The Results 79
The Use of the Housing Starts Equation for Forecasting Purposes 82
Discussion 85
References 92

Chapter 4
A Summary of the Current Financial Intermediary, Mortgage, and Housing Sectors of the FRB-MIT-Penn Econometric Model, *John H. Kalchbrenner* 93

The Behavior of Savings Flows Through Financial Intermediaries 93
The Mortgage Market 103
The Housing Sector 109
Single-family Housing Starts 113
Appendix 4A: Alphabetical Listing of Variables 122
References 124

Chapter 5
Econometric Models of the Residential Construction Sector: A Comparison, *Gary Fromm* 125

Long-Run Considerations 126
Supply and Demand 130
Aggregation and Estimation 132
Conclusion 133
Discussion 135
Appendix 5A: Survey of Private Residential Construction Sectors 137
References 153

Chapter 6
General Discussion of Models and Related Problems 157

Policy Instruments in the Models 157
Macromodels versus Micromodels 159
On Government-Academic Interface for Improved Housing Modeling 171

About the Contributors 177

Index 181

List of Tables

1-1	Peaks and Troughs in Residential Housing Starts	9
1-2	Number of Private Nonfarm Housing Starts	9
1-3	Standard Deviation vs. Standard Error of the Regression of Dependent Variables	30
1-4	Estimates of the Levels of the Predetermined Variables	33
1-5	Housing Starts Forecast by Type	34
2-1	Equation #1: Contributions of Variables	52
2-2	Equation #2: Contributions of Variables	53
2-3	Equation #3: Contributions of Variables	54
2-4	Equation #4: Contributions of Variables	55
2-5	Equation #5: Contributions of Variables	56
2-6	Summary of Comparison of Housing Starts	57
3-1	List and Description of the Variables Used in the Monthly Housing Starts Sector	79
5-1	Variables in Primary Stochastic Starts or Expenditures Function	128

List of Figures

1-1 A Priori Specification of the Econometric Model of U.S. Housing Activity 4
1-2 The Level of Residential Housing Activity 7
1-3 Three Measures of the Level of Total Residential Housing Starts 8
1-4 Actual and Estimated Levels of the Value of Housing Starts (*ICNFR58*) as Estimated by Regression (1.5) 12
1-5 Actual and Estimated Levels of the Number of Housing Starts (*HTTT*) as Estimated by Regression (1.6) 13
1-6 Actual and Estimated Levels of the Number of Housing Starts (*HTT*) as Estimated by Regression (1.8) 17
1-7 Actual and Estimated Levels of the Number of Housing Starts (*HTUS*) as Estimated by Regression (1.9) 18
1-8 The Level of Conventionally Financed Housing Starts (*HC*) 19
1-9 The Level of FHA-Insured Housing Starts (*HFHA*) 19
1-10 The Level of VA-Guaranteed Housing Starts (*HVA*) 20
1-11 The Level of Multiple-Family Housing Starts (*HM*) 20
1-12 The Level of Mobile Homes Shipments (*HMHUS*) 21
1-13 Actual and Estimated Levels of the Number of Conventionally Financed Housing Starts (*HC*) as Estimated by Regression (1.10) 26
1-14 Actual and Estimated Levels of the Number of Multiple-Family Housing Starts (*HM*) as Estimated by Regression (1.16) 27
1-15 Actual and Estimated Levels of the Number of Mobile Home Shipments (*HMHUS*) as Estimated by Regression (1.17) 28
1-16 Actual and Estimated Levels of the Number of Federally Underwritten Housing Starts (*HFED*) as Estimated by Regression (1.14) 29
1-17 Marginal Rates of Substitution Between Instruments for the Policy Model Example 36

Preface

In December 1970, at a conference of the Bank Presidents of the twelve District Banks of the Federal Home Loan Bank System, it was decided that quantitative analysis of supply and demand relationships in national and local housing markets, as a method of research, needed support and strengthening. The twelve District Banks authorized the Office of Economic Research, on behalf of the Bank System, to stimulate the development and dissemination of work in this field, and to encourage the introduction of governmental and Federal Home Loan Bank System policy variables into econometric models currently being constructed as instruments of research.

As the first step in this continuing effort, the Bank System sponsored a conference on housing models, inviting leading researchers concerned with such modeling to attend. This conference was held in Washington on March 4 and 5, 1971. Discussion preceding and following the presentation of papers revealed that academic institutions have inadequate access to existing econometric models, and insufficient opportunity to interact with those who are developing these models. D.C. Heath and Company, recognizing the importance of housing to the economy of the nation and to the well-being of its people, saw the need to have such materials accessible in an organized compilation for classroom and research use. The present volume is the result of this mutual awareness.

This book differs from the usual volume of conference proceedings in that each of the five prepared papers, together with its corresponding oral delivery and informal discussion, is presented as a separate chapter. Following these chapters, there is a general discussion of modeling and related problems. The prepared papers have been heavily edited to reduce each subject to its essentials.

Conference participants were selected by the editor with a view to achieving a balance between the diversity of the econometric approach and the homogeneity of the subject matter. Gene Brady, whose previous work appears extensively in the *Journal of Political Economy,* specializes in the disaggregation of housing starts by type of unit and by type of financing, showing that these markets fluctuate along quite different patterns and that their movements can be explained by correspondingly different sets of variables. In his present paper, Brady concentrates on identification of those independent variables which produce the highest explanatory statistics rather than beginning with a theoretical structural framework and then estimating reduced-form equations from that structural model. His approach is to say, "Let us observe what is happening before we develop a causative theory." Ray Fair has observed, in his research on modeling of the U.S. economy, that the housing sector is extremely difficult to estimate. It is one in which considerably different results are obtained if we use the same variables in different equations – for example, one emphasizing supply, and the other emphasizing demand. He looks at the historical pattern of housing starts as one of regimes, in which supply or credit conditions impose constraints in periods of tight money and high interest rates; and demand factors impose constraints in periods of credit availability. His analysis of the market concentrates on the general level of interest rates. Jim Burnham, at the Federal Reserve Board, extends Governor Sherman Maisel's work which has long focused on the vacancy factor as a critical variable explaining imbalances between supply and demand. In the paper, Burnham investigates the role of vacancies in each of the years 1966 and 1969 when there was a shortage of housing mortgage funds. Jack Kalchbrenner's paper explains the housing and mortgage market sector of the FRB-MIT-Penn large-scale econometric model of the U.S. economy. Gary Fromm, of Data Resources, Inc., provides us with an excellent description of the operations of the housing sector endogenous to a more total economic system. He also performs a real service to future housing researchers by developing a framework for analysis of the current modeling effort and some critiques of the direction it is taking today. His overview provides true insight as to where future work is needed.

Appreciation is expressed to Chairman Preston Martin of the FHLBB, a rare combination of academician, administrator, and government policy maker who has a clear understanding of the strengths and limitations of econometrics as applied to the housing mortgage market area. His strong leadership and support for continued work in this field is truly to be admired and appreciated. John Kleeb was Chairman of the Bank Presidents' Conference during the time of the Banks' initiation of support in this field, and served as host for the conference. John Floyd, of the Office of Economic Research, handled flawlessly the administrative responsibilities of the conference and the compilation and technical work on the publication of the volume. Their services are acknowledged with sincere gratitude.

I hope this volume will stimulate additional work in this field, work that can win recognition and be made accessible in future publications.

R. Bruce Ricks
Chief Economist and Director
Office of Economic Research
Federal Home Loan Bank Board
December 1971

National Housing Models

1 An Econometric Analysis of the U.S. Residential Housing Market

Eugene A. Brady

The long-run demand for residential housing in the decade of the 1970s, as determined by estimated levels of household formation and by geographical and structural changes in the labor force which affect labor migration, is expected to outrun the anticipated supply of housing by a considerable margin. The trend toward multifamily dwellings and to mobile homes in the late 1960s indicates the housing pattern that can be expected to emerge in the 1970s. In recent months, a good deal of congressional attention has been directed to the residential housing market and to the implementation of both long-run and short-run housing policies. The annual volume of residential housing construction is quite small relative to the estimated housing stock – 1.5 million housing starts represents only about 2.5 percent of the stock, and only about 60 percent of these starts represent net additions to the stock of housing. It is estimated that about 40 percent of the gross housing starts in the United States are lost each year through fires, floods, tornadoes, freeway right-of-way demolitions, dilapidation, etc.

The recent and prolonged period of monetary stringency, as reflected in historically high interest rates and by a relatively slow rate of growth of the money supply, has had a strong impact on the level of residential housing starts in the United States. The recent housing troughs of 1966 and 1969–1970 have made it apparent that, in the short run, the housing sector is more strongly affected by changes in the degree of monetary restraint than are other components of gross private domestic investment, and has exhibited cycles of activity greatly exceeding those of other sectors in the economy.

Because the net annual volume of residential construction is quite small in relation to the total housing stock, short-run policies for protecting the housing sector from the effects of monetary stringency are essentially independent of long-run policies designed to achieve particular levels of the housing stock. This paper is concerned with the analysis of short-run fluctuations in the level of residential housing, and relates to the explanatory, predictive, and policy implications that result from models of the housing market with these short-run targets in mind.

In recent years, there have been developed a variety of econometric models which focus on residential housing, either as an independent subset of the economy or within the framework of a model of overall economic activity.[1] For the most part they have tended to treat the housing sector as a single market, and this oversimplification has resulted in models with low explanatory power and poor predictive ability.[2] Hopefully, a series of disaggregated housing models will improve their usefulness as explanatory and predictive devices.

The rather inconclusive results of existing econometric models of the housing sector are a direct reflection of the paucity of quantitative data relating to that market. The data relating to basic demand variables such as net household formation and interregional mobility are relatively poor, and are not available other than on an annual basis. Quarterly interpolations of these data leave much to be desired.

Data series relating to financial variables, such as interest rates, loan-to-value ratios, and amortization periods on mortgages, and to such factors as the volume of savings flows to financial intermediaries and residential construction costs are available on a quarterly basis, and are of better quality than basic demand variables. It is perhaps for this reason that most models of housing, including those that are developed in this paper, tend to rely on financial variables rather than on basic demand variables, and possibly give a misleading impression that variations in housing starts are caused by variations in financial variables rather than by such demographic changes as shifts in interregional mobility of households and household formation. However, shifts in basic demand variables are rather long run in nature, and our analysis of quarterly fluctuations in housing will rely primarily on financial variables that are more closely associated with supply than with demand.

The housing models developed in this paper are based on the structural relationships in the housing market that have been estimated from quarterly data for the decade of the 1960s. It has been assumed that the housing sector has been characterized by arithmetic or logarithmic linear relationships during this forty-observation period.

The Model

Preliminary determination of those variables entering the housing model was made by specifying a series of a priori functional relationships that are presumed to exist as indicated by theoretical considerations. On the demand side, it is assumed that net household formation, interregional migration, housing demolitions, and per capita real disposable income should all be positively related to

1. For the former, see Alberts [1]; Brady [2, 3]; Campbell [6]; and Guttentag [8], pp. 275–298; Lee [11]; Maisel [14]; Mattila [16]; Muth [17]; and Schaff [18]. For the latter, see Klein [10], Liu[12], Malanos [15], and Suits [19].

2. See Brady [3], pp. 147–148.

the demand for residential housing and that as the relative price of housing services declines the demand for housing rises.

A priori specification of supply variables was made in a series of three recursive blocks. The level of per capita disposable income, together with an index of monetary stringency and institutionally imposed rate ceilings on savings deposit interest rates determined the level of savings inputs to the major financial intermediaries who purchase the bulk of mortgages in the economy. These savings inputs, together with institutionally or federally set limitations on mortgages, such as interest rate ceilings and loan-to-value ratio limitations, indicate the extent to which the private sector wishes to add mortgage instruments to its portfolio of assets. The volume of mortgages held by the private sector is supplemented by the public sector through such programs as Federal National Mortgage Association (FNMA) and Government National Mortgage Association (GNMA) net mortgage purchases in the secondary mortgage market and Federal Home Loan Bank (FHLB) advances to member intermediaries which are used to acquire mortgages. This participation of both the public and private sectors in the mortgage market, together with demand variables, determined the terms on which mortgages are acquired. Mortgage terms, together with residential construction costs and FNMA-FHLB interventions in the market, form the final link in the supply-side determination of residential housing activity. Figure 1-1 sketches the a priori causal relationships involved, with those instrument variables which are capable of manipulation by the policy maker noted with an *I*. These instrument variables will be utilized at a later stage in the paper to indicate the levels at which they can be set in order to achieve an optimal level of housing starts. All other variables are considered noncontrollable, with the exception of the target variables – housing starts by type of mortgage.

Both ordinary least squares (OLS) and two-stage least squares (TSLS) regressions were run for the various models of the housing market, with the dependent variables – value of starts in 1957-1959 dollars and number of starts in thousands – regressed as functions of the noted predetermined variables. All computations were made on the Burroughs 5500 computer in Lexington, Massachusetts, through the Data Resources Incorporated time sharing program subscribed to by the FHLBB.

This study is based on quarterly data running from the second quarter of 1952, denoted 52:2, through the second quarter of 1970, denoted 70:2. Nearly twenty years of data have been collected and processed in the FHLBB data bank, and the eighty-five series in that data bank form the foundation for the econometric work done in this study. Since the focus of this study is on the postwar housing market, no attempt was made to collect data before the second quarter of 1952 when real estate credit was controlled by Regulation X prior to its suspension in September of that year.

The data series, together with their symbols, are noted in the appendix to this paper. For ease in pinpointing any particular symbol in the regressions that follow, they are listed alphabetically according to symbol.

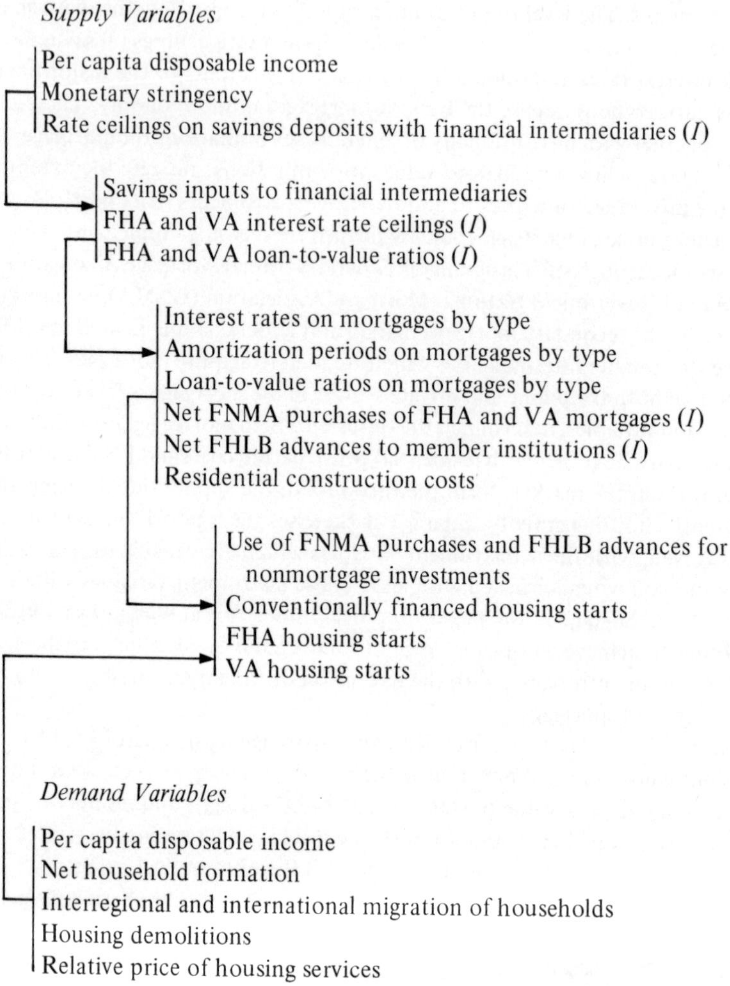
Supply Variables
Per capita disposable income
Monetary stringency
Rate ceilings on savings deposits with financial intermediaries (I)
Savings inputs to financial intermediaries
FHA and VA interest rate ceilings (I)
FHA and VA loan-to-value ratios (I)
Interest rates on mortgages by type
Amortization periods on mortgages by type
Loan-to-value ratios on mortgages by type
Net FNMA purchases of FHA and VA mortgages (I)
Net FHLB advances to member institutions (I)
Residential construction costs
Use of FNMA purchases and FHLB advances for nonmortgage investments
Conventionally financed housing starts
FHA housing starts
VA housing starts
Demand Variables
Per capita disposable income
Net household formation
Interregional and international migration of households
Housing demolitions
Relative price of housing services

Figure 1-1. A Priori Specification of the Econometric Model of U.S. Housing Activity.

Before developing the series of housing models, let us first briefly examine the makeup of the private residential housing market. The market, as measured by the number of dwelling units started, can be decomposed into five major categories as follows:

1. Conventionally financed single-family dwelling units (*HC*)
2. FHA financed single-family dwelling units (*HFHA*)[3]
3. VA financed single-family dwelling units (*HVA*)
4. Multiple-family dwelling units (*HM*)
5. Mobile homes (*HMHUS*)

Three series of total housing units started will be used in this paper. The new commonly accepted series on starts includes all five categories listed above, and is noted as the number of private starts including mobile home shipments:

$$HTTT = HC + HFHA + HVA + HM + HMHUS \tag{1.1}$$

Since the mobile home market and the multiple-family dwelling unit market are different in many respects from the single-family dwelling market, two other housing market totals are considered; dwelling units started with mobile homes excluded, and single-family dwelling units started. Their composition is as follows:

$$HTT = HC + HFHA + HVA + HM \tag{1.2}$$

$$HTUS = HC + HFHA + HVA \tag{1.3}$$

Most studies of the residential housing market have focused attention on one of the three housing series usually considered as "total" starts. The two housing series listed in the financial and business statistics section of the *Federal Reserve Bulletin* have been most widely used as benchmarks of the level of housing construction activity by analysts and policymakers. The physical index of housing starts coincides with our *HTTT* series noted in equation (1.1), and the value series, "investment in private nonfarm residential structures" (*ICNFR*) corresponds roughly with the physical series *HTTT* except that mobile homes are omitted.[4] Stated in terms of 1958 dollars:

$$ICNFR58 = v(HC) + v(HFHA) + v(HVA) + v(HM) \tag{1.4}$$

---

3. A very small proportion of FHA and VA mortgages are used to finance the construction of two- to four-family dwelling units. For simplicity, it is assumed that all federally underwritten mortgages are used to finance single-family dwellings.

4. Again, there is a small discrepancy in that the physical series includes farm residential structures while the value series omits it. The level of residential housing construction on farms is negligible, and for nearly all purposes the slight difference between nonfarm private housing and total private housing can be ignored.

Analysis of Historical Data

Since the housing series noted in equations (1.1) and (1.4) are widely used as indexes of housing activity, we initiate our analysis of the housing market with an examination of these two measures of housing starts. Figures 1-2 and 1-3 indicate the pattern of total housing activity as measured by these two series during the two decades of the 1950s and 1960s. As these Figures and other sources indicate, the total residential housing market has exhibited five and a half cycles in the last twenty years, as measured from peak to peak.[5] The turning points of these cycles are noted in Table 1-1 and the magnitude of housing starts at the turning points can be seen in Table 1-2. Series *HTT* rather than series *HTTT* has been used because mobile homes have been added to the other housing start series only quite recently, and historically, the *HTT* series is the "yardstick" series. It should be noted that postwar housing cycles III through V have been relatively severe; in all three troughs, the level of housing starts fell by nearly 50 percent from its previous peak.

Most housing analysts place the cause of the postwar housing cycle on monetary stringency (as stringency is evidenced by high nominal interest rates). The trough of the third postwar housing cycle immediately followed the period of monetary restraint exercised by the monetary authority during 1956 and 1957, when the Meltzer index of stringency rose from 1.92 in the first quarter of 1955 to 3.57 during the third quarter of 1957.[6] Monetary policy, as viewed by the Meltzer index, was stringent in 1959 and early 1960, leading to housing trough IV. Even more striking is the fourth quarter of 1966 trough in the residential housing cycle, resulting from the tight money period of that year. The trough of housing cycle VI is viewed by most observers as directly following the stringent monetary policies followed in 1968 and 1969, where nominal interest rates reached historic highs, and the Meltzer index of monetary stringency hit a twenty-year peak of 7.53 in the last quarter of 1969.

OLS regressions were run in order to select those predetermined variables which explain the major part of the variation in the number of total housing starts (*HTTT*) and in the value of private housing starts as measured in 1958 dollars (*ICNFR58*). All variables selected by a priori reasoning were included, and those variables which did not have much statistical influence on the level of housing starts were successively eliminated. The goal of this preliminary investi-

5. For an estimate of the months of peak and trough in the housing cycles for the United States between 1947 and 1958, see Guttentag [8], p. 10, and Grebler [7], p. 107.

6. The Meltzer index is calculated as the average rate on new issues of U.S. 91-day government bills, multiplied by one minus the ratio of free to total reserves of the New York and Chicago Central Reserve City Banks. Obviously, this is a "nonmonetarist" index, as contrasted with other measures of stringency such as the proportional rate of growth of the money supply, and an arbitrary one at that. However, it is based on nominal interest rates, which have been presumed to be one of the important influences on residential housing starts.

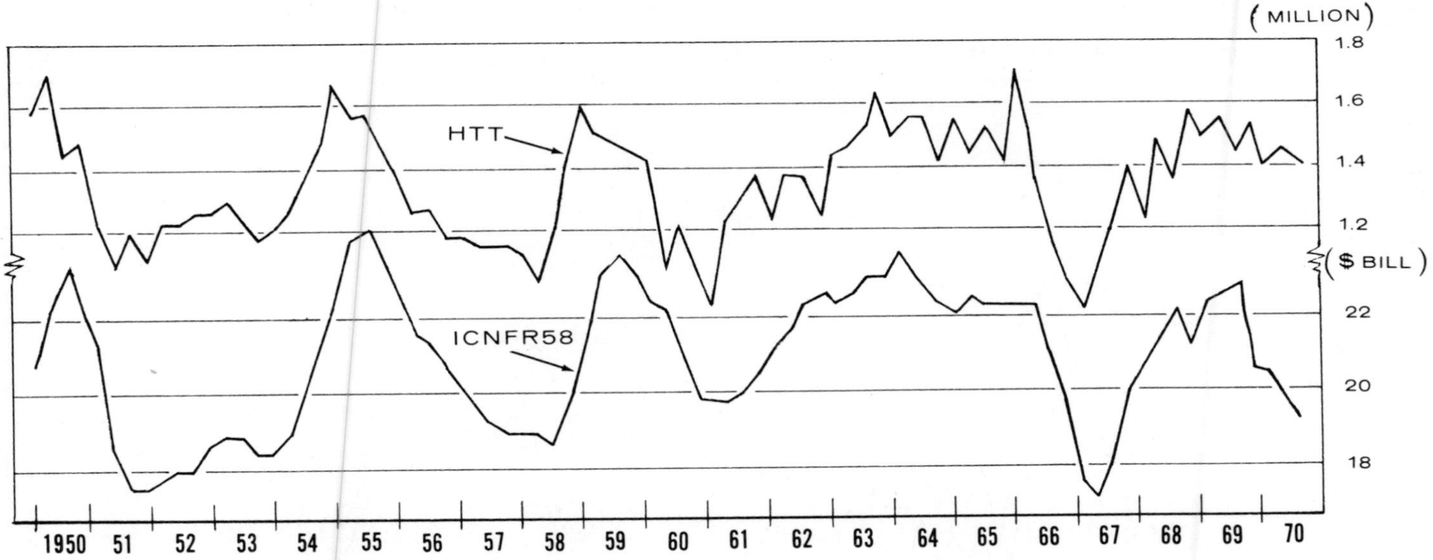

Figure 1–2. The Level of Residential Housing Activity in the United States—1950:1 to 1970:2.

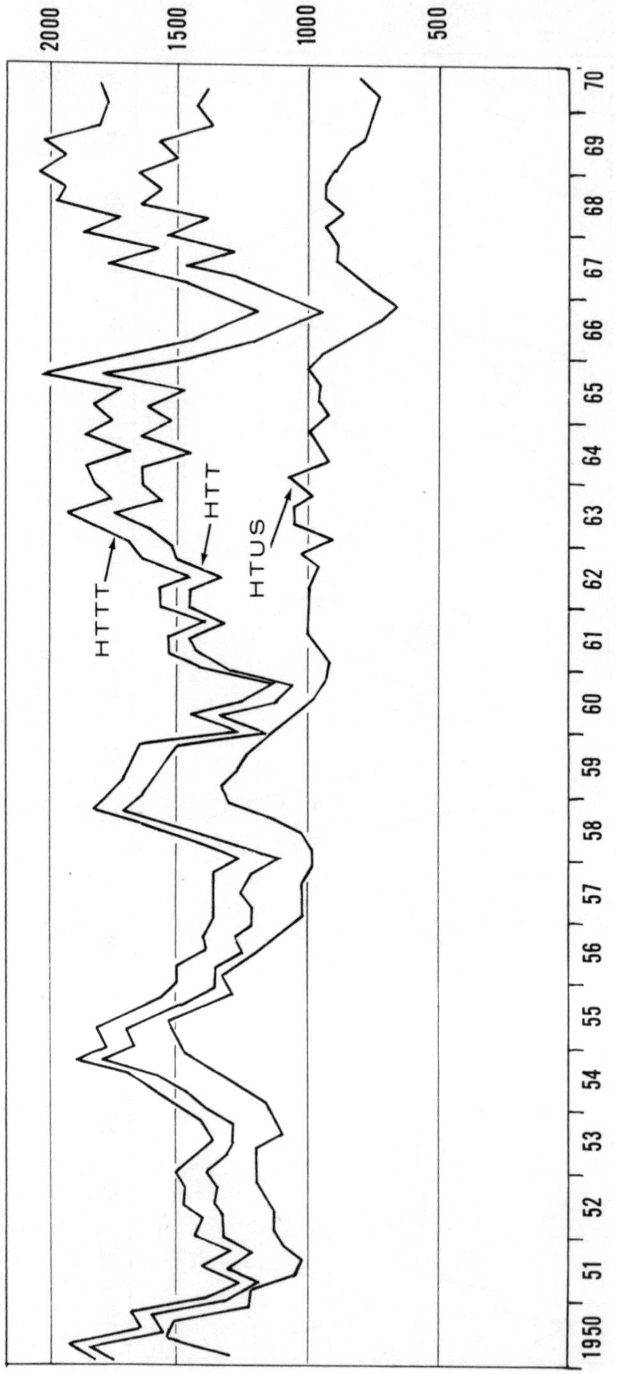

Figure 1–3. Three Measures of the Level of Total Residential Housing Starts in the United States–1950:1 to 1969:4.

Table 1-1
Peaks and Troughs in Residential Housing Starts Between 1950:1 and 1969:4

Postwar Cycle	*Peak*	*Trough*	*Peak*
I	1950:4	1951:2	1953:1
II	1953:1	1953:3	1954:4
III	1954:4	1958:1	1958:4
IV	1958:4	1960:4	1965:4
V	1965:4	1966:4	1968:4
VI	1968:4	1969:4	

Table 1-2
Number of Private Nonfarm Housing Starts in Thousands at Peaks and Troughs of the Housing Cycle (Series *HTT*).

Postwar Cycle	*Peak*	*Trough*	*Peak*
I	1550	1129	1354
II	1354	1235	1732
III	1732	1074	1647
IV	1647	987	1735
V	1735	910	1602
VI	1602	1346	

gation was to eliminate those predetermined variables which, when combined with other predetermined variables, added little to the predicted changes in the level and value of total housing starts. It is interesting to note that in the regressions for both the physical volume and value of housing starts, the basic demand variables dropped out. This either reflects the fact that supply factors are more important in explaining the quarterly variation in housing starts than are demand variables, or that existing statistics for household formation, interregional mobility, etc. are so fragmentary that they lead to poor regression results. We will return to this problem later.

The 20½-year interval running from the first quarter of 1950 through the second quarter of 1970 is a fairly long period, and it seems likely, on a priori grounds, that important structural changes took place during these two decades, both with respect to the U.S. economy and to its residential housing component. For this reason, the period was divided into two ten-year periods, and separate regressions were run for the 1950s and the 1960s, as well as for the entire twenty-year period. The regression results for the decade of the 1960s were statistically much better than those for the 1950s, or for the entire twenty-year period. Regressions were also run with "splice" or dummy variables, which would allow for the loading of structural difference between the two periods on the dummy variable. The results of such a technique indicated that there were important structural differences between the housing market of the 1950s and that of the 1960s.[7] On operational grounds, both with respect to prediction and policy making, this paper concentrates on the decade of the 1960s.

There are serious drawbacks in using the entire 1960 decade for the estimation of the structure of the housing market. One of the most serious is that federal intervention in the housing market was almost nil during the early 1960s, while FNMA-GNMA secondary market purchases and net FHLB advances supported nearly half of the conventionally financed single-family dwelling-unit market in 1969 and early 1970. Obviously, such short-run changes in the structure of the housing market will distort the regression results. The shortcomings of the analysis will be brought out as the models are developed.

Data limitations force us to use the data series for the 1960s to screen out predetermined variables that do not cause much variation in the dependent variables, and then use the same intervals for the data series to derive estimated values for the dependent variables. This raises the possibility that "pretesting bias" exists in the regressions, and some statistical rigor is given up for operationalism. The OLS regression for the value of, and number of housing starts, respectively, are given as follows – using quarterly data for 1960:3, through 1970:2, and with the *t*-statistics in parentheses:

$$\underset{}{ICNFR58} = \underset{(4.6)}{41.206} + \underset{(5.4)}{.398B} - \underset{(4.0)}{3.210IC} + \underset{(7.5)}{.862\,LVC} +$$

$$\underset{(7.5)}{.0024FHLBS} - \underset{(6.8)}{.433T} \qquad (1.5)$$

$$R^2 = .862 \qquad \text{D-W} = 2.43 \qquad \text{SE} = .684$$

$$HTTT = \underset{(3.1)}{-5094.2} + \underset{(4.4)}{60.08B} - \underset{(3.1)}{467.0IC} + \underset{(3.5)}{74.59LVC} +$$

$$\underset{(2.9)}{.1680FHLBS} - \underset{(4.1)}{48.00T} \qquad (1.6)$$

$$R^2 = .701 \qquad \text{D-W} = 1.47 \qquad \text{SE} = 126.8$$

These results indicate that over three-quarters of the variation in both the value of and number of total U.S. housing starts can be explained as a result of

7. Unfortunately, there is no way of untangling these changes in structure, since all structural differences in the relationship between housing starts and the predetermined variables are loaded into the single dummy variable.

variations in the five considered predetermined variables. As a priori theoretical considerations would indicate, housing starts are positively related to loan-to-value ratios and to net Federal Home Loan Bank advances to its member institutions, and are negatively related to the nominal rate of interest on conventionally financed mortgages. The regressions also indicate that the time trend of housing starts was downward during the 1960s. Less clear on a priori grounds is the significant positive relationship between variations in housing starts and variations in the Boeckh index of residential construction costs. Distributed lag forms of the Boeckh index also yielded positive coefficients in alternative forms of these regressions. It can be argued that housing starts are positively related to the Boeckh index for two reasons. First, the Boeckh index, particularly in its distributed lag forms, can be considered a proxy for expected or "permanent" house prices, creating a "buy now" effect on the demand side as well as a stimulus on the supply side. Secondly, rising costs reflect rising house prices, generating a positive real balance effect, since the vast majority of mortgage liabilities offsetting the existing housing stock are fixed in nominal amount.

The standard errors of the regression were about \$875 million (of an average value of housing starts of about \$20 billion) and 121 thousand starts (of an average level of housing starts of about 1.6 million starts), which is not bad as a first approximation. Furthermore, and this is essential for a prediction model, the regressions were able to pinpoint the trough of residential housing activity that took place during the fourth quarter of 1966. This is one distinct advantage of a model that does not use lagged values of the dependent variable as predetermined variables, because models of this sort tend to give a fairly high coefficient for the predetermined variable, and make the model unable to predict turning points.

The actual and estimated values for the value and number of housing starts are given in Figures 1-4 and 1-5, respectively, where the actual and estimated levels are listed on the left and plotted on the right of each figure.

In the initial runs of these regressions, both FHLB net advances to member institutions and FNMA-GNMA net secondary market purchases were included as potential instrument variables. In all cases, secondary FNMA-GNMA purchases of FHA and VA mortgages when used as a predetermined variable gave a negative coefficient, rather than the expected positive one. This suggests that housing starts were inverse to the level of net secondary market purchases by the FNMA-GNMA authorities. This seems to indicate that when the FNMA is purchasing FHA and VA instruments from private financial intermediaries in the secondary market, these private intermediaries are reducing their mortgage portfolios even more rapidly than the FNMA and GNMA are increasing theirs, so that the net result is that FNMA-GNMA net acquisitions of federally underwritten mortgages in the secondary market run counter to the aggregative level of mortgage acquisitions by the four major private financial intermediaries, and hence counter to the level of aggregative housing starts.

DATE	ACTUAL	FITTED
60:3	20.50	20.33
60:4	20.20	20.18
61:1	20.30	20.72
61:2	20.50	20.58
61:3	21.10	22.14
61:4	22.00	21.84
62.1	22.50	22.17
62:2	23.30	22.15
62:3	23.70	24.16
62:4	23.30	23.76
63:1	23.70	22.95
63:2	24.20	24.15
63:3	24.20	24.82
63:4	24.90	24.43
64:1	24.50	24.16
64:2	23.80	23.79
64:3	23.40	23.25
64:4	23.00	23.45
65:1	23.70	23.51
65:2	23.20	23.12
65:3	23.30	22.89
65:4	23.30	22.42
66:1	23.20	22.78
66:2	21.70	22.79
66:3	20.40	19.95
66:4	18.10	18.66
67:1	17.50	17.65
67:2	18.70	19.21
67:3	20.80	22.38
67:4	22.50	21.74
68:1	22.40	23.30
68:2	23.40	22.76
68:3	22.30	22.31
68:4	23.50	22.65
69:1	23.90	23.92
69:2	24.20	23.16
69:3	21.80	23.10
69:4	21.40	21.60
70:1	20.20	20.14
70:2	19.50	19.01

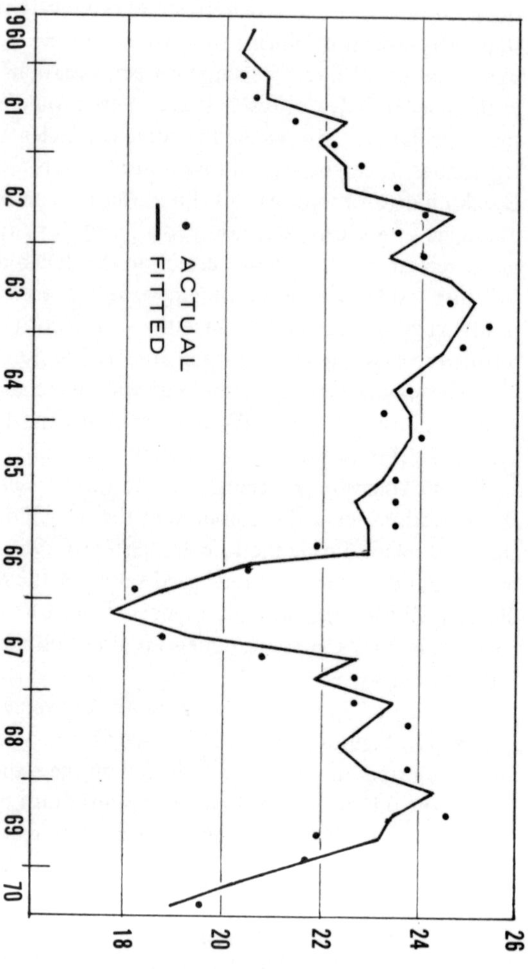

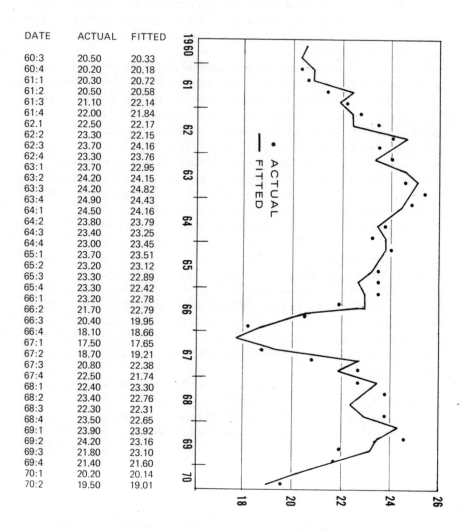

Figure 1–4. Actual and Estimated Levels of the Value of Housing Starts (*ICNFR58*) as Estimated by Regression (1.5) (Billions of 1958 dollars).

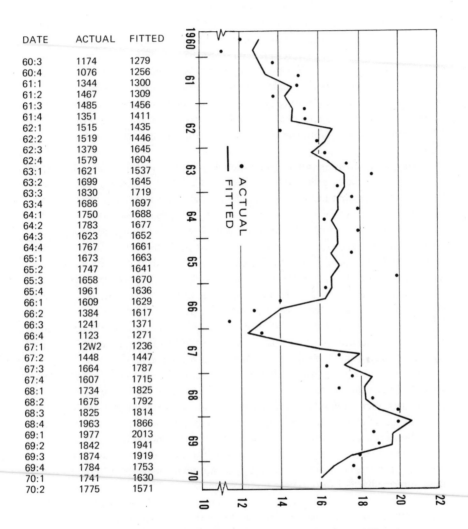

DATE	ACTUAL	FITTED
60:3	1174	1279
60:4	1076	1256
61:1	1344	1300
61:2	1467	1309
61:3	1485	1456
61:4	1351	1411
62:1	1515	1435
62:2	1519	1446
62:3	1379	1645
62:4	1579	1604
63:1	1621	1537
63:2	1699	1645
63:3	1830	1719
63:4	1686	1697
64:1	1750	1688
64:2	1783	1677
64:3	1623	1652
64:4	1767	1661
65:1	1673	1663
65:2	1747	1641
65:3	1658	1670
65:4	1961	1636
66:1	1609	1629
66:2	1384	1617
66:3	1241	1371
66:4	1123	1271
67:1	12W2	1236
67:2	1448	1447
67:3	1664	1787
67:4	1607	1715
68:1	1734	1825
68:2	1675	1792
68:3	1825	1814
68:4	1963	1866
69:1	1977	2013
69:2	1842	1941
69:3	1874	1919
69:4	1784	1753
70:1	1741	1630
70:2	1775	1571

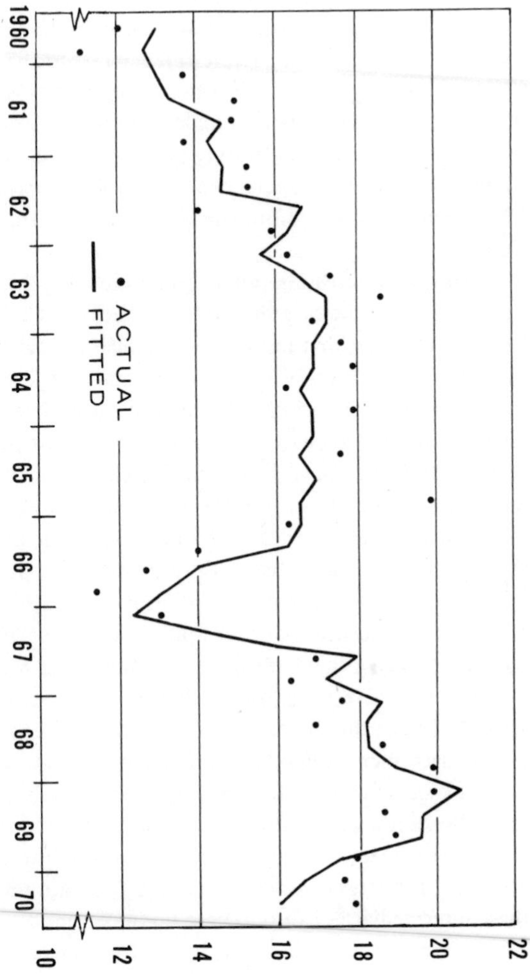

Figure 1-5. Actual and Estimated Levels of the Number of Housing Starts (*HTTT*) as Estimated by Regression (1.6) (Thousands).

This finding exactly corroborates Dwight Jaffee's "rather remarkable" finding that FNMA actions will at least be nearly fully offset by the reactions of the private intermediaries in the housing market.[8]

What are the implications of this finding? This does not mean that FNMA secondary market activities are not proper policy prescriptions. It simply means that the activities of the private financial sector have a tendency to overwhelm FNMA-GNMA operations. For the same reason that the inward collapse of the investment demand function may overwhelm central bank efforts to revive overall economic activity during periods of recession by steps to ease the money supply, the private financial market simply overwhelms the attempts of the FNMA and GNMA to stimulate the housing sector during periods of housing slump.

Another interesting point can be raised by comparing the method by which each of the two major policy intermediations take place in housing sector. We have already seen that net FHLB advances appear to be associated with positive variations in the level of total housing starts. The FHLB system advances funds to its member institutions, of which the vast majority are savings and loan associations. These institutions are, for the most part, single-input single-output firms, in that they have a single major class of assets (mortgages) and a single major class of liabilities (savings and loan share accounts). When the FHLB system makes net advances to its members there are basically only two choices the member institution has with respect to utilization of these funds. It can improve its individual liquidity position by holding these advances in the form of government securities or other liquid investment, or it can improve its earning position by using these advances to make direct mortgage loans.

It is in this respect that net FHLB advances are differentiated from FNMA and GNMA net purchases of mortgages in the secondary market. While both policy instruments operate to supplement private sector willingness to hold mortgage instruments, they may have completely different impacts on the aggregative housing market. On balance, the regressions by themselves indicate FNMA and GNMA operate to allow private financial intermediaries to reduce their holdings of mortgage assets when mortgages are relatively unprofitable, so that these intermediaries can purchase nonmortgage assets. This substitutes FNMA-GNMA ownership of these mortgages for private financial intermediary ownership via the secondary mortgage market. Since these are secondary market purchases, there may be no direct inducement for these private financial intermediaries to purchase new mortgages and stimulate the current level of residential housing. On the other hand, the institutions which borrow funds from the FHLB do not have a wide range of assets from which to select their portfolios. They are locked into mortgages as a dominant class of portfolio asset, so that FHLB advances or FHLB secondary market purchases from its members must

8. Jaffee [9].

either increase the liquidity position of member institutions or result in direct new mortgage lending activity.

As a preliminary conclusion it seems incorrect to view FNMA-GNMA intervention in the private mortgage market as equivalent to FHLB intervention. The difference lies in the nature of portfolio arrangements made by the private financial intermediaries involved.

In equation (1.6) and in all the regressions in which the dependent variable is the number of housing starts, it appears that the elasticity of housing starts with respect to both interest rates and loan-to-value ratios is quite high. As a direct attempt to obtain an elasticity measure for the variables of equation (1.6) it was run in logs as follows:

$$\ln HTTT = \underset{(4.9)}{-29.16} + \underset{(4.7)}{5.68} \ln B - \underset{(3.1)}{2.02} \ln IC + \underset{(3.6)}{4.63} \ln LVC + \underset{(3.5)}{.020} \ln FHLBS - \underset{(4.6)}{.041} \ln T \qquad (1.7)$$

$R^2 = .701$ D-W = 1.423 SE = .084

Since the change in the natural log of the dependent variable associated with the change in the natural log of a predetermined variable is its elasticity coefficient with respect to the variable, equation (1.7) indicates that the interest rate elasticity of housing starts is -2.0 and that the elasticity of housing starts with respect to the loan-to-value ratio is +4.6. Both the sign and the magnitude of both elasticities conform to a priori theory, and indicate that housing starts are quite sensitive to both variables.

Regression (1.6) was used to forecast total housing starts, including mobile homes. The same sets of predetermined variables used in regression (1.6) were used to estimate the structural relationships in the total housing market excluding mobile homes (*HTT*) and in the single-family dwelling unit market (*HTUS*). These regressions follow:

$$HTT = \underset{(2.7)}{-4330.6} + \underset{(3.9)}{52.54}B - \underset{(3.0)}{434.3}IC + \underset{(3.4)}{70.64}LVC + \underset{(2.6)}{.145}FHLBS \underset{(4.2)}{-47.85}T \qquad (1.8)$$

$R^2 = .5693$ D-W = 1.49 SE = 123.6

$$HTUS = \underset{(1.5)}{-820.5} + \underset{(6.2)}{27.59B} - \underset{(5.2)}{251.4IC} + \underset{(3.6)}{25.10LVC} + \underset{(2.0)}{.039FHLBS}$$

$$\underset{(7.7)}{-29.43T} \qquad (1.9)$$

$R^2 = .823$ D-W = 1.64 SE = 41.3

The actual and estimated values derived from regressions (1.8) and (1.9) are plotted and calculated in Figures 1-6 and 1-7, respectively.

The Sectoral Breakdown of the Housing Model

Definitional equation (1.1) described the five major classifications of housing starts in the foregoing section.[9] Figures 1-8 through 1-12 illustrate the pattern of starts for each classification between 1950:1 and 1969:4. Inspection of individual housing sector behavior gives the general impression that no two individual sectors followed the same cyclic pattern over the twenty-year period. This impression is strengthened by the following correlation matrix, derived from quarterly data on housing starts by type for the same period:

	HC	*HFHA*	*HVA*	*HM*	*HMHUS*
HC	1.0000				
HFHA	0.5787	1.0000			
HVA	0.3287	0.4954	1.0000		
HM	-0.2726	-0.3869	-0.5772	1.0000	
HMHUS	-0.5238	-0.5531	-0.4992	0.7237	1.0000

When viewed from the standpoint of a twenty-year period, it is evident that the individual components of the total residential housing market (*HTTT*) behaved sufficiently unlike one another that a sectoral model that separates the overall market into its major components should lead to better structural fits, and, as a result, to better forecasts. The negative correlation between single-family dwelling unit starts and multiple-family dwelling unit and mobile home starts is not too surprising, since it is to be expected that the latter two types of starts would tend to increase when there is excess demand resulting from a decline in single-family dwelling unit starts. Furthermore, multiple-family dwelling units can be considered dependent upon different predetermined variables than are single-family dwelling units, since business investment decisions

9. This is a logical extension of the three-sector model which was published in 1967. See Brady [3].

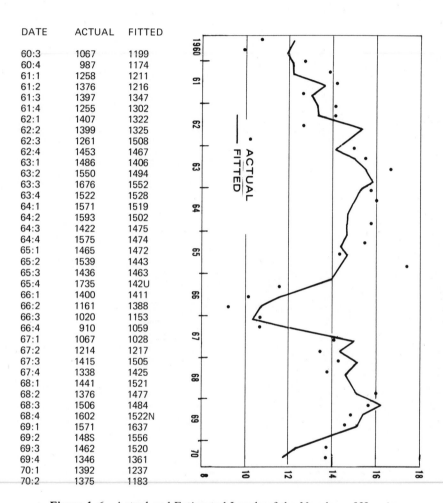

DATE	ACTUAL	FITTED
60:3	1067	1199
60:4	987	1174
61:1	1258	1211
61:2	1376	1216
61:3	1397	1347
61:4	1255	1302
62:1	1407	1322
62:2	1399	1325
62:3	1261	1508
62:4	1453	1467
63:1	1486	1406
63:2	1550	1494
63:3	1676	1552
63:4	1522	1528
64:1	1571	1519
64:2	1593	1502
64:3	1422	1475
64:4	1575	1474
65:1	1465	1472
65:2	1539	1443
65:3	1436	1463
65:4	1735	142U
66:1	1400	1411
66:2	1161	1388
66:3	1020	1153
66:4	910	1059
67:1	1067	1028
67:2	1214	1217
67:3	1415	1505
67:4	1338	1425
68:1	1441	1521
68:2	1376	1477
68:3	1506	1484
68:4	1602	1522N
69:1	1571	1637
69:2	148S	1556
69:3	1462	1520
69:4	1346	1361
70:1	1392	1237
70:2	1375	1183

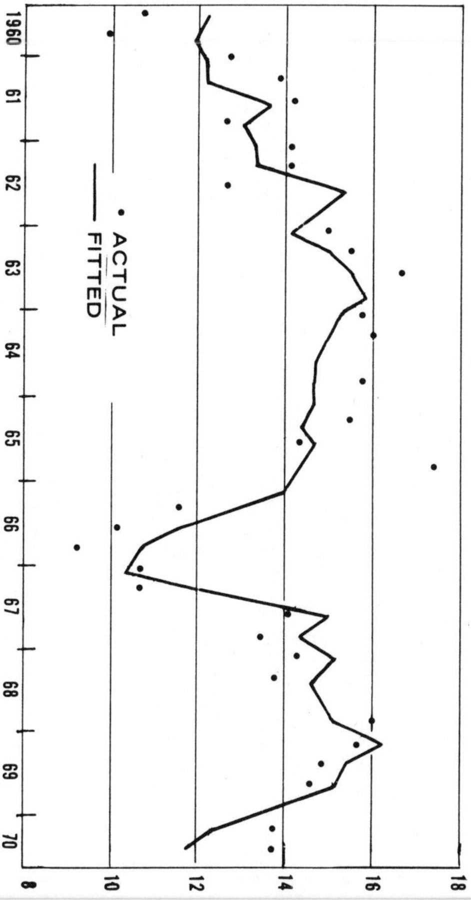

Figure 1-6. Actual and Estimated Levels of the Number of Housing Starts (*HTT*) as Estimated by Regression (1.8) (Thousands).

DATE	ACTUAL	FITTED
60:3	941.2	938.6
60:4	881.0	919.4
61:1	909.2	926.1
61:2	921.9	929.8
61:3	979.6	971.6
61:4	972.1	940.2
62:1	953.4	937.3
62:2	979.9	933.7
62:3	943.9	999.8
62:4	984.4	974.8
63:1	904.0	945.4
63:2	1030	971.8
63:3	1025	989.9
63:4	983.3	976.8
64:1	1013	970.0
64:2	912.0	963.2
64:3	925.1	952.0
64:4	957.4	940.4
65:1	906.9	928.2
65:2	951.5	913.9
65:3	939.2	929.6
65:4	957.4	907.5
66:1	899.8	876.3
66:2	811.6	848.5
66:3	702.6	748.5
66:4	616.8	705.5
67:1	727.0	707.0
67:2	806.8	795.7
67:3	864.4	909.3
67:4	869.5	863.7
68:1	892.9	877.5
68:2	843.7	845.6
68:3	880.1	853.9
68:4	895.5	866.5
69:1	858.1	904.0
69:2	828.0	855.6
69:3	754.3	819.0
69:4	729.0	735.1
70:1	700.1	676.3
70:2	757.4	661.4

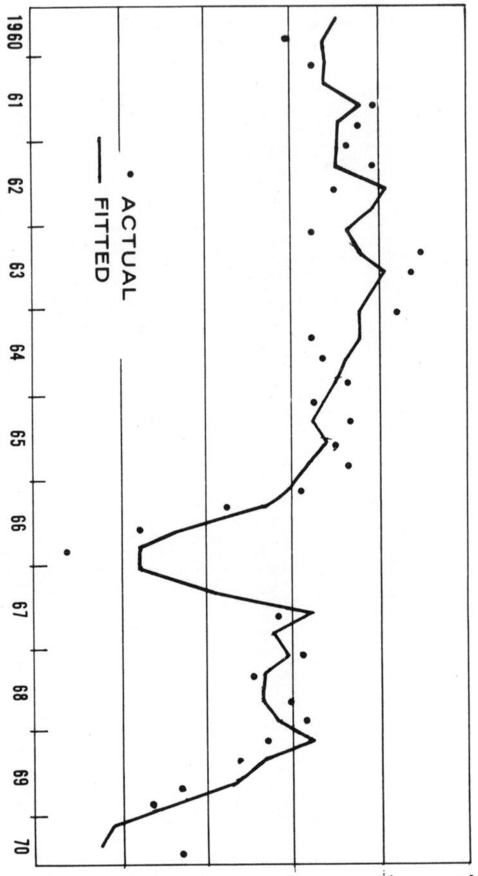

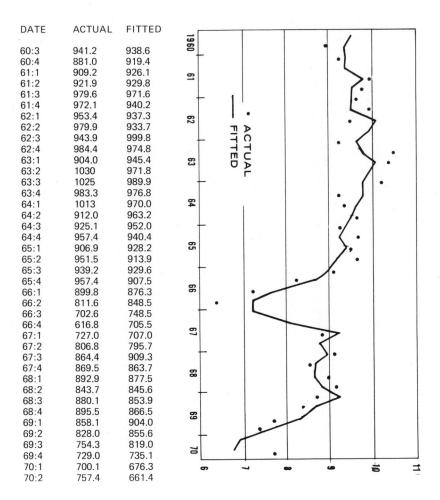

Figure 1-7. Actual and Estimated Levels of the Number of Housing Starts (*HTUS*) as Estimated by Regression (1.9). (Thousands).

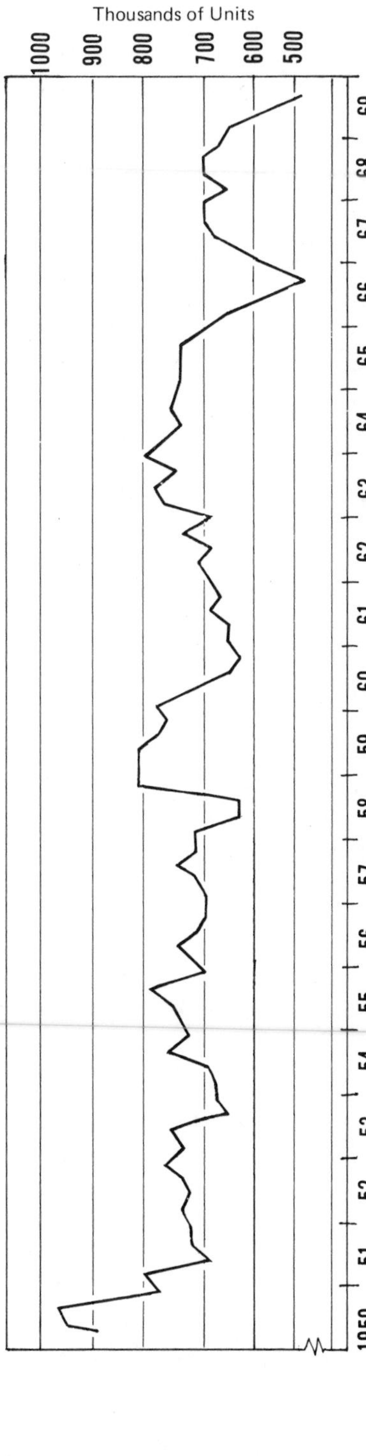

Figure 1–8. The Level of Conventionally Financed Housing Starts (*HC*) in the United States–1950:1 to 1969:4.

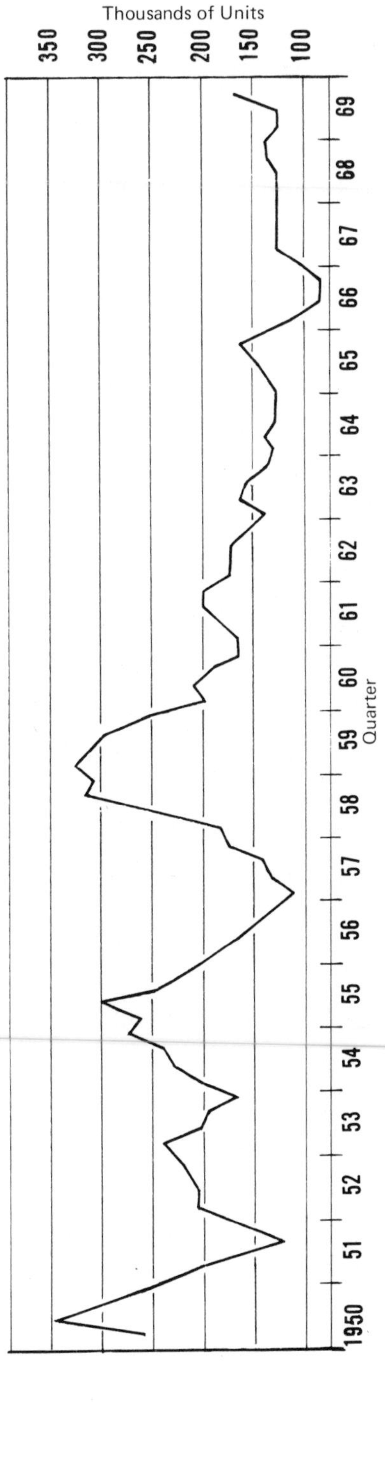

Figure 1–9. The Level of FHA-Insured Housing Starts (*HFHA*) in the United States–1950:1 to 1969:4.

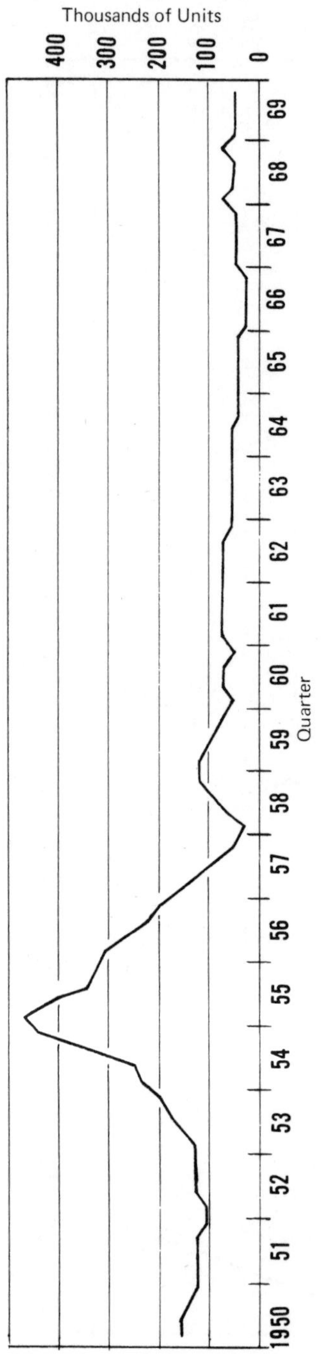

Figure 1–10. The Level of VA-Guaranteed Housing Starts (*HVA*) in the United States—1950:1 to 1969:4.

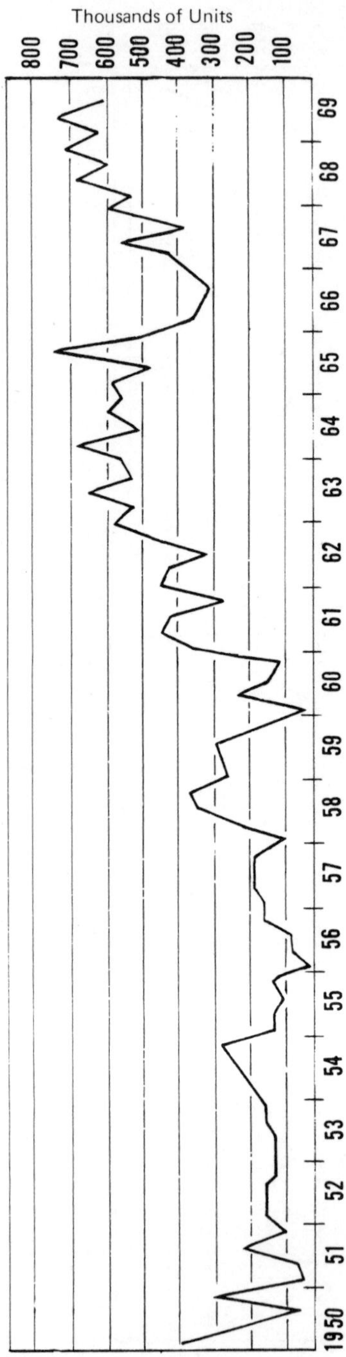

Figure 1–11. The Level of Multiple-Family Housing Starts (*HM*) in the United States—1950:1 to 1969:4.

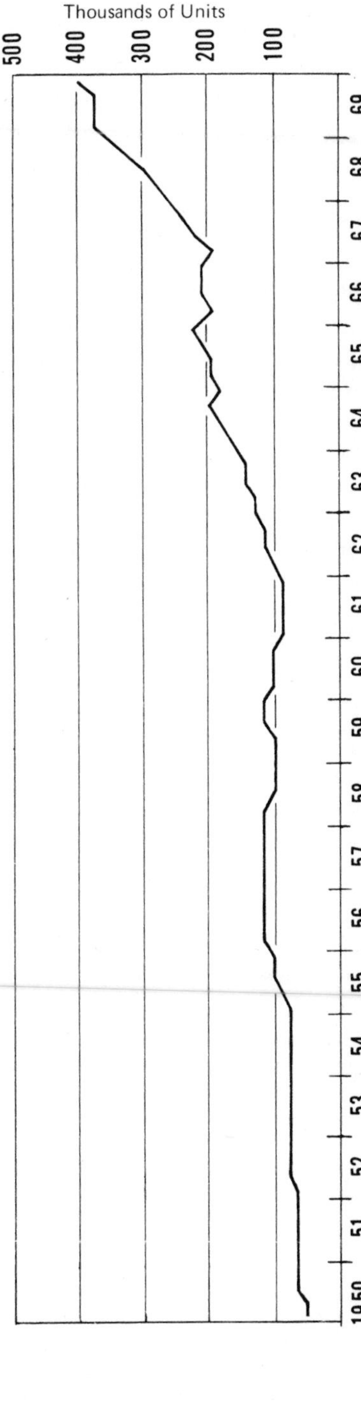

Figure 1–12. The Level of Mobile Home Shipments (*HMHUS*) in the United States–1950:1 to 1969:4.

hinge upon different criteria than decisions relating to home ownership. What is surprising is the low correlation between FHA and VA starts, since the federally underwritten mortgage market has been considered a fairly homogeneous sectoral unit by many students of the housing market. However, a comparison of Figures 1-9 and 1-10 indicates that much of the difference between behavior in the FHA and in the VA markets took place between 1954 and 1959. The VA market showed a strong upturn in the 1954-1955 housing boom and tapered off very sharply during 1956 and 1957. The FHA market, on the other hand, was characterized by a much smaller degree of fluctuation over the period, and moved sharply upward during 1958 and 1959. This indicates that there was a significant shift out of VA instruments and into FHA instruments in late 1957 and in 1958, as a direct result of the fact that the FHA ceiling rate was raised in December of 1956, while Congress rejected the bill to raise the ceiling on the interest rate for VA loans. When activity in the VA market declined drastically in 1958, FHA downpayments were liberalized to support the sagging housing market, and FNMA increased its aid to the housing industry.[10] In any case, it could be argued that the 1954-1958 period was an unusual one,[11] and that the decade of the 1960s would show the two federally supported sectors of the housing market moving together cyclically. For this reason we have constructed an additional correlation matrix for the five sectors for the period 1960:1 through 1969:4.

	HC	*HFHA*	*HVA*	*HM*	*HMHUS*
HC	1.0000				
HFHA	0.3275	1.0000			
HVA	0.3076	+0.7682	1.0000		
HM	0.1349	-0.3038	-0.2821	1.0000	
HMHUS	-0.3904	-0.5246	-0.6077	0.5839	1.0000

The VA-guaranteed market and the FHA-insured market moved closely with one another during the decade of the 1960s with +.77 correlation between the two sectors. The correlation between multifamily starts and mobile home shipments is +.58, conforming to its earlier pattern. However, no other inter-sector correlation coefficient exceeds +.33, suggesting that a four-sector model might prove useful for analysis, with the FHA and VA markets lumped into a single component.

As an initial attempt at constructing a sectoral housing model, the housing market is divided into the components that have already been discussed. With

10. For an excellent detailed analysis of U.S. housing policies during the 1953-1957 period, see Grebler [7], especially pp. 88-111.

11. The correlation coefficient between FHA and VA starts for the period 1950:1 through 1959:4 was +.10.

the simplifying assumption that levels of activity in each individual sector are independent of those in the other sectors, we estimate the structure of the sectoral housing market for the period 1960:3 through 1970:2 using OLS regressions. Successive elimination for each sector, of a priori predetermined variables that did not appear to be important in causing variations in the dependent variables led to the retention of the variables in each market which appeared to explain the major part of the variation in housing starts by type.

The following regressions relate to the conventionally financed single-family housing market. It is interesting to note that, as was the case for the total housing start regressions – equations (1.5) and (1.6) – basic demand variables were eliminated, indicating that the major portion of quarterly variation in conventional single-family housing starts can be explained by variations in supply variables. Estimates of the elasticity of these housing starts follow from the natural log form of the regression.

$$\underset{}{HC} = \underset{(1.9)}{-720.93} + \underset{(6.5)}{20.94B} - \underset{(6.9)}{241.8IC} + \underset{(4.4)}{22.09LVC} + \underset{(2.7)}{.037FHLBS} \underset{(7.0)}{-33.4T} \qquad (1.10)$$

$R^2 = .875$ D-W = 2.26 SE = 29.83

$$\ln HC = \underset{(6.7)}{-21.88} + \underset{(8.0)}{5.26 \ln B} - \underset{(7.8)}{2.78 \ln IC} + \underset{(4.6)}{2.54 \ln LVC} + \underset{(2.6)}{.008 \ln FHLBS} - \underset{(8.7)}{.416T} \qquad (1.11)$$

$R^2 = .890$ D-W = 2.12 SE = .046

Consider some of the implications of the regressions relating to the conventionally financed single-family dwelling market. The level of conventionally financed housing starts is very sensitive to changes in the rate of interest. For example, equation (1.10) indicates that a fall in the interest rate on conventionally financed mortgages of one absolute percentage point will, *ceteris paribus,* lead to a quarter of a million additional conventionally financed single-family dwelling units. When this is compared with the additional 467 thousand total housing starts (including mobile homes) that can be expected to result from a fall of one absolute percentage point in the conventional interest rate as indicated by equation (1.6), it is evident that the bulk of response of housing to a change in the nominal rate of interest will come in the conventionally financed single-family dwelling unit market. Consistent with this result are the elasticities of housing starts with respect to mortgage interest rates in each of the relevant housing markets. Equation (1.11) indicates that a 1-percent proportionate decline in the conventional interest rate will lead to a 2.8 percent proportionate increase in conventionally financed housing starts. These findings support the commonly held view that conventionally financed residential housing is extremely susceptible to changes in the level of monetary stringency and the resultant effect of changing monetary conditions on nominal interest rates.

The relatively high degree of intercorrelation between FHA-insured housing starts and VA-guaranteed starts (+.77) in the decade of the 1960s indicates that it may be possible, even desirable, to lump them together into a federally underwritten starts series without loss of efficiency. Since the true interest rates on FHA and VA mortgages have tended to coincide in the decade of the 1960s, it seems reasonable to suspect that financial intermediaries may have shifted somewhat randomly between these two classes of mortgages to be held as assets in portfolios, and that a regression combining FHA and VA starts would give better results than a model which separates them. For these reasons we distinguish a federal housing market, *HFED*, where

$$HFED = HFHA + HVA \tag{1.12}$$

Lumping FNMA-GNMA net purchases of FHA and VA mortgages in the secondary mortgage market as *AFEDF*, where

$$AFEDF = AFHAF + AVAF \tag{1.13}$$

we run an OLS regression for the major determinants of variations in the federally underwritten mortgage market for the period 1960–1963 to 1970–1972 as follows:

$$\underset{}{HFED} = \underset{(1.9)}{120.50} - \underset{(1.9)}{29.90\,IFHA} + \underset{(1.7)}{.033AFEDF} + \underset{(3.9)}{8.229B} - \underset{(5.9)}{11.257T} \tag{1.14}$$

$R^2 = .670$ D-W = .79 SE = 22.99

$$\ln HFED = \underset{(4.4)}{-17.87} - \underset{(3.8)}{1.01 \ln IFHA} + \underset{(0.8)}{.002 \ln AFEDF}$$

$$+ \underset{(5.9)}{6.055 \ln B} - \underset{(7.3)}{.061T} \tag{1.15}$$

$R^2 = .601$ D-W = .760 SE = .117

We now turn to an analysis of the two remaining sectors which make up total residential housing starts in the United States – the multiple-family dwelling market and the mobile home market. Both of these sectors behaved rather uniquely, and were quite polar, in that it was difficult to make any specification of a priori predetermined variables that gave a good statistical specification of multiple-family dwelling unit starts, while nearly all reasonable combinations of predetermined variables accounted for almost all the variation in mobile home starts.

In an effort to treat both of these sectors in a similar manner, it was postulated that the services of single-family dwelling units would be preferred to those of multiple-family dwellings, and that either of these two types of housing would yield a stream of services preferable in the aggregate to those services provided by mobile homes. Of course this is not true in all circumstances; households in particular regions and/or occupational groups, and households in certain stages of their life cycles may prefer mobile home living or apartment house living to residence in a single-family dwelling, but it does not seem unreasonable to assume that, as a generalization, single-family dwellings are preferred to multiple-family dwellings and mobile homes. Based on these assumptions we have regressed multiple-family dwelling unit starts against the level of "preferred housing starts," and a time trend term. The regression results are as follows:

$$HM = -1434.8 + 1.182HTUS + 14.257T \qquad (1.16)$$
$$(5.2) \quad (5.6) \qquad (8.0)$$

$R^2 = .616$ D-W = 1.617 SE = 97.40

Similarly, it is assumed that the demand for the services of mobile homes is a residual demand, reflecting the inability of the household to obtain conventional housing – either single-family or multiple-family dwellings – because housing costs have priced him out of the market. Accordingly, mobile home shipments are regressed against the Boeckh index of residential construction costs and time trend. The regression results for mobile homes are as follows:

$$HMHUS = -459.25 + 4.077B + 2.965T \qquad (1.17)$$
$$(13.0) \quad (5.5) \qquad (3.0)$$

$R^2 = .950$ D-W = 1.21 SE = 22.4

Figures 1-13 through 1-16 indicate the actual and estimated values for each of the four sectors of the housing model for the third quarter of 1960 through the second quarter of 1970.

A contrast of the standard deviations of the dependent variables and the standard errors of the respective regressions in which they are estimated is

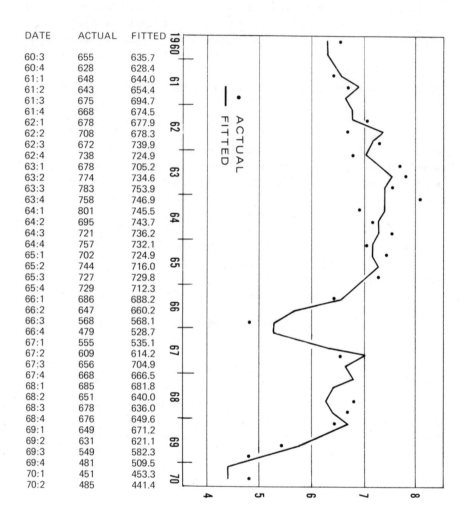

DATE	ACTUAL	FITTED
60:3	655	635.7
60:4	628	628.4
61:1	648	644.0
61:2	643	654.4
61:3	675	694.7
61:4	668	674.5
62:1	678	677.9
62:2	708	678.3
62:3	672	739.9
62:4	738	724.9
63:1	678	705.2
63:2	774	734.6
63:3	783	753.9
63:4	758	746.9
64:1	801	745.5
64:2	695	743.7
64:3	721	736.2
64:4	757	732.1
65:1	702	724.9
65:2	744	716.0
65:3	727	729.8
65:4	729	712.3
66:1	686	688.2
66:2	647	660.2
66:3	568	568.1
66:4	479	528.7
67:1	555	535.1
67:2	609	614.2
67:3	656	704.9
67:4	668	666.5
68:1	685	681.8
68:2	651	640.0
68:3	678	636.0
68:4	676	649.6
69:1	649	671.2
69:2	631	621.1
69:3	549	582.3
69:4	481	509.5
70:1	451	453.3
70:2	485	441.4

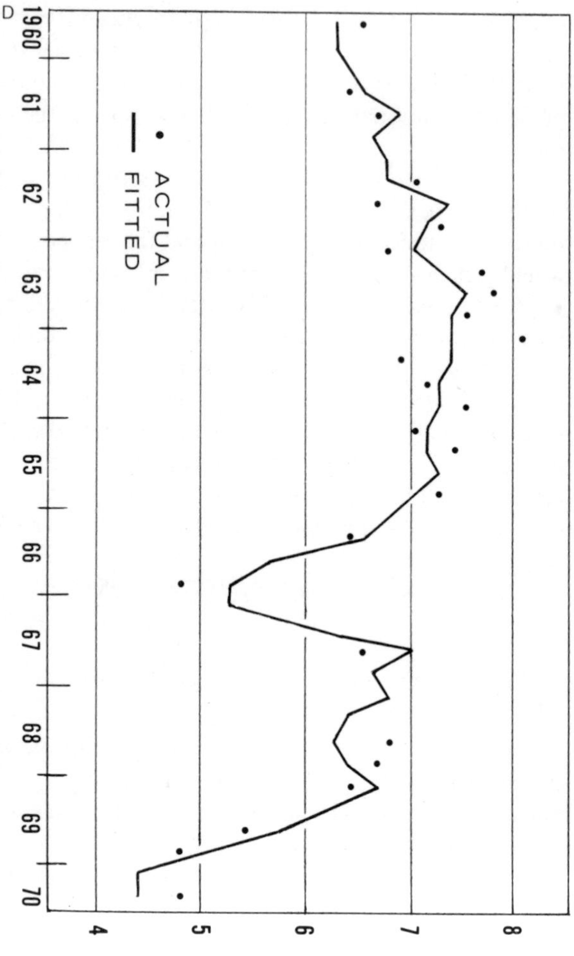

Figure 1-13. Actual and Estimated Levels of the Number of Conventionally Financed Housing Starts (*HC*) as Estimated by Regression (1.10)–Thousands.

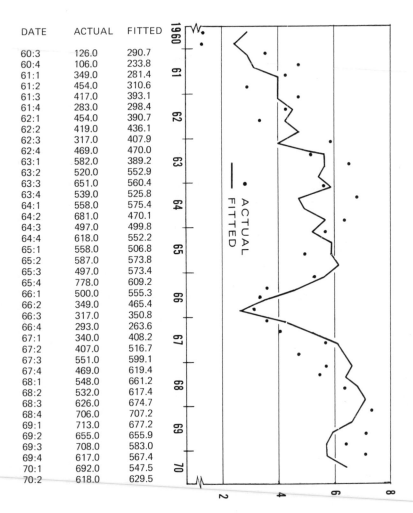

DATE	ACTUAL	FITTED
60:3	126.0	290.7
60:4	106.0	233.8
61:1	349.0	281.4
61:2	454.0	310.6
61:3	417.0	393.1
61:4	283.0	298.4
62:1	454.0	390.7
62:2	419.0	436.1
62:3	317.0	407.9
62:4	469.0	470.0
63:1	582.0	389.2
63:2	520.0	552.9
63:3	651.0	560.4
63:4	539.0	525.8
64:1	558.0	575.4
64:2	681.0	470.1
64:3	497.0	499.8
64:4	618.0	552.2
65:1	558.0	506.8
65:2	587.0	573.8
65:3	497.0	573.4
65:4	778.0	609.2
66:1	500.0	555.3
66:2	349.0	465.4
66:3	317.0	350.8
66:4	293.0	263.6
67:1	340.0	408.2
67:2	407.0	516.7
67:3	551.0	599.1
67:4	469.0	619.4
68:1	548.0	661.2
68:2	532.0	617.4
68:3	626.0	674.7
68:4	706.0	707.2
69:1	713.0	677.2
69:2	655.0	655.9
69:3	708.0	583.0
69:4	617.0	567.4
70:1	692.0	547.5
70:2	618.0	629.5

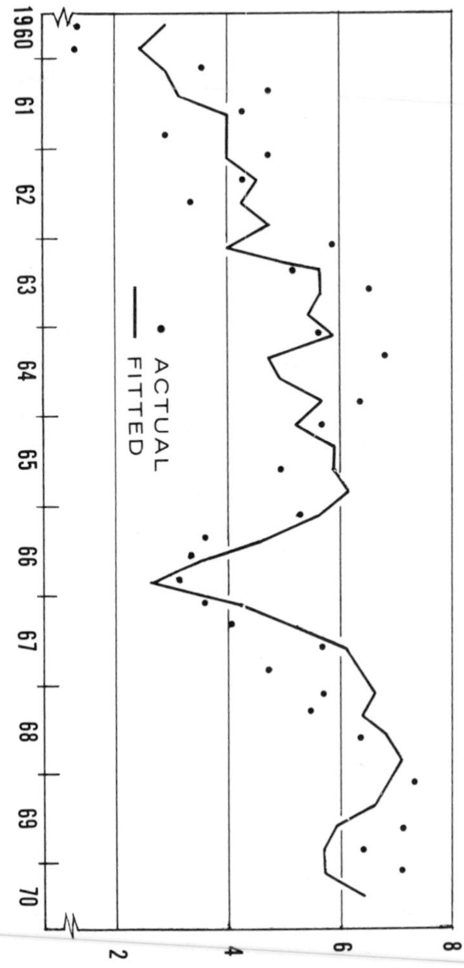

Figure 1-14. Actual and Estimated Levels of the Number of Multiple-Family Housing Starts (*HM*) as estimated by Regression (1.16)–Thousands.

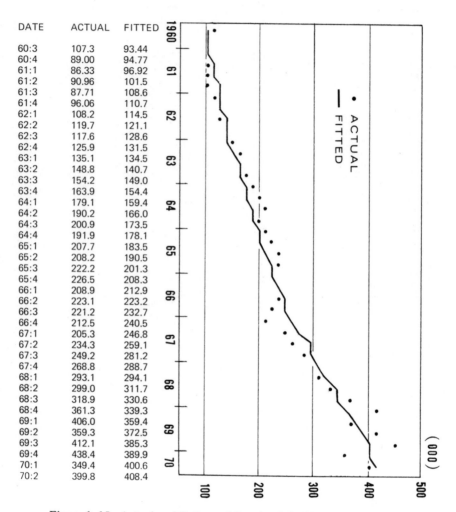

DATE	ACTUAL	FITTED
60:3	107.3	93.44
60:4	89.00	94.77
61:1	86.33	96.92
61:2	90.96	101.5
61:3	87.71	108.6
61:4	96.06	110.7
62:1	108.2	114.5
62:2	119.7	121.1
62:3	117.6	128.6
62:4	125.9	131.5
63:1	135.1	134.5
63:2	148.8	140.7
63:3	154.2	149.0
63:4	163.9	154.4
64:1	179.1	159.4
64:2	190.2	166.0
64:3	200.9	173.5
64:4	191.9	178.1
65:1	207.7	183.5
65:2	208.2	190.5
65:3	222.2	201.3
65:4	226.5	208.3
66:1	208.9	212.9
66:2	223.1	223.2
66:3	221.2	232.7
66:4	212.5	240.5
67:1	205.3	246.8
67:2	234.3	259.1
67:3	249.2	281.2
67:4	268.8	288.7
68:1	293.1	294.1
68:2	299.0	311.7
68:3	318.9	330.6
68:4	361.3	339.3
69:1	406.0	359.4
69:2	359.3	372.5
69:3	412.1	385.3
69:4	438.4	389.9
70:1	349.4	400.6
70:2	399.8	408.4

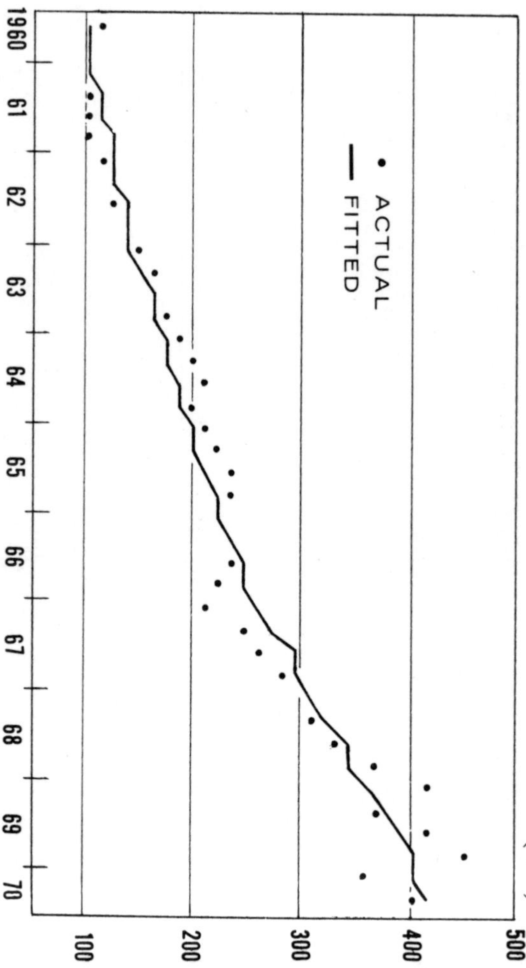

Figure 1-15. Actual and Estimated Levels of the Number of Mobile Home Shipments (*HMHUS*) as Estimated by Regression (1.17)–Thousands.

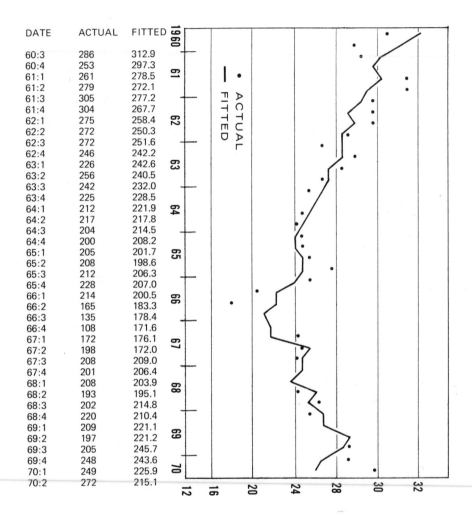

DATE	ACTUAL	FITTED
60:3	286	312.9
60:4	253	297.3
61:1	261	278.5
61:2	279	272.1
61:3	305	277.2
61:4	304	267.7
62:1	275	258.4
62:2	272	250.3
62:3	272	251.6
62:4	246	242.2
63:1	226	242.6
63:2	256	240.5
63:3	242	232.0
63:4	225	228.5
64:1	212	221.9
64:2	217	217.8
64:3	204	214.5
64:4	200	208.2
65:1	205	201.7
65:2	208	198.6
65:3	212	206.3
65:4	228	207.0
66:1	214	200.5
66:2	165	183.3
66:3	135	178.4
66:4	108	171.6
67:1	172	176.1
67:2	198	172.0
67:3	208	209.0
67:4	201	206.4
68:1	208	203.9
68:2	193	195.1
68:3	202	214.8
68:4	220	210.4
69:1	209	221.1
69:2	197	221.2
69:3	205	245.7
69:4	248	243.6
70:1	249	225.9
70:2	272	215.1

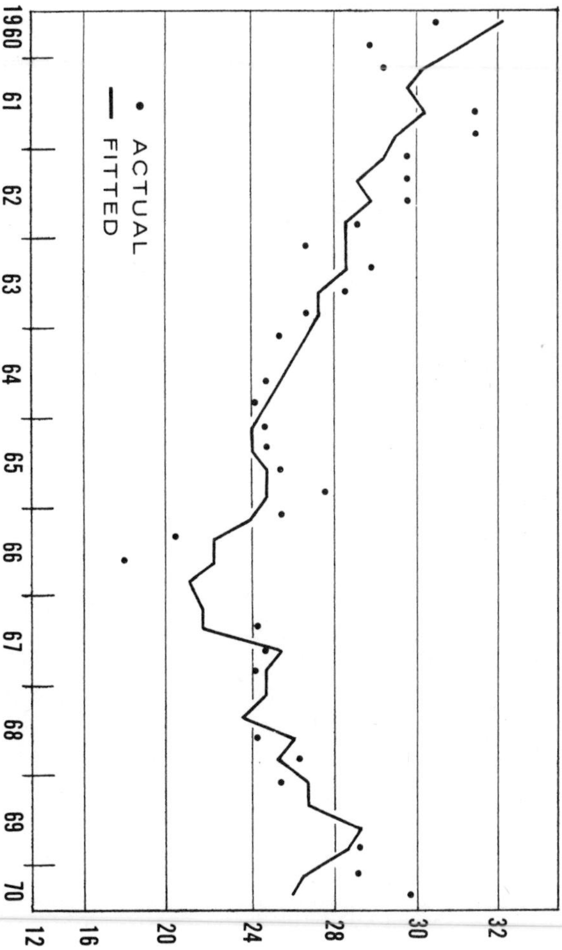

Figure 1-16. Actual and Estimated Levels of the Number of Federally Underwritten Housing Starts (*HFED*) as Estimated by Regression (1.14)–Thousands.

Table 1-3
Standard Deviation vs. Standard Error of the Regression of Dependent Variables

Dependent Variable	*Mean Value*	*Standard Deviation*	*Standard Error of the Regression*
HC	690.6	71.0	29.8
HFED	240.8	58.5	23.0
HM	426.0	166.3	97.4
HMHUS	162.8	55.4	22.4
HTTT	1520.3	215.7	126.8

shown in Table 1-3. Each variable, together with its mean and standard deviation between 1960:3 and 1970:2, is contrasted with the standard error of the regression used to estimate that variable. A glance at Table 1-3 will indicate that the multiple-family housing sector (*HM*) is the one for which the poorest fit has been made. Various attempts were made to respecify the relationships in this sector, but no significant improvements resulted. However, it can be argued that the multiple-family dwelling unit market is somewhat unique, in that it represents investment decisions of firms to produce income yielding assets, rather than household decisions to purchase single-family dwellings and mobile homes. The investment decision takes place in a much more complex way than the household decision (to rent or to purchase), and for this reason multiple-family housing starts are more difficult to explain or predict. We simply note that the standard error in multiple-family housing starts is more than three times as great as that for single-family dwellings financed with conventional mortgages. A model basing multiple-family dwelling unit starts on investment decision criteria may be superior to the one used here.

An Interdependent Intersectoral Model

The assumption of independence between housing sectors is now subjected to test. The two regressions that follow represent a two-equation model of the single-family dwelling unit market, consisting of conventionally financed and federally underwritten components of that market. This model of housing activity is represented by the structural relationships as they appeared in their assumed "independent market" OLS forms of regressions (1.10) and (1.14). Two-stage least squares (TSLS) estimates are made to allow for possible interdependence between the two equations that make up the model.

The method of two-stage least squares takes account of the effects exerted on either single equation in the two-equation model, and is applied directly to each single equation in the model. Essentially, in the TSLS procedure, one regresses the other dependent variables of the model on both the endogenous variables included in the equation in question as well as the variables excluded from the equation but included in the model. Then the fitted (estimated) values for the other dependent variables are included as predetermined variables in the single equation that is being estimated. Identification requires that there are at least as many excluded exogenous variables in the equation as there are included endogenous variables.[12]

The TSLS estimates of OLS regressions (1.10) and (1.14) which make up the model of single-family dwelling unit starts are as follows:

$$\underset{(2.4)}{HC = -1007.7} - \underset{(0.3)}{.169HFED} + \underset{(5.0)}{30.85B} - \underset{(6.6)}{339.8IC} + \underset{(5.2)}{29.71LVC} + \underset{(3.1)}{43.95FHLBS} - \underset{(5.0)}{35.3T} \qquad (1.18)$$

$R^2 = .81$ D-W = 2.52 SE = 34.67

$$\underset{(2.6)}{HFED = 232.12} - \underset{(0.4)}{.048HC} - \underset{(2.6)}{53.29IFHA} + \underset{(2.2)}{.036AFEDF} + \underset{(4.2)}{9.30B} - \underset{(5.8)}{12.369T} \qquad (1.19)$$

$R^2 = .815$ D-W = .99 SE = 19.46

A comparison of regressions (1.10) and (1.18) and of regressions (1.14) and (1.19) indicates that the simplifying assumption of intersectoral independence is reasonable. The estimated coefficients for the dependent variables of the model exogenous to any single equation in it are quite small, and their low *t*-values make them statistically insignificant.[13] It appears that we can proceed to base our predictions on OLS regressions without worrying too much about the fact that simultaneous estimation bias will give us misleading estimates.[14]

---

12. For a very simple discussion of simultaneous estimation bias inherent in OLS and the rationale for the TSLS procedure, see Brennen [4].

13. TSLS estimates were made for the three-sector model of conventionally financed single-family dwelling units, federally underwritten housing, and multiple-family dwelling units and similar conclusions apply.

14. These findings support those noted by Professor Huang in his analysis of disaggregated components (FHA, VA, conventional) of the housing market. He found that TSLS estimates were not significantly better than OLS estimates. See David S. Huang, "Effect of Different Credit Policies on Housing Demand," *Study of the Savings and Loan Industry*, prepared for the FHLBB and directed by Irwin Friend, July 1969, pp. 1126–1127.

Forecasting Housing Starts with the Model

This section contains predictions for the various types of housing starts quarterly through 1971:4. They are made on the basis of the following expected levels for the predetermined variables. It is assumed that the Boeckh index of residential construction costs will rise at an annual rate of 5 percent; that the effective interest rate on conventionally financed mortgages will fall steadily to a level of 7.9 percent by the end of the fourth quarter of 1971; that the loan-to-value ratio on conventionally financed mortgages will rise steadily to .75 by the end of the fourth quarter of 1971; that the Meltzer index of monetary stringency will decline steadily from its second quarter of 1970 level of 6.91 to a level of 5.00 by the first quarter of 1971, and then return to 5.50 by the end of that year; that the interest rate on FHA mortgages will fall steadily to 8.3 percent by the fourth quarter of 1971; that net FNMA-GNMA acquisitions in the secondary mortgage market will be approximately $4 billion during 1971; and that FHLB increase in advances run to about $1 billion over the same period. More specifically, the predetermined variables of the model are assumed to take on the values through the fourth quarter of 1971 that are noted in Table 1-4.

In Table 1-5, forecasts of housing starts by type are based on the parameters of the previously discussed regressions, together with the estimated levels of the predetermined variables.

A few comments on these forecasts are in order. First, the poorest of the structural fits was for the regression estimating the level of multiple-family dwelling unit starts. Some of the problems involved have been mentioned, but it should be remembered that the multiple-family dwelling unit series is a residual series, obtained by subtracting conventionally financed single-family dwelling unit starts and FHA-VA starts from the *HTT* series on total starts. As a residual series, it is subject to random fluctuation as a result of the manner in which it is obtained, and is a possible source of the relatively poor fit. In addition, multiple-family dwelling unit starts moved sharply upward during the decade of the 1960s while single-family dwelling unit starts had a slight downward trend over the same period. While this may correctly depict the structural relationships that existed in the 1960s, it seems unlikely that multiple-family dwelling unit starts will be able to maintain this strong trend relative to single-family starts, and that projections past the second quarter of 1971 may be too high for multifamily housing.

Policy Making with the Model

This section contains the basic structural equations upon which the forecasts of the foregoing section have been made. We now form a policy model of the U.S. conventionally financed single-family dwelling unit market to introduce

Table 1–4
Estimates of the Levels of the Predetermined Variables in the Model Between 1970:4 and 1971:4

	Period				
Predetermined Variable	*1970:4*	*1971:1*	*1971:2*	*1971:3*	*1971:4*
Boeckh index of residential construction costs	161.7	164.2	166.6	169.1	171.7
Contract interest rate on conventional mortgages	8.30	8.10	8.00	7.95	7.90
Loan-to-value ratio on conventional mortgages	72.6	73.2	73.8	74.4	75.0
Meltzer index of monetary stringency	5.36	5.00	5.25	5.25	5.50
True interest rate on FHA mortgages	8.90	8.60	8.40	8.35	8.30
Net FNMA-GNMA purchases of FHA-VA mortgages (in 1958 dollars)	900.	956.	803.	652.	504.
Net FHLB advances (in 1958 dollars)	50.	144.	-213.	351.	415.

Table 1-5
Housing Starts Forecast by Type

Item	*Forecast Period*				
	1970:4	*1971:1*	*1971:2*	*1971:3*	*1971:4*
	Forecasted Level of Investment (billions)				
ICNFR58	$22.04	$23.79	$24.15	$26.51	$27.74
	Forecasted Number of Housing Starts (x1000)				
Type of Housing Start					
HTTT	2022	2248	2352	2587	2744
HTT	1577	1777	1868	2071	2207
HTUS	855	949	1001	1077	1136
HC	606	694	741	809	862
HFED	253	269	276	277	280
HM	773	899	974	1078	1162
HMHUS	441	452	464	475	486

the mechanism by which the consequences of alternative policies with regard to the housing sector can be evaluated.

Models such as those we have presented have been commonly used to examine the expected outcomes of various policies. For example, regression (1.10) would enable one to predict that if the rate of interest on conventionally financed single-family mortgages were to fall from 8 to 7 percent, other things unchanged, the level of conventionally financed housing starts would rise by 242,000 units. These models have generally been used to deduce, from the regressions representing the structure of the housing sector, the end result of changes in policy variables. However, it is usually more straightforward to be able to tell the policy maker the best way in which he could achieve a given target once the level of the particular target to be achieved is specified. This involves reversing the causal ordering of ordinary forecasting models; instead of predicting what will happen to conventional single-family housing starts as a result of a reduction in the conventional mortgage rate, one forecasts how much the interest rate on conventional mortgages must be lowered in order to effect a given increase in the level of housing starts. The housing starts variable, which had been an unknown in the forecasting model, is reformulated as a known target, and the level of interest rates on conventional mortgages, which had been treated as given, is now reformulated as an unknown. The changed causal ordering of the model is the essential difference between a forecasting model and a policy model. Let us turn our simple example – consisting of regression (1.10) – inside out, transforming it into a policy model. As an arbitrary target, we have chosen the desired level of conventionally financed housing starts to be 750,000 for the fourth quarter of 1970. Assume that the policy maker has the power to manipulate either the rate of interest on conventional mortgages, or the loan-to-value ratio on them as arbitrary instruments. As the number of instruments in this case now exceeds the single target for the sector, the policy model is underdetermined, and there is more than one way to achieve the target. The policy maker has two choices. He can either take into account the comparative advantage of the two instrument variables at his command and match his target with that instrument which is the most effective in achieving it, or fix one instrument at an arbitrary level and calculate the optimal level of the remaining instrument so that the target level will be achieved. Since it is quite difficult to assess the relative merits of interest rate changes vs. loan-to-value changes as a means of effecting housing starts, the second method is used.[15]

In generic form, the regression (1.10), which stated

$$HC = a_0 + a_1 B + a_2 IC + a_3 LVC + a_4 FHLBS + a_5 T$$

is reformulated to

$$IC = b_0 + b_1 B + b_2 LVC + b_3 FHLBS + b_4 T + b_5 HC$$

Setting the target level of *HC* at 750 for 1970:4, and using the parameters of regression (1.10) together with the forecasts for the predetermined variables under expected conditions, the model yields a solution interest rate of 7.9 percent, assuming that the loan-to-value ratio is set at its predetermined level of 72.6.

Alternatively, the conventional rate can be assumed to attain its predetermined set rate of 8.3 percent as was assumed under expected conditions, and a solution can be derived for the loan-to-value ratio as a policy instrument which would induce 750,000 conventionally financed housing starts in 1970:4. In this case, regression (1.10) is reformulated to:

$$LVC = c_0 + c_1 B + c_2 IC + c_3 FHLBS + c_4 T + c_5 HC$$

The loan-to-value ratio which will be required to maintain conventionally financed housing starts at a level of three-quarter of a million by 1970:4 would be 75.2 percent.

There is also the possibility of setting combinations of both instruments so that the target of 750,000 starts is achieved. Line *TT* on Figure 1-17 traces out the locus of points indicating combinations of *IC* and *LVC* for which the target can be attained, of which points *a* and *b*, respectively, are the two solutions discussed above. By reexamining these two solutions, one can determine the linear barter terms-of-trade between them and settle for a combination of the two instruments to achieve the given target. If the target level were higher, this

15. If both instruments have a common denominator then the first choice is possible. For example, the relative efficiency of FHLB advances, as compared with FNMA-GNMA secondary market purchases, can be calculated, since they are both measured in dollars.

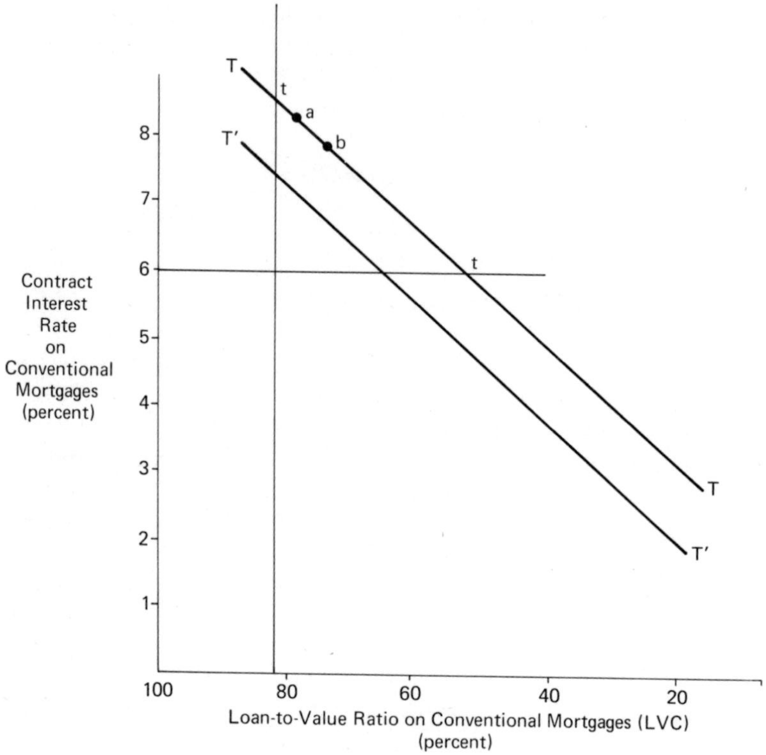

Figure 1-17. Graphical Depiction of the Marginal Rates of Substitution Between Instruments for the Policy Model Example.

would reflect a new locus of points such as that shown by line $T'T'$, lying parallel to and to the left of line TT. The slope of line TT reflects the barter terms-of-trade between the two instruments of housing policy – Figure 1-17 indicates that an absolute 1 percent fall in the conventional mortgage interest rate will have the same effect on conventionally financed housing starts as an increase in the loan-to-value ratio of 11.5 absolute percentage points.[16]

The policy maker now has flexibility in his choice of instrument combinations; he can select his target (e.g., 750,000 conventionally financed housing starts) and calculate the rates of substitution between instruments (e.g., a point on line TT). The locus of instrument combinations available to the policy maker may have a particularly defined finite span. For example, the setting of loan-to-value ratios greater than 80 percent may violate portfolio restrictions on financial intermediaries; and for the same reason, contract interest rates on conventional mortgages may not be allowed to fall below 6 percent. By specifying the limited range of instruments, we have defined the "boundary conditions" that must be met. Therefore, in the example of Figure 1-17, range tt of line TT specifies the range of instrument levels that cannot be exceeded. The boundary conditions can be structural, social, or economic.[17]

The above analysis was simply an attempt to get at the mechanics of policy formulation based on regression results, and is far too simple for the pragmatic use of housing policy. One major shortcoming is that neither the loan-to-value ratio nor the contract interest rate on conventional mortgages is a direct instrument variable in the sense that it can be directly controlled by those agencies responsible for housing policy in the United States. We must now go to a more complex policy model to get at those direct instruments available to policy makers.

Consider the more operational example of a two-instrument two-target policy model. The two targets to be achieved are desired levels for conventionally financed single-family housing starts and for federally underwritten housing starts. The two instruments of housing policy are net FHLB advances to member institutions and net FNMA-GNMA purchases of federally underwritten mortgages in the secondary mortgage market. The structural regressions for these two

---

16. An alternative way of calculating the marginal rates of substitution between instruments (equal to the average rates in our linear regressions) would be to calculate the partial derivatives of the target with respect to each instrument as given by the regression coefficients, and solve for the ratios to find the marginal rates of substitutions between instruments. For example, regression (1.10) indicates that $\delta HC / \delta IC = -333.9$, and that $\delta HC / \delta LVC = +29.03$. Since $\delta LVC / \delta IC = (\delta HC / \delta IC) / (\delta HC / \delta LVC)$, it can be calculated as -11.501.

17. These limitations can be applied to the targets as well, as a result of capacity constraints, and will be limitations on the maximum level of the target or targets under usual conditions. In terms of our example, line $T'T'$ may be the maximum level of conventionally financed housing starts that can be attained, regardless of how stimulating the level at which the instrument variables are set.

housing markets are variations of regressions (1.10) and (1.14), which are amended to include both policy instruments as predetermined variables in the regressions. The structural parameters of these regressions are based on data from 1960:3 through 1970:2 – when FNMA-GNMA secondary market purchases were limited to federally underwritten mortgages. Since the major impact of FHLB advances is on the conventionally financed mortgage market, it is to be expected that these advances should have more impact on that market than on the FHA-VA housing market, and FNMA-GNMA operations should have a greater impact on federally underwritten housing starts than on conventionally financed starts. However, for completeness, both instruments are included in both markets. The regressions for this two-sector policy model follow:[18]

$$\underset{}{HC} = \underset{(1.3)}{-643.93} + \underset{(5.4)}{24.60B} - \underset{(5.1)}{267.01IC} + \underset{(3.2)}{21.35LVC} + \underset{(2.0)}{.0369FHLBS}$$

$$- \underset{(0.6)}{.0207AFEDF} - \underset{(5.6)}{24.29T} \tag{1.20}$$

$R^2 = .775$ D-W = 1.689 SE = 37.95

$$HFED = \underset{(4.0)}{192.93} + \underset{(5.4)}{9.09B} - \underset{(3.7)}{49.96IFHA} - \underset{(0.7)}{.007FHLBS}$$

$$+ \underset{(2.3)}{.0418AFEDF} - \underset{(7.4)}{12.20T} \tag{1.21}$$

$R^2 = .820$ D-W = .965 SE = 19.18

18. The conclusions of the preceding section also apply to the relationships between the OLS regressions and their TSLS counterparts. For comparative purposes, the TSLS estimates follow:

$$\text{HC} = \underset{(0.8)}{-495.96} + \underset{(0.4)}{0.544HFED} + \underset{(1.2)}{18.84B} - \underset{(2.2)}{230.50IC} + \underset{(1.4)}{17.45LVC}$$

$$+ \underset{(1.8)}{0.0372FHLBS} - \underset{(0.6)}{0.0422AFEDF} - \underset{(0.8)}{16.53T} \tag{1.20a}$$

$R^2 = 0.746$ D-W = 1.420 SE = 40.945

$$HFED = \underset{(0.7)}{76.80} + \underset{(1.2)}{0.161HC} + \underset{(2.6)}{6.869B} - \underset{(1.1)}{27.02IFHA} - \underset{(0.9)}{0.010FHLBS}$$

$$+ \underset{(2.3)}{0.047AFEDF} - \underset{(4.0)}{10.11T} \tag{1.21a}$$

$R^2 = 0.798$ D-W = 0.896 SE = 20.61

Given regressions (1.20) and (1.21), which are presumed to represent the structures of the two components of the single-family dwelling unit market, assume we have two fixed targets. We wish to set out instruments at a level which will yield a million annual single-family housing starts as of 1970:4, of which 750,000 starts will be financed by conventional mortgages while the remaining 250,000 starts will be financed by federally underwritten mortgages. Regressions (1.20) and (1.21) yield forecasts for conventionally financed starts and federally underwritten starts of 618,000 and 239,000 respectively, which are close to those starts forecasted from the parameters listed on Table 1-2.

The problem now is to set the levels of the two instrument variables so that we can simultaneously achieve the two targeted levels of housing starts. Regressions (1.20) and (1.21) indicate a given linear relationship between each instrument variable and each given target. If the change in any particular target variable (ΔX_i) is defined as due to the change in a particular instrument variable (Δz_j), the ratio $(\Delta X_i) / (\Delta z_j)$ will estimate the efficiency of that instrument. The reciprocal of this ratio will represent the partial differential coefficient of each instrument with respect to each target variable. Using this notation to analyze our policy problem, let us assume that

Δx_1 = an increase in conventionally financed housing starts of 1000 units

Δx_2 = an increase in federally underwritten housing starts of 1000 units

Δz_1 = an increase in net FHLB advances outstanding of \$1 million in 1958 dollars

Δz_2 = an increase in net secondary market purchases by FNMA-GNMA of \$1 million in 1958 dollars

Deriving the relevant partial differential coefficients from regressions (1.20) and (1.21), we obtain

$$\frac{2x_1}{2z_1} = .0369 \quad \frac{2x_1}{2z_2} = -0207 \quad \frac{2x_2}{2z_1} = -.007 \quad \frac{2x_2}{2z_2} = .0418.$$

These values are now inserted into an equation system where the set levels of FHLB advances and FNMA-GNMA purchases are unknown and dependent on the known desired level of the targets. In terms of the above notation, the equation system becomes

$$\Delta x_1 = a_{11}\Delta z_1 - a_{12}\Delta z_2 \qquad \Delta x_2 = a_{21}\Delta z_1 + a_{22}\Delta z_2$$

where the a_{ij}'s are generic representations of the relevant partial derivatives of the system. Replacing these coefficients by the values for their respective partial derivatives as obtained from the two regressions, where

$$a_{ij} = \frac{2x_i}{2z_j}.$$

Solving this system for Δz, and z_2, we obtain

$$\Delta z_1 = 29.92\Delta x_1 + 14.812\Delta x_2 \tag{1.22}$$

$$\Delta z_2 = 5.009\Delta x_1 + 26.404\Delta x_2. \tag{1.23}$$

The estimated forecast of conventional housing starts is 668,000 while the target level is 750,000. For federally underwritten starts, the estimated level is 219,000 while the target level is 250,000. Our solution thus requires that

$$\Delta x_1 = 82 \qquad \Delta x_2 = 31.$$

Inserting these required values into equations (1.22) and (1.23) and solving for Δz_1 and Δz_2 we obtain

$$\Delta z_1 = 724.6 \qquad \Delta z_2 = -10973.0.$$

This indicates that we should increase the levels of both instruments to achieve the two targets simultaneously. The results follow from taking *AFEDF* as an instrument which is presumed to affect *HC*, and *FHLBS* as an instrument as operating on *HFED*. The regression results appear to indicate that conventional housing starts are influenced by net FNMA-GNMA purchases and federally underwritten starts are likewise affected by FHLB advances. However, the poor statistical fits for net FNMA-GNMA purchases in the conventionally financed market, and for FHLB net advances in the federally underwritten market, would strengthen the view that these two predetermined instrument variables have very little effect on those markets. In pursuing this view further, one could ignore coefficients a_{12} and a_{21} and base the optimal instrument levels on a_{11} and a_{22}. On the basis of this assumption, the optimal levels of the z's would be

$$\Delta z_1 = 2222 \qquad \Delta z_2 = 742$$

In this example, therefore, the target levels of housing starts could be achieved if the FHLBB advanced a net \$2.22 billion in 1958 dollars to its member institutions, and if the FNMA-GNMA operated to purchase a net of \$742 million in 1958 dollars of FHA-VA mortgages in the secondary mortgage market.

Discussion

Mr. Ricks: Good morning gentlemen. Welcome to the first FHLB Model Conference. Gene Brady will make the first presentation.

Gene had worked for us last spring and summer at the Board on leave from Iowa State. He has gone back to Iowa State and continued to work on a consulting basis. We had said to Gene, "There is no model work being done at the FHLBB: get us some." And we had constrained Gene to get some modelling work up and running without taking the time to go through a structural model, so that he has simply taken a group of variables and said, "What kind of regression results can I get with it." And we are now beginning to look and see whether those variables make any sense.

The problems incident to approaching a subject that way are imposed on Gene by us. He has also done work for the last few days on applying his modeling work to small areas. He will be presenting that as part of his presentation.

Mr. Brady: I would like to make a very few comments on both papers. I came to the Board from Iowa State the middle of March of last year, and spent approximately four months on housing analysis. Of that four months, very close to three months was spent grubbing for data, which is rather unpleasant business, and a little over three weeks was spent in preliminary analysis of the data. I consider the relative merits of these two lines of research effort roughly proportional to the time I spent on them.

We have some 85 housing series,[19] all quarterly, in the DRI data bank. The ones that do show seasonal variation have been adjusted, and all value series are in 1958 dollars.

The fragmentary nature of the data is one of the real shortcomings of existing housing models, and we have made a considerable effort to improve the existing housing series. Many of these series are available now and have been since the early 1960s, but time series analysis requires more observations and the real problem was to go back as far as possible. In some cases we couldn't go any further back than 1952, so many of the series start second-quarter, 1952; and the rest go back to first-quarter, 1950.

The "Maisel" adjustment was made on the housing start data, since the National Housing Inventory in 1960 indicated the housing start series had been seriously underestimated. The other adjustment I had nothing to do with concerns the "Maisel" household formation series. Again, this is an attempt to obtain a reasonable net household formation series, undertaken by John Birnbaum. I take no credit or debit for that. (Laughter.)

19. *The Quarterly National Housing Market Data Bank of the Federal Home Loan Bank Board,* Working Paper No. 22, March 3, 1971. Available from the Office of Economic Research, Federal Home Loan Bank Board.

As you get a chance today to look through the data I will be glad to explain where we got it and how we manipulated it. I would be appreciative of any criticism you have of it or things you think we can do to improve it.

Now, in terms of the paper, itself, this is the sort of model that Harry Havens was talking about yesterday, very inelegant and uncomplicated in approach. I think it is useful in a policy context when you are dealing directly with policy makers, such as Preston Martin, who want to see the direct way that various instrument variables affect housing starts.

It is quite interesting to note that the demand variables for the most part dropped out, in that they explained little of the variation in housing starts; variations in demand variables explained only 6 to 8 percent of the variation in housing starts. I don't believe it is because demand variables aren't important, but because they have been rather poorly specified.

The household formation series, for example, is an interpolation between two ten-year Census benchmarks (1950 and 1960). The interregional household migration series is also quite fragmentary. Various people, notably Mike Sumichrast, have estimated the magnitude of housing demolitions. None of these variables did a very good job of explaining variations in housing starts in our models.

I think the formal paper is too long to go through in any great detail, but there are some interesting issues raised in it.

For example, the contrast of Fannie-May/Ginny-Mae operations in the secondary mortgage market relative to Federal Home Loan Bank advances is a case in point. Both these Federal intermediations in the mortgage market have tended to support the housing sector, but I believe their impacts on the housing market are quite different.

I have tried to separate the housing market into five sectors with varying degrees of success. In the decade of the fifties, it seems that even the FHA and VA markets behaved quite differently from one another, due to the fact that Congress refused to raise the ceiling on VA mortgages in 1956, which caused a strong downturn in the VA housing market. But in the sixties the FHA and VA markets seem to have moved together, since the ceilings on federally underwritten mortgages seem to have been changed about the same time. I believe the FHA-VA sector could now be considered a unified market, which has behaved differently in the postwar period than the conventional market.

As you can see, the multifamily dwelling unit market is the most poorly behaved of all the sectors.

The elasticity of housing starts with respect to both interest rates and loan-to-value ratios seems to be high; the model indicates that a decline in the mortgage rate of one absolute percentage point would lead to an increase of about 250 thousand housing starts.

The section on policy making considers a two-sector, two-instrument, two-target case, and it seems to indicate that the secondary market activity of

Fannie-Mae/Ginny-Mae is a less efficient instrument in terms of its impact on housing starts than advances of the Home Loan Bank System.

We are attempting to improve on housing models by shifting our analysis to smaller regions. We started with a pilot study of the L.A./Long Beach SMSA, and contrasted it with the San Diego SMSA. The pattern of housing starts in each region was completely different; and, since they are separated by less than 300 miles, it leads one to believe that the poor quality of national housing models is due at least partially to the fact that different regions are experiencing different patterns of housing start fluctuations at the same time. The Office of Economic Research at the FHLBB has so far collected twenty or twenty-five series for each of 14 SMSA regions.

Mr. Ricks: Are there any very brief points of clarification you would like?

Mr. Silber: I wanted to ask – you found it also – there seems to be a tremendous difference in the results you get when you start with 1960 as opposed to 1952. Does somebody want to explain that to me?

Mr. Brady: I think the decade of the 1960s is different in terms of the quality of houses than those built from the 1950s. The housing constructed in the 1950s was pretty much postwar "ticky-tacky," and the 1960s was a decade of higher quality construction.

Mr. Silber: You said that you tried money supply, or whatever.

Mr. Brady: I took changes in M–1, the narrowly defined money supply.

Mr. Silber: If you allow for distributive lag – however you want to explain it, say rates of growth – that explains a tremendous amount of this stuff. I don't know whether you want to call that endogenetive policy, but it does work very, very well.

Mr. Kimball: Another question, again you have the problem of the two periods. Through 1964, M–1 does not –

Mr. Silver: The M–1 does extremely well.

Mr. Kimbell: Bill Gibson has recently published a series of articles on the distributive lag model. He finds there may be an initial period during which rates drop, but it may be that if you don't have a specified lag, you are sort of comingling, in effect, and may need to be disentangled here.

Appendix 1A
Alphabetical Listing of Variables

All value series are stated in millions of 1958 dollars, and the number of housing starts by type are stated in thousands of units.

Symbol	*Title*
AFEDF	Net acquisition of FHA and VA mortgages by the Federal National Mortgage Association
AFHAF	Net quarterly acquisition of FHA mortgages by the Federal National Mortgage Association
AVAF	Net quarterly acquisition of VA mortgages by the Federal National Mortgage Association
B	Boeckh index of residential construction costs
FHLBS	Net quarterly change in Federal Home Loan Bank advances outstanding, seasonally adjusted
HC	Number of conventionally financed single-family housing starts at seasonally adjusted annual rates
HFED	Federal housing market: number of FHA- and VA-financed housing starts
HFHA	Number of FHA-financed housing starts at seasonally adjusted annual rates
HM	Number of private nonfarm multiple-family housing starts at seasonally adjusted annual rates
HMHUS	Number of mobile home shipments at seasonally adjusted annual rates
HTT	Number of private nonfarm housing starts at seasonally adjusted annual rates
HTTT	Number of private nonfarm housing starts plus mobile home shipments at seasonally adjusted annual rates
HTUS	Total number of private nonfarm single-family housing starts at seasonally adjusted annual rates
HVA	Number of VA-financed housing starts at seasonally adjusted annual rates
IC	True interest rate on conventional mortgages
ICNFR	Investment in private nonfarm structures
IFHA	True interest rate on FHA mortgages
LVC	Loan-to-value ratio on conventional mortgages
T	Time trend term

References

1. Alberts, W.W. "Business Cycles, Residential Construction Cycles and the Mortgage Market." *Journal of Political Economy* 70, no. 3 (June 1962): 263–281.
2. Brady, Eugene A. "Regional Cycles of Residential Construction and the Interregional Mortgage Market: 1954–1959." *Land Economics* vol. 39, No. 1 (February 1963): 15–30.
3. Brady, Eugene A. "A Sectoral Econometric Study of the Postwar Residential Housing Market." *Journal of Political Economy* (April 1967): 147–158.
4. Brennen, Michael J. *Preface to Econometrics.* 2nd Ed. Cincinnati, South-western Publishing Co., 1965. Pp. 400–407.
5. Brownlee, Oswald. "The Effects of Monetary and Credit Policies on the Structure of the Economy." *Journal of Political Economy* 76, no. 4, pt. II (July/August 1968): 786–795.
6. Campbell, B.O. "Long Swings in Residential Construction: The Postwar Experience." *American Economic Review* Papers and Proc. (May 1963).
7. Grebler, Leo. *Housing Issues in Economic Stabilization Policy.* Occasional Paper #72. National Bureau of Economic Research, 1960.
8. Guttentag, J.M. "The Short Cycle in Residential Construction, 1946–1959," *American Economic Review* 51, no. 3 (June 1961).
9. Jaffee, Dwight M. "An Econometric Model of the Mortgage Market: Estimation of Simulation." Mimeographed. Revised April 1, 1970, pp. 56–57.
10. Klein, L.R. "A Postwar Quarterly Model: Description and Applications." *Studies in Income and Wealth* 28 (1964).
11. Lee, T.H. "The Stock Demand Elasticities of Nonfarm Housing." *Review of Economics and Statistics* 46, no. 1 (February 1964): 190–196.
12. Liu, T.C. "An Exploratory Quarterly Econometric Model of Effective Demand in the Postwar U.S. Economy." *Econometrica* 31, no. 3 (July 1963): 301–348.
13. Maisel, S. J. "The Effects of Monetary Policy on Expenditures in Specific Sectors of the Economy." *Journal of Political Economy* 76, no. 4, pt. II (July/August 1968): 796–814.
14. Maisel, S.J. "A Theory of Fluctuations in Residential Construction Starts." *American Economic Review* 53, no. 3 (June 1963): 359–383.
15. Malanos, G.T., and H. Thomassen. "An Econometric Model of the U.S., 1947-1958." *Southern Economic Journal* 27 (July 1960): 18–27.
16. Mattila, J.M. "An Econometric Analysis of Construction." Wisconsin Commerce Reports, vol. IV, no. 1 (April 1955).
17. Muth, R.F. "The Demand for Nonfarm Housing." In Arnold C. Harberger (ed.), *The Demand for Durable Goods.* Chicago: University of Chicago Press, 1960.

18. Schaff, A.H. "Federal Mortgage Interest Rate Policy and the Supply of FHA-VA Credit." *Review of Economics and Statistics* 40 (November 1958): 384–389.
19. Suits, D.B. "Forecasting and Analysis with an Econometric Model." *American Economic Review* 52 (March 1962): 104–132.

2 Housing Starts in 1966 and 1969: A Comparison Using an Econometric Model

James B. Burnham

The performance of housing starts in 1966 and 1969 has aroused considerable interest. During both periods similar pressures were at work in the nation's financial markets: interest rates rose rapidly and flows of funds to depositary institutions dropped substantially. It was widely believed that such a set of circumstances would result in a sharp fall in the number of housing starts; and, in fact, during both periods the number of starts did fall considerably. But the fall between 68:4 and 69:4 was less than half that experienced between 65:4 and 66:4. The number of starts in 69:4 was 68,000 less than in 68:4; whereas in 66:4 it was 146,000 less than in 65:4. This paper uses a well-known econometric model of the housing market to investigate the reason for the significantly different behavior in housing starts during these two periods.[1]

Adverse financial trends were present in roughly equal intensity in both periods. In 1969 the conventional mortgage interest rate rose 93 basis points while the FHA secondary rate rose 115 points. In 1966 the conventional rate rose 67 points and the FHA rate 125 points. The net flows to deposit institutions, plus lending by the Home Loan Banks to savings and loan associations were on the order of $20.3 billion in 1966 and minus $0.4 billion in 1969. If we disregard commercial bank time deposits, the figures are $7.1 billion in 1966 and $10.6 billion in 1969. Given these roughly comparable data, it would be surprising if financial variables alone could explain the different behavior of housing starts in the two periods.

The Maisel model of the housing market attempts to explain the quarterly level of private housing starts in four separate equations using independent variables for the cost of mortgage financing, the availability of such financing, inventory factors, the relationship between the returns and costs of building or owning houses, and household income. The fifth equation attempts to predict the change in starts using a similar set of variables.

Tables 2-1 to 2-5 examine the performance of each of these equations in the fourth quarters of 1965, 1966, 1968, and 1969, and compare the predicted

1. The model itself and a fuller explanation of the theory behind it have appeared in articles by S. J. Maisel in the *American Economic Review* (June 1963), and the *Journal of Political Economy* (July/August 1968, Pt. II).

level of housing starts in each quarter with the actual number. Table 2-6 summarizes these results.

Table 2-6 groups the independent variables into three categories: monetary (interest rates and financial flows), inventory (vacancy rates and the change in inventory under construction), and "all other" (income and relative prices). It is readily apparent that while the impact of the monetary variables was even more severe in 1969 than in 1966, inventory factors more than offset the increased severity of monetary factors. According to Table 2-6, monetary factors would have accounted for a decline of 68,000 private starts (annual rate) in 1966, holding other factors constant and 102,000 starts in 1969. However, the vacancy situation, which contributed a negative 17,000 starts in 1966, became a powerful impetus to starts in 1969, with an impact equal to 51,000 additional starts more than offsetting the severe impact of monetary factors. All other variables contributed, in aggregate, insignificantly.

Clearly, it is the impact of the different vacancy levels in each period which exerts the major influence preventing the level of starts from falling as drastically in 1969 as it did in 1966. In 1966 the average rental vacancy rate was 2.5 percent; by 1969 this had fallen to 1.7 percent. The individual equations (see Tables 2-1 to 2-5) respond forcibly to these altered circumstances. In Equation 1, whereas in 1966 the vacancy variable had a positive impact of only 2,000 starts over the period, in 1969 this jumped to 81,000, more than compensating for the adverse impacts from changes in the cost and availability of financing. The same pattern is repeated in Equation 2 with *VX3* (a net increase of 70,000 starts), Equation 4 (a net increase of 78,000 starts), and in Equation 5 (a net increase of 61,000 starts).

Tables 2-1 to 2-5 are arranged so that the impact of each variable within each equation may be evaluated and then the total performance of each equation compared to the actual results may be studied. Note that the four level equations consistently tended to underpredict the extent of the drop in both 1966 and 1969, although the 1969 performance was better overall.

It might be argued that this examination has failed to give proper consideration to the activities of the FHLBB and FNMA in the two periods. Both of these organizations drastically increased their net lending in 1969 as compared to 1966: FHLBB from \$0.9 billion to \$4.0 billion, and FNMA from \$1.9 billion to \$3.9 billion. However, 1969, unlike 1966, was marked by a massive CD run-off at commercial banks which offset, to a certain degree, these moves by the two federal institutions. Furthermore, the activities of the FHLBB are considered in equations with the variable *FIN3.*[2] (The FNMA variable is designed to mirror,

2. The value of *FIN3,* the three-quarter moving average of the weighted sum of mortgage-related inflows to deposit institutions, dropped by roughly equivalent amounts in the two periods: from \$4.388 billion in 65:4 to \$2.875 billion in 66:4, and from \$4.013 billion in 68.4 to \$2.514 billion in 69:4.

with an opposite sign, the fall-off in the flow of funds to savings institutions. Because recent changes in the magnitude and method of operations of FNMA have probably introduced a structural shift, the variable probably overstates the actual monetary impact.)

The conclusion which is suggested by these results is that while variations in the flow of financing through depositary institutions are important factors in generating the housing "cycle," basic demand factors will tend to put a floor to cyclical troughs, and that the extent of the decline from peak to trough is strongly influenced by the vacancy level at the peak.

Table 2–1
Equation #1: Contributions of Variables

	65:4	*66:4*	*Change*	*68:4*	*69:4*	*Change*
FNMA3	-15	-62	-47	-78	-155	-77
FHA3	-286	-329	-43	-376	-429	-53
VX3	-249	-247	+2	-107	-26	+81
RC3	-299	-291	+8	-270	-256	+14
DIHXL	-8	-8	0	-8	-8	0
All Variables:						
Constant	1222	1222		1222	1222	
Calculated	366	285	-81	382	347	-35
Actual	375	229	-146	407	339	-68
Percent of actual decline accounted for		55%			51%	

Note: Data are expressed in thousands of private housing starts at seasonally adjusted rates.

Table 2–2
Equation #2: Contributions of Variables

	65:4	*66:4*	*Change*	*68:4*	*69:4*	*Change*
INT3	-382	-402	-20	-449	-502	-53
FNMA3	-9	-39	-30	-49	-97	-48
VX3	-217	-215	+2	-94	-22	+72
RC3	-43	-42	+1	-39	-37	+2
DIHXL	+15	+16	+1	+16	+16	0
STL1	+168	+124	-44	+176	+164	-12
STL3	-122	-121	+1	-122	-140	-18
All Variables:						
Constant	948	948		948	948	
Calculated	359	269	-90	388	331	-57
Actual	375	229	-146	407	339	-68
Percent of actual decline accounted for		62%			84%	

Note: Data are expressed in thousands of private housing starts at seasonally adjusted rates.

Table 2–3
Equation #3: Contributions of Variables

	Change 65:4–66:4	*Change 68:4–69:4*
DFHA	-56	-51
DFNMA3	-45	-75
DRC3	+8	+16
X52	+7	+29
All Variables:		
Constant	1	1
Cumulative	-85	-80
Actual	-146	-68
Percent actual decline accounted for	58%	118%

Note: Data are expressed in thousands of private housing starts at seasonally adjusted rates.

Table 2–4
Equation #4: Contributions of Variables

	65:4	*66:4*	*Change*	*68:4*	*69:4*	*Change*
INT3	-371	-391	-20	-436	-488	-52
FIN 3	+116	+73	-43	+113	+73	-40
VXL2	-321	-325	-4	-200	-126	+74
RC3	+150	+146	-4	+135	+128	-7
DIHXL	-7	-8	-1	-8	-8	0
All Variables:						
Constant	786	786		786	786	
Calculated	352	282	-70	390	365	-25
Actual	375	229	-146	407	339	-68
Percent of actual decline accounted for		48%			37%	

Note: Data are expressed in thousands of private housing starts at seasonally adjusted rates.

Table 2–5
Equation #5: Contributions of Variables

	65:4	*66:4*	*Change*	*68:4*	*69:4*	*Change*
INT3	-290	-305	-15	-340	-381	-41
FIN3	+64	+41	-23	+63	+41	-22
VXL2	-253	-256	-3	-158	-100	+58
RC3	+215	+209	-6	+194	+184	-10
DIHXL	+99	+102	+3	+107	+107	0
STL1	+178	+132	-46	+186	+174	-12
STL3	-131	-130	+1	-132	-150	-18
All Variables:						
Constant	477	477		477	477	
Calculated	359	270	-89	396	352	-44
Actual	375	229	-146	407	339	-68
Percent of actual decline accounted for		61%			65%	

Note: Data are expressed in thousands of private housing starts at seasonally adjusted rates.

Table 2–6
Summary of Comparison of Housing Starts 1966 vs. 1969

	Monetary Impact		*Inventory Impact*		*All Other Variables Impact*		*Totals*	
	1966	*1969*	*1966*	*1969*	*1966*	*1969*	*1966*	*1969*
Equation #1	-90	-130	+2	+81	+8	+14	-80	-35
Equation #2	-50	-101	-41	+42	+2	+2	-89	-57
Equation #3	-101	-126	+7	+29	+8	+16	-86	-81
Equation #4	-63	-92	-4	+74	-5	-7	-72	-25
Equation #5	-38	-63	-48	+28	-3	-10	-89	-45
Average	-68	-102	-17	+51	+2	+3	-83	-49
Average net change from 1966		-34		+68		+1		
					Actual		-146	-68
					Percent of decline accounted for		57%	72%

Note: Data are expressed in thousands of private housing starts at seasonally adjusted rates. Totals may differ slightly from those in the equation tables due to rounding.

Discussion

Mr. Ricks: We are very fortunate in having Jim Burnham present the work that he and FRB Governor Sherman Maisel did. Sherm is in Los Angeles, and regrets that he can't be here, but he is well represented by Jim Burnham.

Mr. Burnham: Thank you, Bruce. Before I begin, I would like to footnote the household series that Gene Brady put in the DRI data bank. It is based on interpolation between ten-year census benchmarks, using the March Census Bureau survey on the estimated number of households, then an annual change estimate which is put into a three-year moving average, and then interpolated on a quarterly basis. The interpolation remains an eyeball exercise, because I haven't been able to find any quarterly series which seems reasonable enough to use as a basis for interpolation for the annual average levels.

I will talk to whoever is in charge of keeping those series up-to-date, and give them an update when the 1970 benchmark comes out.

The remarks that I am presenting here today are my own, though you will detect a flavor of Sherm Maisel's philosophy and approach, and as in a lot of cases like this, you will probably find me more Papist than the Pope.

But I would like to spend most of my time by placing the model which was analyzed and used for a specific purpose in the previously distributed paper in a more general context.

Specifically, I would like to raise the question about the desirability of using what are essentially long-run equilibrium arguments to explain short-run variations in housing starts. It is not a novel issue, but I think very relevant for the purposes of this conference to bring it up. In bringing it up, however, I don't want to criticize certain econometric models of the housing market for not doing something they weren't designed to do.

But there is a trade-off here, in terms of whether or not we are going to concentrate on the historical, structural relationships in the housing market, or are really interested in building medium-term forecasting models. I simply take it as a starting assumption that for policy makers such as the boards of the Home Loan Bank System and the Federal Reserve System, that the specification of the model most relevant to them is the medium forecasting model, and they are only interested in the past insofar as it will help them to make correct decisions about the future.

I think the policy makers are entitled to ask that the model be theoretically acceptable as well as operationally useful. In terms of determining whether it is operationally useful, I think two questions should be up front. First, how much effort is going to have to be spent on forecasting exogenous variables? This consideration makes the use of large-scale econometric models highly attractive to the housing specialist, since many of the important variables exogenous to the housing sector can be endogenous to the model as a whole.

At the same time, this consideration makes me leery of using dummy variables in models, since the dummy variables are used mainly for highly unusual periods, when demands on the policy maker are greatest. It does him little good if, after the year is over, the econometrician tells him the forecast would have been on target if they had had the foresight to use a dummy variable for the past twelve months.

Secondly, the medium-term forecasting model should include as many policy instruments as possible, and they should, if at all possible, be contained in equations which deal with those sectors of primary concern to policy makers. It seems reasonable to assume that the further removed policy variables are from the relationships that policy is trying to influence, the more "noise" and probability of accumulation of error.

Let me return to the question of theoretical acceptability. The explanation of short-run movements in the level of housing starts calls for a theory of adjustment in a situation where the path toward the long-run equilibrium solution has a questionable influence on current periods and the arguments relevant to determining long-run equilibrium are not necessarily helpful in explaining short-run movements, particularly in the case of housing starts.

At the same time, there are arguments which, although not necessary in the specification of long-run models, are probably necessary in the specification of short-run models. One of these arguments, I believe, is the vacancy rate.

The vacancy rate, more than any other variable, provides a measure of the degree to which the existing housing stock is being utilized, and is thus a fairly good indicator of the current state of excess demand in terms of units. There is a value question implicit here. Are you interested in producing units, or are you interested, in the dollar value of construction? If you are a four-walls-and-a-roof man, as I consider myself, and you aren't worried about two-car garages, central air conditioning, five bedrooms, and three baths, then I think that as a housing specialist and policy maker you generally should be concerned with the number of units rather than the dollar value of construction.

In the long run, the relationship between housing asset prices and housing construction costs should also be able to express the excess demand relationship, but for short-run analytical and forecasting purposes, it is difficult to see why relative prices, particularly in view of the compound statistical and measurement difficulties involved, should be used in place of more direct measures of utilization of the existing available stock and the excess demand for housing.

A word about the nature of the residential construction process. Only about 25 percent of private starts are nonspeculative, in the sense that the ultimate occupier of the dwelling has agreed to live in it before the foundation is dug. The other three-quarters of starts are speculative, risk-taking ventures by builders who are betting that a sufficient number of their newly constructed single-family and multifamily units will be occupied by owners or renters in the near future to return a profit on their investment.

Given the necessarily long lag between starts and occupancy, builders' imperfect knowledge of housing markets, and the generally atomized nature of the residential construction industry, the existence of a cyclical pattern of behavior in housing starts should not be surprising. Indeed, the delegation of pig farmers parked outside the White House just a few weeks ago, trying to make a case for government help to their industry, reminded me that just about a year ago it was the homebuilders making the same sort of pilgrimage.

Some people have suggested a rather interesting hypothesis to explain how expectations and the monetary policy cycle operate together to produce a pro-cyclical pattern of housing starts in certain areas. Assume a part of the country were the long-run demand for housing, based on population growth, is steadily increasing. When lenders have plenty of funds to invest, they can accept a lower probability of full occupancy or sale on a given project for a given future date than the developer. But since the developer puts up only a fraction of the cost of the project, and if he is a risk lover—as most developers are reputed to be—the proposed deal will be attractive. If full occupancy or sale is not achieved and the developer is not able to meet his cash flow commitments, the lender assumes ownership of the project at a discount price, and can afford to wait the extra year or two for the project's cash flow to grow up to expectations. Thus, the ample availability of funds can quite logically contribute to a short-run disequilibrium situation.

But clearly, cyclical movements in housing starts are far more complicated than cyclical movements in hog production, if only because farmers are far less affected by the monetary policy cycle than homebuilders. I think that my prepared paper can be interpreted to show this. However, I certainly don't want to claim that the Maisel model as now specified is going to offer a really good test of this. I think the SMSA data Gene Brady spoke of earlier will provide a very interesting set of data in which to test this out.

The 1966 decline in housing starts was far more drastic than that which occurred in 1969 (39 percent vs. 17 percent), because a restrictive monetary policy period coincided with the down phase of the home-building cycle. In 1969, however, because the builders' cycle typically has a longer period than the interval between these two episodes of monetary restraint, the two cycles, monetary and builder, offset, rather than complemented each other. Parenthetically, I believe that we are now being set up, once again, for a period during which a policy of monetary restraint is going to coincide with the down phase of the building cycle. The result, once again, will be a sharp downturn in starts followed by the cyclical pilgrimage of the homebuilders' representatives to Washington.

Let me now turn to a more specific discussion of the prepared paper. The Maisel model of the housing market consists of a single equation which is specified in five slightly different ways. Four equations attempt to explain the quarterly level of starts using independent variables for the cost and availability of mortgages, inventory factors, the relative return to building or owning housing, and household income. The fifth equation attempts to predict the change in starts using a similar set of variables.

What I did in this paper parallels somewhat what Craig Swan did in his paper for the Brookings reports.

As measured by the average of the five equations, the impact of monetary policy (as measured by interest rate and financial flow variables) on starts was even more severe in 1969 than in 1966. This impact, however, was more than offset by the positive impact resulting from the inventory of vacant housing units. In other words, monetary policy "took away" 68,000 starts in 1966 and 102,000 starts in 1969. But the inventory impact, which took away 17,000 starts in 1966, "added" 51,000 in 1969, more than offsetting the increased negative impact of monetary policy.

Now, in conclusion, before the afternoon's session gets underway, I would like to prepare a fallback position, first, by describing some of the improvements in the Maisel model which are underway, but which were not ready in time for this conference.

First, it is clear that using total private new starts as the critical dependent variable is no longer acceptable in this day of mobile homes and increasing activity in multiunit construction. A greater degree of disaggregation is necessary if we are to properly assist policy makers. Consequently, we have developed the necessary data series so that the approach used in this paper can be applied to a split between single and multiunits.

Preliminary results are quite encouraging for the multiunit sector, but less so for the singles. Part of the reason for problems with the single sector may lie in the fact that almost 50 percent of single-family starts are spoken for by the final occupant before the foundation is dug, and therefore may fall outside the basic theoretical approach used in the model.

Second, we have developed data series which should reflect more accurately occupancy rates and builders' inventory under construction. The procedure used in this paper attempts to approximate builders' inventory by using the lagged dependent variable, a method fraught with considerable statistical caveats. Finally, we are experimenting with lag structures for the independent variables in place of the three-quarter moving averages currently used.

In conclusion, I would like to endorse Ray Fair's point about not using level adjustments at the end of your estimation period, since either you have to assume that your error term is normally distributed or you should be using more sophisticated estimating technique.

Mr. Friedman: You painted the scenario about the builder being a risk lover–but it is the lender that is the true risk taker, and the builder is out of it one way or another. If the house is not sold, he is not taking much risk.

Mr. Burnham: From the lender's point of view, he can count on a much longer time for the cash flow of the project to build up. The developer is really behind the eight ball. The lender can afford to wait; the builder can't.

Mr. Ricks: Don't you think they are both risk averters, and one pays the penalty of a mistake more than the other?

Mr. Burnham: Everybody, to some extent, is a risk taker, but I think the lender and the builder can have different views of the future as to when the project is going to pay off.

Mr. Smith: Can I ask about the basic model? The interest rates that were used, are they nominal or real?

Mr. Burnham: Nominal rates.

Mr. Smith: Did you try expected real rates in this, because it would seem to me that the decline in expected real rates during the period—'69 would be a lot less than in '66—or the increase would be a lot less, so you would expect a lot smaller housing decline from that factor.

Mr. Burnham: Do you have a series on expected real rates?

Mr. Smith: We are working with one in Canada. Any kind of loose thing may show a difference. It may not.

Mr. Ricks: I will give Karl Fox thirty seconds to rebut Jim Burnham's remark on behalf of the hog farmers, if he wants.

Mr. Fox: Just a comment that the hog farmers established their cyclical response, which I guess, as Henry Wallace once said, implies the persistence of damn foolishness. They initiated this kind of response a long while ago, and they are still more or less at it.

Mr. Ricks: But you can kill hogs, and people haven't destroyed housing starts yet. Right?

Mr. Fox: Henry Agard Wallace does have something like 16 million porkers on his conscience for 1934. During the OPA meat-rationing days there was some conservative newspaper columnist who used to hark back to that. The answer was, "Did you ever try eating an eighteen-year-old hog?" (Laughter.)

Mr. Ricks: So, with a more serious and less entertaining point, I wonder why you don't use net starts less demolitions.

Mr. Burnham: The demolitions, and such, are taken care of. When we estimate the vacancy rate we are also estimating the stock.

Mr. Ricks: Why don't you have as your dependent variable the net additions?

Mr. Burnham: I have tried along those lines, taking gross starts and making them net, in a sense, of additions to households and removals without much luck.

Mr. Fair: You found much less effect of the Federal Home Loan Bank activities than I did in my work. I wonder if you could explain this in terms of 1966 versus 1969, in that in 1966 there were much larger vacancies–right?

Mr. Burnham: Right.

Mr. Fair: And if you believed in 1966 that there was really a supply constraint, I guess, more so than in 1969, then I think that you could explain the fact that the Federal Home Loan Bank System had more of an effect in 1969 in boosting up the demand, keeping it from falling, in a sense that there was the demand there to be met, that the demand wasn't the constraint; whereas, in 1966 they may have tried the same thing to some extent, and did not have as much luck because the demand was not there.

Mr. Burnham: The really distinctive feature, in addition to the FNMA and Home Loan Bank activities of 1966, is the fact you had a tremendous CD run-off in 1969, and to my mind that may well have offset a good deal of the Home Loan Bank advances to the S & L's. Commercial bank lending dropped considerably.

Mr. Burnham: The fact is that the Home Loan Bank advances can be interpreted up to the 1966 requirements as simply providing liquidity reserves for the S & L's. . . .

Mr. Branson: On your point about the CD run-off–commercial bank lending offsets. . . .

Mr. Burnham: The financial variable used in the model covers this. It consists of the historical percentage of savings flows to S & L's, life insurance company net financial acquisitions, and commercial bank time deposits which go into residential mortgages, plus 100 percent of the Home Loan Bank advances; so within that variable we have covered both the Home Loan Bank advances and the commercial bank time deposits.

Mr. Branson: You seem to make the assumption that the dollar CD against the dollar Home Loan Bank loan has the same effect on the mortgage.

Mr. Kimbell: I have strong support for your interpretation and also some support for Maisel's emphasis on household formation and inventories in general, as found by looking at the regional data. The 1966 episode, which has been analyzed by several people, with emphasis on the California situation, supports the vacancy interpretations; and much of the decline in 1966 was concentrated in the western states, themselves. I found, in effect, that it seemed to be operating very strongly in 1966 to exaggerate the impact of monetary policy in housing in general. It was a sort of coherence effect analogous to a laser, which meant that in 1964 there was considerable incoherence in the local fluctuations, considerable instability in the sense that some areas were booming and some areas falling apart; but the national data was largely offsetting, so the percentage changes were substantial before that period.

In 1966 they were almost uniformly downward, but they were knocked downward by magnitudes that were considerably greater than what they were down in 1964. Some places were dropping by 20 percent in 1964; others were going up by 20 percent; in 1966, both were going down by 25 percent.

What you say, then, is sort of a coherence of local inventory cycles which produced in the national data much larger response than is apparent when you look at the local data. And especially the household formation net migration across all states of course sums to zero; whereas, at the local level it is very demanding.

With reference to your methods of estimating household formation, I found an acute problem in looking at demand variables, and it is that most of our methods for estimating these smooth over or interpolate in some fashion.

The only State, to my knowledge, that takes a census every year is Kansas. I have looked at actual census data for Kansas for metropolitan areas–Wichita, in particular–and estimated the household formation on a crude basis, and I found that when I plotted the household formation against the wild gyrations and starts that it looked as if the builders were stabilizing, if anything, that actually the oscillations in household formation were larger than the starts variations, even though the starts variations appear to be extremely dramatic in isolation.

I think frequently we are taking the household formation at the local area and smoothing across it by interpolation. It is a much more energetic variable, so I think especially if you are concerned with regional fluctuations, some of Maisel's emphasis is much more relevant than might be nationally.

Mr. Burnham: The existence of this large SMSA data bank that you have got now is going to be very helpful. When you do get this coherence of cycles, that is when the situation is really bad.

Mr. Ricks: We have a slish/slash variables and energetic variables. The language of economists is improving. (Laughter.)

We are very much excited about some migration data that is in OBE, I believe, coming from Social Security data. Does someone want to take a moment to explain that? Let's defer to Dr. Graham.

Dr. Graham: Well, I can explain what we have. We simply take a 1 percent sample from the Social Security Board of the labor force that covers the old-age security program. A 1 percent sample is tabulated quarterly. We have done nothing except on an annual basis, but it can be handled quarterly.

Once a person is in the sample, he or she remains there as long as he is in the labor force, and therefore you can trace over time and with the following demographically economic characteristics: age, race, sex, industry of occupation, county of work, and level of earnings.

The data begin in 1957. That is the first year, and we now have it through–I am not sure whether 1966 or 1967. There is a fair lag there, but special arrangements have been made to get data for the first quarter of 1970 as a one-shot affair. That will bring us up to date.

So this way it is possible to trace migration into and out of an area and also the point of origin and the point of the destination of outflow.

Mr. Fox: You talk about migration in following the 1 percent sample from one place to another. How about, say, where you would have a cross-section of most of the employed members of the labor force who are living in a certain place and at a certain time? I can't articulate this very well.

Dr. Graham: That is a much larger part of the whole tabulation–the people who did not migrate. They are stay-putters.

Mr. Fox: Let's say you have 100,000 people in a certain commuting field. A normative experiment–if they will put that into a priori coefficients, how would the demand for housing change, or the fit of 100,000 people to an existing stock of housing, how would that fit change if you varied the composition of 100,000 by age, sex, occupation, etc?

Mr. Ricks: Are you asking the question, what the results would be?

Mr. Fox: It is an intriguing thing to do there. Does a cross-section base exist?

Dr. Graham: Yes.

Mr. Ricks: Absolutely, yes.

Mr. Friend: Are the data adequate for getting an SMSA basis built on wage income?

Dr. Graham: It is a 1 percent sample. That is all I can say.

Mr. Ricks: Thank you very much.

Appendix 2A
Listing of Variables

Cost of Mortgage Financing

FHA3[a]	Yield of FHA-insured section 203 new-home mortgages sold in the secondary market
INT3	Contract rate of conventional first mortgages on new homes, as reported by the FHLBB

Availability of Mortgage Financing

FNMA3	Dollar volume of offerings of mortgages by private holders to FNMA for purchase for its secondary market portfolio—less sales from same portfolio[b]
FIN3	Sum of seasonally adjusted net inflows to financial institutions—adjusted to historic proportion of such funds invested in mortgages, and for FHLBB advances

Inventory Factors

VX3	Number of housing units available and fit for use—adjusted downwards by a cumulated factor of 0.04 percent increase in households
VXL2	Number of vacant housing units
STL1, STL3	Starts lagged one and three periods, respectively—together, an estimate of the change in inventory under construction X52 VXL2, plus the change in inventory under construction

Returns/Cost of Building/Owning Houses

RC3	Ratio of the BLS consumer price index rent component to the Boeckh residential construction cost index

Household Income

DIHXL[c]	Disposable personal income per household—seasonally adjusted

---

[a]The number suffix *3* indicates that a three-quarter moving average, lagged one period, is used.

[b]Due to series discontinuation, comparable values for 1969 have been estimated.

[c]In Equation 3, the letter prefix *D* indicates that a first difference, lagged one period, is used.

3 Monthly Housing Starts

Ray C. Fair

In order to use the housing investment equation in the money GNP sector for forecasting purposes, housing starts have to be explained within the model or else forecast exogenously. The theoretical and empirical work explaining the level of housing starts is still in its infancy [6,7], and only limited success has been achieved in developing reliable housing starts equations. The approach taken in this study is to treat the housing market as a market that is not always in equilibrium and to estimate supply and demand schedules of housing starts under this assumption. It seems to be a widespread view that the housing and mortgage market is not always in equilibrium,[1] and one of the advantages of the technique used in this chapter is that this view can be tested.

The outline of this chapter is as follows. In the next section the basic model of the housing market is presented and discussed. The technique that has been used to estimate the model is then described in Section 3.2. The technique is based on the work in Fair and Jaffee [4] and Fair [2]. The data are discussed in Section 3.3, and the results of estimating the model are presented in Section 3.4. The chapter concludes with a discussion in Section 3.5 of how the housing starts equations can be used for forecasting purposes.

3.1 A Model of the Housing and Mortgage Market

The housing and mortgage market is a difficult market to specify. The interaction between the financial (mortgage) side of the market and the real side of the market is complex, and it does not as yet appear to be well understood. In this section an attempt is made at a reasonable specification of the housing and mortgage market and of the interaction between the two sides of the market, but a number of simplifying assumptions have been made in order to keep the analysis as tractable as possible. To begin with, the present model is concerned only with the market for *new* houses (i.e., housing starts) and for the mortgage funds associated with these houses.

This article is Chapter 8 of *A Short-Run Forecasting Model of the United States Economy* (Lexington, Mass: Heath-Lexington Books, D. C. Heath and Company, 1971).

[1] See, for example, de Leeuw and Gramlich [1], pp. 482–483.

Looking first at the demand side of the market, let HS_t^D denote the demand for housing starts (new houses) during period t. Then the demand schedule for housing starts is taken to be

$$HS_t^D = f(X_t^D, \epsilon_t^D), \tag{3.1}$$

where X_t^D denotes the vector of variables that determine HS_t^D and where ϵ_t^D is an error term. The variables that have been included in the X_t^D vector in the present model will be discussed below, but in general the X_t^D vector should include such variables as population, income, the number of houses already in existence, the purchase price of new houses, and the cost of obtaining mortgage funds to finance the purchase of a house (i.e., the mortgage rate).

An important simplifying assumption will now be made concerning the relationship between the demand for housing starts and the demand for the mortgage funds associated with these starts. Let $MORT_t^D$ denote the demand for mortgage funds associated with HS_t^D. Then it is assumed that

$$\frac{MORT_t^D}{HS_t^D} = a_0 + a_1 t, \tag{3.2}$$

where t is a time trend. Equation (3.2) states that the ratio of the demand for new mortgage funds to the demand for housing starts is equal to some constant value plus a time trend. The time trend is designed to pick up any trend increase in the average size of mortgages per housing start. The assumption made in (3.2) is admittedly a highly simplifying one, since the mortgage-fund–housing-starts ratio is likely to fluctuate in the short run in response to such things as the mortgage rate, but for purposes of this study, ignoring these fluctuations may not be too serious. Equations (3.1) and (3.2) imply that the demand for new mortgage funds is, aside from a trend term, merely a function of the variables in X_t^D and the error term ϵ_t^D.

Turning next to the supply side of the market, let HS_t^S denote the supply of housing starts during period t. Then the supply schedule of housing starts is taken to be

$$HS_t^S = g(X_t^S, \epsilon_t^S), \tag{3.3}$$

where X_t^S denotes the vector of variables that determines HS_t^S and where ϵ_t^S is an error term. In general, the X_t^S vector should include such variables as the price of houses, the cost of building houses (materials and supplies plus labor costs), and the cost of short-term credit. Home builders, in other words, are likely to decide how many new houses to build on the basis of the price of houses vis-à-vis their building cost and on the basis of the cost of short-term credit. Note that it is the cost of short-term credit that is likely to affect the supply of housing starts and not the cost of long-term credit, as reflected in, say, the mortgage rate. Home builders generally need a mortgage commitment from one of the financial intermediaries before they can get short-term loans from commercial banks; but, providing that commitments are available, the mortgage rate associated with these commitments should not directly concern them. The mortgage cost is incurred by the person who buys the house and takes out the mortgage, not by the person who builds the house.

Finally, let $MORT_t^S$ denote the supply of new mortgage funds during period t. Then the supply schedule of mortgage funds is taken to be

$$MORT_t^S = h(Z_t^S, \eta_t^S), \tag{3.4}$$

where Z_t^S denotes the vector of variables that determines $MORT_t^S$ and where η_t^S is an error term. The variables that have been included in the Z_t^S vector in this study will be discussed below; but in general the vector should include such variables as deposit flows into financial intermediaries, the mortgage rate, and interest rates on competing assets. Since mortgages are supplied primarily by financial intermediaries, deposit flows into these intermediaries should have a positive effect on the supply of mortgages. Also, for a given flow of deposits, financial intermediaries are likely to put more of the flow into the mortgage market the higher is the mortgage rate relative to other interest rates.

The demand and supply sides of the housing and mortgage market differ in that the people who demand new houses are essentially the same people who demand mortgage funds, whereas the people who supply (build) new houses are in general not the same people who supply mortgage funds. There are thus three groups of people or institutions under consideration: the consumers, the home builders, and the financial intermediaries. If the housing and mortgage market were always in equilibrium, then it would be the case that:

$$HS_t = HS_t^D = HS_t^S, \tag{3.5}$$

and

$$MORT_t = MORT_t^D = MORT_t^S, \tag{3.6}$$

where HS_t is the actual number of housing starts during period t and MORT_t is the actual value of new mortgage funds during period t. In equilibrium, the purchase price of houses would clear the housing side of the market, as in (3.5), and the mortgage rate would clear the mortgage side of the market, as in (3.6). Note that the assumption made in (3.2) above implies that in equilibrium,

$$\frac{MORT_t}{HS_t} = a_0 + a_1 t.$$

If the housing and mortgage market is not always in equilibrium, then (3.5) and (3.6) obviously do not always hold, and the question arises as to how the disequilibrium aspects of the market should be specified. In this study the specification is as follows. It is first assumed that the actual ratio of new mortgage funds to housing starts is always equal to $a_0 + a_1 t$. It was seen above that, given (3.2), the ratio is equal to $a_0 + a_1 t$ in equilibrium; and it is now assumed that the actual ratio is equal to $a_0 + a_1 t$ even if the market is not in equilibrium. Because of this assumption, the supply of mortgages from the financial intermediaries in (3.4) can be translated into an equivalent supply of housing starts. The equivalent supply is $MORT_t^S/(a_0 + a_1 t)$. There are thus two supply schedules of housing starts under consideration – the supply schedule from the home builders and the supply schedule from the financial intermediaries. It is finally assumed that the observed quantity of housing starts is equal to the minimum of the *ex ante* demand and supply schedules:

$$HS_t = \min \left\{ HS_t^D, HS_t^S, \frac{MORT_t^S}{a_0 + a_1 t} \right\}. \tag{3.7}$$

Equation (3.7) implies that there are three possible constraints in the housing market. Either demand is the constraint (HS_t^D is the minimum) so that home builders and financial intermediaries go unsatisfied at prevailing prices, or supply from the home builders is the constraint (HS_t^S is the minimum) so that demanders and financial intermediaries go unsatisfied, or supply from the financial intermediaries is the constraint ($MORT_t^S/(a_0 + a_1 t)$ is the minimum) so that demanders and home builders go unsatisfied. It appears to be commonly accepted that most of the "supply" constraint in the housing market comes from the financial sector, and thus as a simplifying approximation in this study, HS_t^S is assumed always to be greater than or equal to the minimum of HS_t^D and $MORT_t^S/(a_0 + a_1 t)$. This assumption simplifies matters in that the supply schedule of home builders in (3.3) does not have to be specified. In a more detailed study of the housing market it would, of course, be desirable to specify and estimate the home builders' side of the market as well.

What remains to be done, then, is to specify equations (3.1) and (3.4). With respect to equation (3.1), the demand for housing starts is assumed to be a function of (1) population growth and trend income, both of which are approximated by a time trend; (2) the number of houses in existence or under construction during the previous month; (3) the mortgage rate lagged two months; and (4) seasonal factors.

Let H_t denote the number of houses in existence or under construction during month t and let HS_t continue to denote the number of housing starts during month t. Then H_t is approximated as follows. It is assumed that the number of houses removed (i.e., destroyed) each month is constant from month to month, which implies that

$$HS_t = H_t - H_{t-1} + b_0, \tag{3.8}$$

where b_0 is the constant number of removals each month. Equation (3.8) then implies that for any base period 0:

$$H_t = H_0 + \sum_{i=1}^{t} HS_i - b_0 t, \tag{3.9}$$

where H_0 is the number of houses in the base period. In other words, the number of houses at the end of month t is equal to the sum of past housing starts less the sum of past removals, the sum of past removals being approximated by a time trend, as implied by the assumption in equation (3.8).

With respect to seasonal factors, the housing starts series does have a pronounced seasonal pattern in it, due in large part to the weather, and in an attempt to account for this pattern eleven seasonal dummy variables were included in the equation.[2] An alternative approach would have been to use the seasonally adjusted housing starts series that is published by the Department of Commerce, but the Department of Commerce does not adjust the series for the number of working days in the month. This causes the month-to-month changes in the seasonally adjusted series to be mroe erratic than is really warranted. In an attempt to account in this study for the influence of the number of working days in the month on the number of housing starts for that month, a working-day variable was included in the equation. The variable was constructed by adding up all of the weekdays in the month less any holidays that fell on these days. The holidays were excluded in the following manner. One day was always excluded for January, September, November, and December, and one day was also excluded for May and July unless May 30 or July 4 respectively fell on a Saturday.

The demand schedule for housing starts is thus taken to be

$$HS_t^D = \sum_{I=1}^{11} d_I DI_t + d_{12} W_t + b_1 H_{t-1} + b_2 t + b_3 RM_{t-2} + \epsilon_t^D, \tag{3.10}$$

where DI_t is the seasonal dummy variable for month I, $b_2 t$ is the trend term, and

2. Dummy variable 1 being equal to one in January, minus one in December, and zero otherwise; dummy variable 2 being equal to one in February, minus one in December, and zero otherwise; and so on. A constant term was included in the equation, which is the reason why only eleven dummy variables were included. The values for December were set equal to minus one instead of zero so that the seasonal factors could be more readily identified from the estimates of the coefficients of the dummy variables.

RM_{t-2} is the mortgage rate lagged two months. Using the definition of H_t in equation (3.9), equation (3.10) becomes

$$HS_t^D = \sum_{I=1}^{11} d_I DI_t + d_{12} W_t + (b_1 H_0 + b_1 b_0)$$

$$+ b_1 \sum_{i=1}^{t-1} HS_i + (b_2 - b_1 b_0)t + b_3 RM_{t-2} + \epsilon_t^D, \qquad (3.11)$$

which introduces the constant $b_1 H_0 + b_1 b_0$ in the equation and changes the interpretation of the coefficient of the time trend. The data that have been used to estimate equation (3.11) will be discussed below.

It should be noted that the purchase price of houses has not been included as an explanatory variable in the demand equation. Theoretically the price of houses (or, more specifically, the price of houses deflated by some general price index) should be included in the equation, but this was not done for the work here because of the difficulty that would be involved in forecasting the price of houses exogenously. To the extent that the influence of the (relative) price of houses on the demand for housing starts is not picked up by the time trend in equation (3.11), the equation is misspecified, but for short-run forecasting purposes this misspecification is not likely to be too serious. It should also be noted that various lagged values of the mortgage rate were tried in the work below, and the mortgage rate lagged two months gave the best results for the demand equation.

With respect to equation (3.4), the supply of new mortgage funds is assumed to be a function of (1) lagged deposit flows into Saving and Loan Associations (SLAs) and Mutual Savings Banks (MSBs), (2) lagged borrowings by the SLAs from the Federal Home Loan Bank (FHLB), (3) the mortgage rate lagged one month, and (4) seasonal factors. Let DSF_t denote the flow of private deposits into SLAs and MSBs during month t, and let DHF_t denote the flow of borrowings by the SLAs from the FHLB during month t. Various lags and moving averages of *DSF* and *DHF* were tried in the work below, and the best results were achieved by using the six-month moving average of *DSF* lagged one month (denoted by $DSF6_{t-1}$) and the three-month moving average of *DHF* lagged two months (denoted as $DHF3_{t-2}$). The results were not very sensitive, however, to slightly different specifications. The six-month moving average of *DSF* has the advantage of eliminating the monthly fluctuations in the series due to the quarterly interest payments by the SLAs and MSBs and the switching of funds at the beginning of each quarter. The current and various lagged values of the mortgage rate were also tried in the supply equation, and the one-month lagged value gave the best results. Seasonal factors were assumed to enter the supply equation in the same way in which they entered the demand equation. The supply of new mortgage funds is thus taken to be

$$MORT_t^S = \sum_{I=1}^{11} d_I' DI_t + d_{12}' W_t + c_1 DSF6_{t-1} + c_2 DHF3_{t-2}$$

$$+ c_3 RM_{t-1} + \eta_t^S. \tag{3.12}$$

The equivalent supply of housing starts from the financial sector was defined above to be $MORT_t^S/(a_0 + a_1 t)$. Let HS_t^{FS} denote this equivalent supply. Then $MORT_t^S = (a_0 + a_1 t)HS_t^{FS}$. As a further simplifying assumption, $t \cdot HS_t^{FS}$ will be approximated by $t + HS_t^{FS} + c_0$, where c_0 is a constant. This then implies that

$$HS_t^{FS} = \frac{1}{a_0 + a_1} (-a_1 c_0 - a_1 t + MORT_t^S).$$

Using equation (3.12) and ignoring the $1/(a_0 + a_1)$ multiplier, the equation determining HS_t^{FS} can thus be written

$$HS_t^{FS} = - a_1 c_0 - a_1 t + \sum_{I=1}^{11} d_I' DI_t + d_{12}' W_t + c_1 DSF6_{t-1}$$

$$+ c_2 DHF3_{t-2} + c_3 RM_{t-1} + \eta_t^S. \tag{3.13}$$

In other words, equation (3.12) explaining the supply of mortgage funds can be transformed into an equation explaining the equivalent supply of housing starts from the financial sector. The latter differs from equation (3.12) only in that a constant term and a time trend have been added to the equation. The time trend is designed to pick up any trend in the mortgage-fund–housing-starts ratio.

Equations (3.11) and (3.13) thus determine the demand and supply of housing starts respectively, and the model is closed by equation (3.7), which from the above assumption about home builders can be written

$$HS_t = \min\left\{HS_t^D, HS_t^{FS}\right\}. \tag{3.14}$$

The technique that was used to estimate equations (3.11) and (3.13) will now be discussed.

3.2 The Estimation Technique[3]

In Fair and Jaffe [4] four techniques for estimating disequilibrium markets were developed. Three of the techniques were designed to separate the sample period into demand and supply regimes so that each schedule could be fitted against the observed quantity for the sample points falling within its regime. The fourth technique was designed to adjust the observed quantity for the effects of rationing so that both schedules could be estimated over the entire sample period using the adjusted quantity. The fourth technique has been used in this study, and it will be briefly outlined below. All four of the techniques developed in [4] were used to estimate the present model, and two of the four techniques gave good results. These results are presented and compared in [4], Section III. The fourth technique was chosen to be used in this study because it appeared to be somewhat more suited for forecasting purposes.

The technique used here is based on the following assumption about how prices (or, in this case, interest rates) are determined:

$$\Delta RM_t = q(HS_t^D - HS_t^{FS}), \qquad 0 \leqslant q \leqslant \infty. \tag{3.15}$$

Equation (3.15) states that the change in the mortgage rate is directly proportional to the amount of excess demand in the market. q equal to zero is the polar case of no adjustment, and q equal to ∞ is the polar case of perfect adjustment. Equation (3.15) is consistent with many theories of dynamic price setting behavior.

Solving equation (3.15) for excess demand yields:

$$HS_t^D - HS_t^{FS} = \frac{1}{q} \Delta RM. \tag{3.16}$$

If q can be estimated, then the actual amount of excess demand or supply can be determined directly from the change in the mortgage rate, and thus both the demand and supply schedules can be estimated over the entire sample period. The procedure described below simultaneously estimates q and the parameters of the two schedules.

First consider a period of rising rates. From equation (3.16) it is known that this will be a period of excess demand; and thus, from equation (3.14), the observed quantity will equal the supply. Consequently, the supply function can be directly estimated using the observed quantity as the dependent variable:

$$HS_t = HS_t^{FS}, \qquad \Delta RM_t \geqslant 0, \tag{3.17}$$

---

3. Some of the discussion in this section follows closely the discussion in [4], Section II.

where HS_t^{FS} is given in (3.13). Furthermore, because the supply equals the observed quantity, equation (3.16) can be rewritten as

$$HS_t = HS_t^D - \frac{1}{q} \Delta RM_t, \qquad \Delta RM_t \geqslant 0, \tag{3.18}$$

where HS_t^D is given in (3.11). Thus the parameters of the demand function can also be estimated, using the observed quantity as the dependent variable, as long as the change in the mortgage rate is included in the equation as an implicit adjustment for the amount of rationing.

In periods of falling rates essentially the same principles apply. The supply and demand functions will then be estimated as, respectively:

$$HS_t = HS_t^{FS} - \frac{1}{q}|\Delta RM_t|, \qquad \Delta RM_t \leqslant 0, \tag{3.19}$$

and

$$HS_t = HS_t^D, \qquad \Delta RM_t \leqslant 0. \tag{3.20}$$

Indeed, the system of equations (3.17) to (3.20) can be reduced to a single demand equation and a single supply equation, each to be estimated over the entire sample period, by making the appropriate adjustment for the change in the mortgage rate:

$$HS_t = HS_t^D - \frac{1}{q}/\Delta RM_t/, \tag{3.21}$$

where

$$/\Delta RM_t/ = \begin{cases} \Delta RM_t & \text{if } \Delta RM_t \geqslant 0 \\ 0 & \text{otherwise} \end{cases}$$

and

$$HS_t = HS_t^{FS} - \frac{1}{q}\backslash \Delta RM_t \backslash, \tag{3.22}$$

where

$$\backslash \Delta RM_t \backslash = \begin{cases} -\Delta RM_t & \text{if } \Delta RM_t \leqslant 0 \\ 0 & \text{otherwise} \end{cases}$$

It is apparent that equation (3.21) is equivalent to the two demand equations (3.18) and (3.20) and that equation (3.22) is equivalent to the two supply equations (3.17) and (3.19).

Equations (3.21) and (3.22) can thus be estimated directly, given the specifications of HS_t^D and HS_t^{FS} in (3.11) and (3.13) respectively, but two problems occur in the estimation. One problem is that the same coefficient $1/q$ appears in both equations. The second problem is the likelihood of simultaneous equation bias due to the endogeneity of $/\Delta RM_t/$ and $\backslash\Delta RM_t\backslash$. The introduction of equation (3.15) above makes RM_t an endogenous variable, and even though RM enters with a lag in (3.11) and (3.13), RM_t still enters in equations (3.21) and (3.22) through the $/\Delta RM_t/$ and $\backslash\Delta RM_t\backslash$ variables. These two problems are heightened in the present case by the fact that the error terms ϵ_t^D and η_t^D, which enter equations (3.21) and (3.22) respectively, are assumed to be serially correlated.

Ignoring the fact that $1/q$ appears in both equations, the problem of simultaneous equation bias can be handled in the manner described by Fair and Jaffee [4]. Essentially the two-stage least squares technique can be used, but the step function characteristic of $/\Delta RM_t/$ and $\backslash\Delta RM_t\backslash$ makes the application of the technique somewhat more complicated than usual. In addition, if the error terms are serially correlated, the technique described in Fair [3] must be used in place of the standard two-stage least squares technique. Ignoring the problem of simultaneous equation bias, the constraint across equations can be taken into account by using the technique developed in Fair [2]. This technique is designed for the estimation of models with restrictions across equations and serially correlated errors. In Fair and Jaffee [4], both of these techniques were used to estimate the present model, and both yielded reasonable results. Since techniques are not yet available for dealing with simultaneous equation bias and restrictions across equations at the same time, it is not clear theoretically which technique should be used. One sacrifices efficiency to gain consistency, while the other gains efficiency at a cost of consistency. The decision was made in this study to ignore possible simultaneous equation bias and use the second technique to account for the restriction across the two equations. This technique is somewhat easier to use than the other one, and this is the main reason for its use here.

It should be pointed out that the technique used here is based on the assumption that the error terms in the two equations (i.e., ϵ_t^D and η_t^S in (3.11) and (3.13) above) are each first order serially correlated, but are uncorrelated with one another. While it may not be too unrealistic to assume that the demand and supply error terms are uncorrelated, it may be unrealistic to assume that the error terms in equations (3.21) and (3.22) are uncorrelated. This is because HS_t may be measured with error. If HS_t is measured with error, this same error will be included in both (3.21) and (3.22), and thus the error terms in the two equations will be correlated. To the extent that this is true, the technique used here loses efficiency by not taking the correlation into account.

Table 3-1. List and Description of the Variables Used in the Monthly Housing Starts Sector.

HS_t	=	Private Nonfarm Housing Starts in thousands of units.
RM_t	=	FHA Mortgage Rate series on new homes in units of 100 (beginning-of-month data).
$DSLA_t$	=	Savings Capital (Deposits) of Savings and Loan Associations in millions of dollars.
$DMSB_t$	=	Deposits of Mutual Savings Banks in millions of dollars.
DSF_t	=	$(DSLA_t + DMSB_t) - (DSLA_{t-1} + DMSB_{t-1})$.
$DSF6_t$	=	Six-month moving average of *DSF*.
$DHLB_t$	=	Advances of the Federal Home Loan Bank to Savings and Loan Associations in millions of dollars.
DHF_t	=	$DHLB_t - DHLB_{t-1}$
$DHF3_t$	=	Three-month moving average of *DHF*.
W_t	=	Number of working days in month t.
DI_t	=	Dummy variable I for month t, $I = 1, \ldots, 11$.

3.3 The Data

The data that have been used to estimate the demand and supply equations are presented in Table 3-1. All of the variables listed in the table are seasonally unadjusted. Data on HS_t are currently published in *Economic Indicators,*[4] and data on the three deposit variables and the mortgage rate are currently published in the *Federal Reserve Bulletin.* Data on the RM_t series were not directly available for January 1959 through April 1960, and the figures used here were constructed from an FHA series on the average of new and existing conventional mortgage rates. The data on RM_t and W_t are presented in Appendix A for the January 1959 to December 1969 period. (See *A Short-Run Forecasting Model of the United States Economy,* p. 250.) The other data used in this chapter are easily obtainable from *Economic Indicators* or the *Federal Reserve Bulletin.*

3.4 The Results

Equations (3.21) and (3.22) were estimated by the above technique for the June 1959 to December 1969 period, with the following results:[5]

4. Actually, the HS_t series was discontinued in December 1969. Beginning in 1970 the breakdown of private housing starts into farm and nonfarm was no longer made. The number of nonfarm housing starts was always a small fraction of the total number of housing starts, and the decision was made by the Department of Commerce to discontinue the breakdown into farm and nonfarm. This change does not affect the work in this study, but for future purposes the published figures on total housing starts will have to be adjusted downward slightly.

5. The steel and automobile strikes appeared to have little effect on the level of housing starts, and so no observations were omitted from the period of estimation for the housing starts equations because of the strikes.

$$HS_t = \sum_{I=1}^{11} \hat{d}_I DI_t + \underset{(4.63)}{2.70}\, W_t + \underset{(2.46)}{112.95} - \underset{(2.27)}{.0709} \sum_{i=1}^{t-1} HS_i + \underset{(2.31)}{8.48}\, t$$

$$- \underset{(1.54)}{.127}\, RM_{t-2} - \underset{(2.81)}{.412}\, /\Delta RM_t/ \qquad (3.23)$$

$\hat{r} = \underset{(17.54)}{.841}$

$SE = 8.98$

$R\Delta^2 = .790$

127 observ.

$$HS_t = \sum_{I=1}^{11} \hat{d}_I DI_t + \underset{(4.42)}{2.84}\, W_t - \underset{(1.75)}{49.22} - \underset{(2.63)}{.164}\, t + \underset{(8.07)}{.0541}\, DSF6_{t-1}$$

$$+ \underset{(5.27)}{.0497} DHF3_{t-2} + \underset{(2.67)}{.100}\, RM_{t-1} - \underset{(2.81)}{.412}\, \backslash \Delta RM_t \backslash \qquad (3.24)$$

$\hat{r} = \underset{(6.64)}{.507}$

$SE = 8.30$

$R\Delta^2 = .822$

127 observ.

$\hat{d}_1 = -34.44$ (12.52)	$\hat{d}_6 = 19.84$ (7.22)	$\hat{d}'_1 = -34.38$ (14.21)	$\hat{d}'_6 = 20.69$ (8.54)
$\hat{d}_2 = -33.72$ (11.46)	$\hat{d}_7 = 15.16$ (5.56)	$\hat{d}'_2 = -38.85$ (14.36)	$\hat{d}'_7 = 12.03$ (5.14)
$\hat{d}_3 = -9.67$ (2.87)	$\hat{d}_8 = 11.97$ (4.27)	$\hat{d}'_3 = -7.33$ (2.83)	$\hat{d}'_8 = 8.46$ (3.24)
$\hat{d}_4 = 18.62$ (5.47)	$\hat{d}_9 = 8.55$ (2.91)	$\hat{d}'_4 = 20.97$ (7.88)	$\hat{d}'_9 = 6.57$ (2.57)
$\hat{d}_5 = 23.72$ (7.76)	$\hat{d}_{10} = 11.61$ (3.85)	$\hat{d}'_5 = 36.68$ (11.20)	$\hat{d}'_{10} = 10.01$ (3.83)
	$\hat{d}_{11} = -4.88$ (1.53)		$\hat{d}'_{11} = -7.74$ (3.16)

$\hat{r}$ in equations (3.23) and (3.24) denotes the estimate of the first order serial correlation coefficient. The R-squared is again the R-squared taking the dependent variable in first differenced form and is a measure of the percent of the variance of the change in HS_t explained by the equation. Note that because of the constraint that has been imposed on the model, the estimate of the coefficient of $/\Delta RM_t/$ in (3.23) is the same as the estimate of the coefficient of $\backslash\Delta RM_t\backslash$ in (3.24).

The dummy variables are in general highly significant in equations (3.23) and (3.24), which indicates the pronounced seasonality in the series. The working-day variable, W_t, is also significant in the equations, and thus the number of working days in a month does appear to influence the number of housing starts for that month. All of the other coefficient estimates in the two equations are of the expected sign, and all but the estimate of the coefficient of RM_{t-2} in (3.23) and the estimate of the constant term in (3.24) are significant. The time trend has a positive effect in the demand equation (3.23) and a negative effect in the supply equation (3.24), and the mortgage rate (RM_{t-2} or RM_{t-1}) has a negative effect in the demand equation and a positive effect in the supply equation. The time trend is expected to have a positive effect in the demand equation, since it is mainly proxying for population growth and trend income. The deposit flow variables are highly significant in the supply equation, and the housing stock variable is moderately significant in the demand equation. The fact that the time trend and the mortgage rate have opposite effects in the two equations (using the same dependent variable) certainly supports the hypothesis that (3.23) represents a demand equation and (3.24) a supply equation.

The estimate of the coefficients of $/\Delta RM_t/$ and $\backslash\Delta RM_t\backslash$ in (3.23) and (3.24) is of the expected negative sign and is significant. The significance of the estimate indicates that the housing market is not always in equilibrium and that rationing does occur. When equations (3.23) and (3.24) were estimated separately without imposing the constraint (by the standard Cochrane-Orcutt technique), the estimate of the coefficient of $/\Delta RM_t/$ in (3.23) was -.408 and the estimate of the coefficient of $\backslash\Delta RM_t\backslash$ in (3.24) was -.438. These compare with the restricted estimate of -.412. It is remarkable that the unconstrained estimates are so similar, which perhaps provides further support to the view that rationing does occur in the housing market.

The estimate of the serial correlation coefficient is larger in the demand equation (.841) than it is in the supply equation (.507), and the fit of the demand equation is somewhat worse than that of the supply equation (SE = 8.98 vs. 8.30).

A number of other variables were tried in the two equations, especially in equation (3.24); and some of these results should be mentioned. First, different lags of the mortgage rate were tried in the two equations, and while RM_{t-2} and RM_{t-1} gave the best results in (3.23) and (3.24) respectively, the results were not substantially changed when slightly different lags were used. Theoretically, of course, it is not the absolute size of the mortgage rate that should matter, but the size of the mortgage rate relative to rates on alternative assets. A number of yield differential variables were tried in the equations, but with no success. While theoretically not very satisfying, it definitely appeared to be the absolute level of rates that mattered and not rate differences.

As mentioned above, different lags of the deposit flow variables in (3.24) were tried, and the ones presented in (3.24) gave the best results. Deposit flows into Life Insurance Companies and Commercial Banks were also tried in (3.24), but these flows added almost no explanatory power to the equation. Deposit and mortgage *stock* variables of the SLAs and MSBs were also tried in (3.24), and again with no real success. The flow variables always dominated the stock variables, which probably indicates that the adjustment of SLAs and MSBs to changing conditions is fairly rapid. The flow variables of the SLAs and MSBs were also tried separately in (3.24), and the coefficient estimates were close enough so that it was decided to consider only the sum of two flow variables. Notice also that in (3.24) the coefficient estimate of DHF_{t-2} is nearly the same as the coefficient estimate of $DSF6_{t-1}$. The lag seemed to be slightly different for the *DHF3* variable than for the *DSF6* variable, however, and it was decided to treat these two variables separately.

Finally, the mortgage holdings of the Federal National Mortgage Association (FNMA) was tried as an explanatory variable in equation (3.24), but with no success.[6] Both stock and flow variables were tried and various moving averages and lags were tried, and none of these variables was significant. Most of the time the estimates were even of the wrong sign. The results in this study thus indicate that for policy purposes, the Federal Home Loan Bank lending activity (as reflected through $DHF3_{t-2}$ in (3.24)) has much more of an effect on the level of housing starts than does the activity of FNMA.[7] These results are, of course, not conclusive, since the level of aggregation is so high, but they do seem to indicate the importance of the FHLB relative to FNMA. It should be noted, however, that not even the FHLB will have an effect on housing starts if demand and not supply is the constraint.

3.6 The Use of the Housing Starts Equation for Forecasting Purposes

There are two basic ways in which equations (3.23) and (3.24) can be used for forecasting purposes. One way is to treat ΔRM_t as exogenous. Assuming

6. In 1968 FNMA was split into two groups (the new FNMA and the Government National Mortgage Association), but in this study the two groups were treated as one.

7. Jaffee [5] in a detailed study of the mortgage market has found that the activity of FNMA has little effect on the total stock of mortgages, which is consistent with the conclusions reached in this study.

ΔRM_t to be exogenous, let $\overline{HS}_t$ denote the predicted value of HS_t from equation (3.23), let $\widetilde{HS}_t$ denote the predicted value of HS_t from equation (3.24), and let $\widehat{HS}_t$ equal a weighted average of the two predicted values: $\widehat{HS}_t = \lambda \overline{HS}_t + (1 - \lambda) \widetilde{HS}_t$. It is easy to show that if the error terms in equations (3.23) and (3.24) are independent and if the desire is to choose λ so as to minimize

$$\sum_{t=1}^{T} (HS_t - \widehat{HS}_t)^2,$$

then the optimum value of λ is $\sigma_1^2/(\sigma_1^2 + \sigma_2^2)$, where σ_1^2 is the variance of the error term in equation (3.24), σ_2^2 is the variance of the error term in equation (3.23), and T is the number of observations. From estimates of σ_1^2 and σ_2^2, therefore, an estimate of λ can be used for forecasting purposes. In the present case the estimate of λ is $(8.30)^2/[(8.30)^2 + (8.98)^2] = .46$.[8] In other words, the predictions from equation (3.23) are weighted slightly less than those from (3.24), since the estimate of the variance of the error term is slightly larger in (3.23).

The other way in which (3.23) and (3.24) can be used for forecasting purposes is to treat ΔRM_t as endogenous. Let $\widehat{HS}_t^D$ denote the predicted value of demand, and let $\widehat{HS}_t^{FS}$ denote the predicted value of supply. $\widehat{HS}_t^D$ is obtained from (3.23) by ignoring the $/\Delta RM_t/$ term, and $\widehat{HS}_t^{FS}$ is obtained from (3.24) by ignoring the $\backslash \Delta RM_t \backslash$ term. [See (3.21) and (3.22).] Then given $\widehat{HS}_t^D$ and $\widehat{HS}_t^{FS}$, the predicted value of ΔRM_t (denoted as $\Delta\widehat{RM}_t$) can be obtained from equation (3.15), using as the estimate of q the reciprocal of the estimate of the coefficient of $/\Delta RM_t/$ and $\backslash \Delta RM_t \backslash$ in (3.23) and (3.24). $\Delta\widehat{RM}_t$ can be used to compute $/\Delta\widehat{RM}_t/$ and $\backslash \Delta\widehat{RM}_t \backslash$, and the predicted value of the actual number of housing starts, HS_t, can then be computed as

$$\widehat{HS}_t = \widehat{HS}_t^D - .412/\Delta\widehat{RM}_t/.$$

From equations (3.15), (3.21), and (3.22), it can be seen that the latter expression is the same as $\widehat{HS}_t^{FS} - .412\backslash \Delta\widehat{RM}_t \backslash$. Since RM also enters equations (3.23) and (3.24) with a lag (as RM_{t-1} and RM_{t-2}), in a dynamic simulation or forecast the values for $\widehat{RM}_{t-1}$ and $\widehat{RM}_{t-2}$ can be taken from the $\Delta\widehat{RM}_t$ series.

Treating ΔRM_t as endogenous thus yields one predicted value of HS_t, whereas treating ΔRM_t as exogenous yields two. There are, in other words, two

8. The question of degrees of freedom has been ignored in this discussion. The estimates of the standard errors in (3.23) and (3.24) have been adjusted for degrees of freedom, whereas the variances that result from the above minimization are not so adjusted. Since the number of variables in equation (3.23) is only one less than the number in (3.24), however, the difference between adjusting or not adjusting for degrees of freedom is trivial.

independent pieces of information in the system of equations (3.15), (3.23), and (3.24). The decision was made in this study to treat ΔRM_t as exogenous and generate the two predictions of HS_t. Some initial experimentation was done treating ΔRM_t as endogenous, and while the static simulation predictions of ΔRM_t from equation (3.15) were fairly good, the equation was sensitive to dynamic error accumulation and to errors made in forecasting the exogeneous variables. The results seemed to indicate that ΔRM_t could be more accurately forecast exogenously than by the use of equation (3.15).

Given that ΔRM_t is to be taken as exogenous, the question arises as to how the two predictions from (3.23) and (3.24) are to be weighted. The derivation at the beginning of the section suggested that the predictions should be weighted by the estimates of the variances of the error terms in the two equations. The derivation was based on the assumption that the errors in the two equations are uncorrelated. To the extent that the errors are positively correlated, it can be seen that the above minimization approach implies that even more weight should be attached to the equation with the smaller variance. In the limit, if the errors were perfectly correlated, it can be shown that all of the weight should be given to the equation with the smaller variance. The error terms in the two equations are in fact positively correlated (as a regression of one set of error terms on the other revealed), which is probably due in part to errors of measurement in the HS_t series. In spite of this, in the work below the predictions from the two equations have been weighted equally: equation (3.24) with the smaller variance has not been weighted more. For actual forecasting purposes, the better fit of equation (3.24) is somewhat illusory, since the equation includes the two important variables, $DSF6_{t-1}$ and $DHF3_{t-2}$, which must be forecast exogenously. In equation (3.23) the only exogenous variable that is not trivial to forecast is the mortgage rate. On these grounds, then, equation (3.23) should be given more weight, and in the final analysis the simple compromise of treating both equations equally was made.

Discussion

Mr. Ricks: The next speaker is Ray Fair. We are very fascinated with the housing market disequilibrium work Ray is doing. We also respect the way he has concerned himself with the interaction of supply and demand variables.

Mr. Fair: If I were going to title this talk other than Chapter 8, it would be something like, "A Way of Looking at the Housing and Mortgage Market." The housing and mortgage market is a difficult market to specify, and the interaction between the financial side of the market and the real side of the market does not appear from my reading of the literature to be well understood. There also appears to be some confusion on whether the equations that are estimated to explain housing starts or mortgage flows are demand equations, supply equations, or reduced form equations incorporating both demand and supply variables. My approach to the specification of the housing and mortgage market is as follows:

I conceive of three basic participants in the housing and mortgage market, two demand curves, and two supply curves. The first group of participants are the people who actually buy the houses. These people generally demand both houses and the mortgage funds needed to finance housing purchases. The second group of participants are the people who actually build the houses – the construction sector or the real supply side of the market. The third group of participants are the people who supply the money to finance the housing purchases. This group – the financial supply side of the market – primarily includes savings and loan associations and mutual savings banks, with life insurance companies and commercial banks playing a somewhat smaller role.

What I have tried to do in my work is to specify in as reasonable a way as possible the two demand curves and the two supply curves and then to develop a model of how the three groups of participants interact in the housing and mortgage market. There are many factors that indicate that the housing and mortgage market is not always in equilibrium, and in the specification of the model an attempt has been made to incorporate disequilibrium aspects. What I would like to do here in the next few minutes is to outline the model briefly and then to make a few general comments.

Since my work was primarily concerned with forecasting total housing starts, I made a number of simplifying assumptions that should be relaxed in a more detailed study of the housing and mortgage market. These simplifying assumptions will be evident in what follows. Looking first at the demand side of the market, the demand for housing starts, HS_t^D is specified to be:

$$HS_t^D = f(X_t^D, \epsilon_t^D), \tag{1}$$

where X_t^D is a vector of variables that determine HS_t^D and where ϵ_t^D is an error term. The variables that affect HS_t^D are well known and include such variables as population growth, normal or trend income, the number of houses already in existence, the mortgage rate, and the price of houses relative to some general price index. If desired, the price of houses can be looked upon as including mortgage costs, in which case the mortgage rate would not enter as a separate variable.

With respect to the demand for mortgages, I made the following assumption:

$$\frac{MORT_t^D}{HS_t^D} = a_0 + a_1 t, \tag{2}$$

where $MORT_t^D$ is the demand for mortgage funds associated with HS_t^D. Equation (2) states that the mortgage value per housing start is a simple linear function of time: short-run fluctuations in the mortgage-fund–housing-starts ratio are ignored. While this assumption is quite simple, it did not appear to me to be overly restrictive.

Turning next to the supply side, the real supply side of housing starts, HS_t^S is specified to be:

$$HS_t^S = g(X_t^S, \epsilon_t^S), \tag{3}$$

where X_t^S is a vector of variables that determine HS_t^S and where ϵ_t^S is an error term. The variables that affect HS_t^S are likely to include the selling price of houses relative to their building cost and the cost of short-term credit. Note that it is the cost of short-term credit that should affect HS_t^S and not the mortgage rate. Provided that a home builder can get a mortgage commitment from one of the financial intermediaries, the borrowing cost to the builder is the short-run cost of financing the building of the house until it is sold. The mortgage cost is incurred by the person who eventually buys the house.

Finally, the supply of mortgage funds, $MORT_t^S$ is specified to be:

$$MORT_t^S = h(Z_t^S, \eta_t^S), \tag{4}$$

where Z_t^S is a vector of variables that determine $MORT_t^S$ and where η_t^S is an error term. The variables that affect $MORT_t^S$ are likely to include deposit flows into financial intermediaries, the mortgage rate, and interest rates on competing assets.

We are now in a position to put these demand and supply schedules together and discuss how the three groups of participants interact. If the housing and mortgage market were always in equilibrium, then it would be the case that:

$$HS_t = HS_t^D = HS_t^S \quad \text{and} \quad MORT_t = MORT_t^D = MORT_t^S, \tag{5}$$

where HS_t is the actual number of housing starts and where $MORT_t$ is the actual value of mortgage funds associated with HS_t. In equilibrium, the purchase price of houses would clear the housing side of the market and the mortgage rate would clear the mortgage side of the market.

Since the housing and mortgage market does not always appear to be in equilibrium, an alternative assumption to (5) will be made. In order to do this, one further simplifying assumption has to be made. Note first that if assumption (5) were true, then (2) would imply that

$$\frac{MORT}{HS_t} = a_0 + a_1 t. \qquad (6)$$

Even though (5) is not necessarily true, I will assume that

$$\frac{MORT_t^S}{HS_t^{FS}} = a_0 + a_1 t, \qquad (7)$$

where HS_t^{FS} is the *equivalent* supply of housing starts from the financial sector. Equation (7), which is the supply side equivalent of equation (2), is merely a simple way of converting the supply of new mortgage funds, $MORT_t^S$, into an equivalent supply of housing starts, HS_t^{FS}.

The disequilibrium aspect of the housing market is now specified as follows. It is assumed that the actual number of housing starts is equal to the minimum of the one demand and the two supply schedules:

$$HS_t = \min\left\{HS_t^D, HS_t^S, HS_t^{FS}\right\}, \qquad (8)$$

where again HS_t is the actual number of housing starts. Equation (8) implies that there are three possible constraints in the housing market. Demand may be the constraint, in which case home builders and financial intermediaries go unsatisfied at prevailing prices; or supply from the home builders may be the constraint, in which case demanders and financial intermediaries go unsatisfied; or supply from the financial intermediaries may be the constraint, in which case demanders and home builders go unsatisfied.

So this is the basic way that I look at the housing and mortgage market: three groups of participants, two demand schedules, two supply schedules, and three possible disequilibrium constraints. In the actual empirical work for my forecasting model, I made a number of simplifying approximations, but since I am primarily concerned here with presenting my basic theoretical framework, I will not discuss my empirical work in any detail.

The technique that I used to estimate the disequilibrium model is described in a paper I did with Dwight Jaffee, "Methods of Estimation for Markets in Disequilibrium," which is forthcoming in *Econometrica,* May 1972. In that paper we developed four techniques for estimating disequilibrium markets, one of which I used in Chapter 8 of my book on the forecasting model. The basic assumption upon which three of the four techniques are based is that prices rise in periods of excess demand and fall in periods of excess supply. From this assumption, one can then break up the sample period into supply regimes, where the price is rising, and demand regimes, where the price is falling, and estimate each schedule over the relevant sample period. There is also a way to adjust quantitatively for the amount of rationing involved, and this method we called the "quantitative method." This method, which is the one I used in Chapter 8, has the advantage of being able to test for the existence of disequilibrium in the market. If a particular variable, which has come to be called the slish-slash variable, has a significant coefficient estimate, then this indicates that there is disequilibrium; otherwise if the estimate is not significant, this indicates that the market is always in equilibrium.

The empirical results turned out fairly well. They definitely seem to indicate that both a demand equation and a supply equation have been estimated. The demand and supply equations both have the same left-hand-side variable, HS_t, and yet in the demand equation the mortgage rate (the price variable in the model) has a negative effect and the time trend has a positive effect; whereas in the supply equation the mortgage rate has a positive effect and the time trend has a negative effect. These signs are as expected, and it is encouraging that the demand and supply equations appear to be identified enough to get the correct opposing signs with the same left-hand-side variable.

The slish-slash variable was significant, which I interpret as indicating that there is some disequilibrium in the housing and mortgage market.

I would like to emphasize one important policy issue that arose from my work. I found that the flow of advances of the Federal Home Loan Bank to savings and loan associations has a significant effect on the equivalent supply of housing starts from the financial sector. This in itself is not too surprising, but it is important to note that this effect will be significant in influencing actual housing starts only if supply from the financial sector is the constraint. If either demand or the supply from the construction sector is the constraint, then increasing FHLBB advances will not affect actual housing starts. For most of the 1960s it does appear that supply from the financial sector has been the constraint: the mortgage rate was rising during most of the period and FHLBB advances did appear to have a significant effect on actual housing starts.

An interesting question now, I think, is whether, given the tremendous flow of deposits into savings and loan associations and mutual savings banks in the past few months, there is enough demand so that it is still the case that supply is the constraint. The mortgage rate has begun to fall, which indicates that we may be in the beginning of a period in which there are plenty of mortgage funds available and demand is the constraint. If this is the case, then the FHLBB does not have to worry about the expected rapid repayment of outstanding advances because this should have little effect on actual housing starts.

The last point I want to make relates to my forecasting work. I have an explicit policy with respect to my model of not engaging in constant term adjustments or other "fine tuning" devices. My forecasts from the model, including the forecasts of housing starts, are thus more objective than forecasts from models that have been extensively fine tuned. Only time will tell whether my approach is a fruitful one, but it does seem to me that if econometrics is going to be of significance for forecasting purposes it must be the case that models be used in a fairly mechanical way to generate forecasts. Otherwise, if models must be substantially fine tuned in order to produce reasonable forecasts, then econometrics has a very limited role to play in terms of forecasting.

Mr. Fromm: The FHA rate has been falling. Is it demand or supply?

Mr. Fair: We are on the demand function, according to me – I am not as optimistic on my forecasts of housing starts as some others, because demand is now becoming the constraint. I am not picking up all of the effect of the tremendous inflow of funds into S & L's and mutal savings banks because according to me not all of these funds are going to be translated into housing starts.

Question: Does the model well enough represent the deferred demand built up over the past?

Mr. Fair: That is a good question. The demand equation is simpler and does not fit as well as the supply equation. I have the stock of houses in there – or an approximation for the stock of houses – and so that should be picking up some of this, but I don't know, really. There is a lot more work that could be done in specifying both functions, in fact.

Mr. Friedman: You might never get your demand function. When demand is the constraint, houses are built, anyway, and vacancy rates increase.

Mr. Fair: I haven't thought much until lately about the vacancy question. I guess that is conceivable, though many houses, I understand, are initiated by the person who wants the house built as opposed to being initiated by the builders. Your question is of relevance for contractors who build even when demand prospects do not look very promising.

Mr. Friedman: It did happen once before.

Mr. Fair: The vacancy question is something that has not been captured very well in here. I am only picking up the vacancy through the stock of houses in the demand equation.

Mr. Smith: I have a couple of points. One has to do with when the mortgage rate is changing, then you decide whether you are on supply or demand function. What would happen in the case like the last year, where substantial easing in financial policy and in financial variables would probably tend to bring down the mortgage rate quite apart from what is happening in the housing market, itself? So even if there was a strong housing demand, that would just widen the gap between the mortgage and the bond rate, but the general trend would be determined by what is happening in financial markets.

Mr. Fair: I am not sure I follow that. If you have an easing of policy in terms of falling mortgage rates . . . .

Mr. Smith: Bond rates, they will pull the mortgage rate down, even though within the housing market, itself, there may be strong demands so that you could still have a strong demand for housing starts.

Mr. Fair: I am not arguing that there would not be a strong demand for housing starts, but I am arguing that there would be more supply available than would meet the demand, not necessarily that the demand would be small. You could have a buoyant demand; it just means that supply is more buoyant than demand. I am saying nothing about the level of these variables.

Right now it is the case that we have a very large demand for housing. The question is whether we even have more supply available, so that, in effect, demand is the constraint.

Mr. Smith: There are certain assumptions about financial institution behavior, that they are pretty well – that the rates are going to operate in a different manner – that you start out in an equilibrium.

Let's assume for a moment you are right at the intersection point, start at a point of equilibrium. Within the housing market, income rises. At the same time there is a shift, or something like that. At the same time the economy is slowing down. Financial institutions then have lots of funds to place. They will put a lot more funds into houses and supply of mortgage money will increase.

Mr. Fair: Right, and demand will meet it.

Mr. Smith: But you are in a period of falling mortgage rates, even though the demand is moving up and is actually your constraint.

Mr. Fair: That is right. That would be consistent with my model. You would observe increasing housing starts and yet a falling mortgage rate. Both curves would be shifting up, only the supply curve would be shifting faster than the demand curve.

Mr. Ricks: Let me insist on the Chairman's prerogative and make a comment. I noticed that the District Bank people and Home Loan Bank people were smiling and Arnold Diamond of HUD was smiling when you were talking about excess supply, and the inadequacy of demand to absorb those funds. There has been a fair amount of work in Washington on that specific point.

Our small-area analysis in some areas, particularly Los Angeles, San Diego, Houston, and Dallas, shows this to be the case. We are concerned about the accumulation of liquidity. The associations are paying back Home Loan Bank advances of $289 million in January. The FHLMC finds it is unable to buy mortgages – FNMA also – and has begun selling mortgages at the rate of $50 million a week, so that the types of disequilibria we are talking about are obvious to us in our nonmodelling look at the area.

There is another factor thst is very strong here that doesn't show up in the models, and that is the *repayments,* which do change quite a bit from periods of monetary stringency to monetary ease – repayments on existing mortgages, prepayments, actually.

Another factor is the financing of existing units. That is bigger than new starts by, I believe, some two and a half times. So there is a substantial effect that is going on there.

The third point is the question of the composition of housing starts, the translation between units and dollars of expenditure. I think that is far less stable in the short-run than you indicate, particularly in view of some substitution effects on subsidy programs where a subsidy unit is not a net addition, but rather an acquisition of a lower priced unit.

We are seeing some tremendous shifts in builders' plans to provide town houses this year, so that the quarter-to-quarter shift in that type is quite dramatic. A townhouse uses up both less total dollars, less GNP. The housing price uses up less mortgage funds, so there are some very significant shifts between starts and dollars that are concerning us quite a bit.

References

1. de Leeuw, Frank, and Edward M. Gramlich, "The Channels of Monetary Policy." *Federal Reserve Bulletin* 55 (June 1969): 472–491.
2. Fair, Ray C., "The Estimation of Equation Systems with Restrictions Across Equations and Serially Correlated Errors." Mimeographed.
3. Fair, Ray C., "The Estimation of Simultaneous Equation Models with Lagged Endogenous Variables and First Order Serially Correlated Errors." *Econometrica* 38 (May 1970): 507–516.
4. Fair, Ray C. and Dwight M. Jaffee, "Methods of Estimation for Markets in Disequilibrium." *Econometrica* (forthcoming, 1972).
5. Jaffee, Dwight M., "An Econometric Model of the Mortgage Market: Estimation and Simulation." Mimeographed.
6. Maisel, Sherman J., "Nonbusiness Construction." In Duesenberry et al., *The Brookings Quarterly Econometric Model of the United States* (Chicago: Rand McNally, 1965), pp. 178–201.
7. Sparks, Gordon R., "An Econometric Analysis of the Role of Financial Intermediaries in Postwar Residential Building Cycles." In Ferber, *Determinants of Investment Behavior* (New York: National Bureau of Economic Research, 1967), pp. 301–331.

4 A Summary of the Current Financial Intermediary, Mortgage, and Housing Sectors of the FRB-MIT-Penn Econometric Model

John H. Kalchbrenner

Since this conference dealt not only with the housing sector, but with the role of the Federal Home Loan Banks in housing, we felt it desirable to include a summary which encompasses more than just the housing sector of the FRB-MIT-Penn econometric model. Although the behavior of the housing sector is obviously related to the behavior of the economy generally, the behavior of financial intermediaries and the mortgage market assume particular importance in explaining housing. Consequently, summaries of the existing financial intermediary and mortgage sectors of the overall model are also included.[1]

The Behavior of Savings Flows Through Financial Intermediaries

The discussion in this section summarizes the recent revisions to the financial-intermediary–liquid-asset sector of the model made by Professor Franco Modigliani.[2] The analysis of savings flows through the financial intermediaries includes estimates of the determinants of the following: (i) passbook savings at commercial banks; (ii) savings deposits at savings and loan associations and mutual savings banks; and (iii) life insurance reserves net of policy loans. After the description of these demand equations, we present a summary of the equations for the rates of return offered on each of these liquid assets. These are the supply equations since it is assumed that the supply of deposits is infinitely elastic for any given rate of return.

Demand Equations

The theoretical treatment of the demand for these categories of liquid assets is based upon portfolio theory. The theoretical model explains the propor-

1. For those interested, complete discussions of these sectors, alternative versions thereof, specific estimated equations and simulation experiments are available in Gramlich and Jaffee [3].

2. For the complete description, see Modigliani, in [3], ch. 3. The author wishes to thank Professor Modigliani for his suggestions for improving an earlier version of this summary.

tion of total net worth allocated to each of the assets in question as a function of expected own and other rates of return, the covariance of return among the assets, and a measure of risk aversion. That is

$$\frac{A_i}{V} = \alpha_i(\ ) \tag{4.1}$$

where A_i is a liquid asset, V is net worth, and α_i is the long-run equilibrium proportion, a function of expected rates of return and risk.

However, a cursory inspection of the data leads to the conclusion that the actual ratio

$$\frac{A_i}{V} \equiv a_i$$

adjusts quite slowly toward the equilibrium ratio α_i. In earlier empirical studies this phenomenon generally has been attributed to the fact that portfolios adjust but slowly to the desired ratio. An alternative explanation, which forms the basis of the model's formulation, is that the portfolio adjusts promptly to the desired composition as perceived at any given point of time, but that this perceived optimum ratio, say a_i^* adjusts but gradually toward the long-run ratio α_i. This gradual adjustment is approximated by

$$a_t^* = a_{t-1}^* + g(\alpha_t - a_{t-1}^*) \tag{4.2}$$

where g is the speed of adjustment (percent per quarter). Furthermore, on the assumption that the portfolio adjusts promptly to the perceived optimum, a_i^* in (4.2) can be replaced by the observed ratio a_i. (A broader hypothesis incorporating both a portfolio adjustment and a perception lag was also formulated and tested; but, in part because of multicollinearity problems, there was no adequate ground for perferring it to the simpler model.)

Define S as the quarterly saving flow into asset A, $A_t - A_{t-1}$ (the subscript i being understood hereafter). Then from (4.2), $a^* = a$, and some simple algebra one can infer

$$S_t = a_{t-1}\ \Delta V + g(\alpha_t - a_{t-1})V \tag{4.3}$$

that is, the current addition can be expressed as the sum of the increment in wealth multiplied by the lagged share, and a portfolio rebalancing term which is a fraction g of the existing imbalance $(\alpha_t - a_{t-1})V$.

Some changes in net worth accrue as capital gains on existing asset holdings (in the postwar period, about 2/3 of V is due to capital gains and only 1/3 to personal savings). It is assumed that these accruals will not be liquidated and reallocated quickly; i.e., that only some fraction, m, will be redistributed currently. Further, the assets in question here are not subject to capital gains by their nature, so it is only necessary to account for the distribution into these assets of capital gains accruing from other portfolio holdings.[3]

Taking this additional factor into account yields the principal equation form used in the empirical estimation

$$\frac{S_t}{V_t} = ba_{t-1}\frac{SP_t}{V_t} + ma_{t-1}\frac{CG_t}{V_t} + g\alpha - ga_{t-1} \qquad (4.4)$$

where the newly introduced notation is as follows:

SP = personal saving

CG = capital gains

m = the fraction of capital gains currently reallocated

a_{t-1} = the observed actual proportion of net worth held in a given asset, lagged one quarter.

Empirical Applications

Time deposits other than large certificates of deposit at commerical banks. For purposes of defining the determinants of α in the commercial bank time and savings deposit equation, the following assumptions are made. Time deposits of this type are viewed as partial substitutes for demand deposits, other savings deposits and other money-fixed assets (short-term market assets primarily). Substitution with equities and physical assets is assumed to be considerably lower. Covariance terms are ignored on the assumption of constancy over time. Thus

$$\alpha_{TP} = a_0 + a_1(RTD - RM) + a_2(RTD - RSL) + a_3(RTD - RMS)$$
$$+ a_4(RTD - RTB) + a_5(RTD - RCB) + a_6(RTD - RR) \qquad (4.5)$$

where

RTD = the time deposit rate

RM = the rate on demand deposits

RSL = the savings and loan rate

3. In his paper, Modigliani also derives the expression for assets to which capital gains do accrue.

RMS = the mutual savings bank rate

RTB = the Treasury bill rate

RCB = the corporate bond rate

RR = the rate of return on equities and physical assets.

All of the a_i are assumed positive. RM is assumed constant over the period of estimation and is included in the constant. In addition, in an effort to reduce multicollinearity, the two rates RMS and RSL were replaced by a single rate RA, computed as an average of the two components weighted by recent inflows into the two types of deposits. Thus the second and third terms of (4.5) collapse into a single term $(RTD - RA)$. Finally, conceptual and measurement problems made it advisable to drop the variable RR in the empirical estimates.

In the context of broader portfolio behavior, consistent behavior implies certain constraints. The following variables were assumed to have the same coefficients (in absolute value) in the time deposit equation and in the savings deposit equation for (combined) savings and loan associations and mutual savings banks:

(i) $(RTD - RA)$ (iii) $a_{t-1}SP_t$

(ii) $a_{t-1}CG$ (iv) g (with less certainty).

Consequently, the empirical estimates were obtained by estimating the two equations simultaneously applying these constraints. Also, to allow for the increased competition for saving deposits between commercial banks and other intermediaries since the early 1960s, the coefficient of $(RTD - RA)$ was allowed to rise in the later period by adding a term $[a_7 + a_8(RTD - RA)]$ where Q is a dummy variable with value 0 up to 1962:2 and 1 thereafter. The coefficient a_8 again was constrained to have the same value (except for sign) in the time deposit and the other savings deposit equation, and was found to be highly significant. By contrast, the spread $(RTD - RA)$ was totally insignificant up to 1962:2, and was finally dropped.

In addition, the empirical estimates incorporate an attempt to measure the influence of transactions demands, measured by disposable income (Y). This variable was included on the assumption that time deposits are a close substitute for demand deposits as a temporary abode of purchasing power, and, therefore, should vary like demand deposits with transaction volume.

Deposits at mutual savings banks and savings and loan associations. These two types of deposits were combined for estimation purposes on the grounds that the differences that exist between them are primarily geographical (and in terms of the speed of growth in the areas in which the two are situated) rather than economic. It is assumed that the relevant α for these two types of deposits depends upon the same factors as those listed for time deposits, but that there is less substitution between these deposits and demand deposits or short-term market instruments, and greater substitution with longer-term money-fixed claims.

Otherwise, the underlying model and the empirical equations are substantially the same as in the time deposit discussion. In the empirical equation, the income variable is included for symmetry with the time deposit equation. Consistent with the assumption that these deposits are more sensitive to rates on longer-term claims, the corporate bond rate appears in this equation, unlike the time deposit equation. As indicated above, this relationship was estimated simultaneously with the time deposit equation, applying the same constraints.

After estimating the joint intermediary deposit equation, it is necessary to separate the two deposit types for use in the mortgage sector. This allocation is accomplished by replacing – in the basic model (4.3) – total wealth V by the total amount of deposits at savings and loan associations and mutual savings banks, and estimating the savings and loan share of that total.

Given that the two assets are virtually identical, the principal variable is an Almon lag on the rate spread $(RSL - RMS)$, with the lag reflecting inertia and a lag on the spread of information. To add some measure of the institutional changes that fostered a faster growth of savings and loan shares, a time trend was entered, and to reflect the fact that the more rapid rate of growth tapered off by the mid-1960s, a second degree time trend was used, terminating in 1966.

Thus, the allocation equation is of the form

$$\frac{\Delta MSL\$ - a_{t-1}\Delta MS\$}{MS\$} = b_0 + g\sum_{i=0}^{11} b_i (RSL - RMS)_{t-i} - ga_{t-1} + b_{13}\,\text{time} + b_{12}\,\text{time}^2 \tag{4.6}$$

where $MS\$$ = deposits at savings and loan associations $(MSL\$)$ + deposits at mutual savings banks $(MMS\$)$, and time begins in 1955:1 and ends in 1965:4.

Life insurance reserves. A somewhat different basic model is used to explain life insurance reserves. Due to their contractual nature, only small effects are expected from transient changes in income or capital gains and losses. Further, it is argued that the demand for life insurance should be a function of permanent income rather than net worth or wealth. In the empirical equation, permanent income is represented by the model definition of consumption expenditures which is broader and less volatile than that of the National Income Accounts.

The long-run equilibrium relationship is written in fashion similar to the equations presented in the earlier sections.

$$MIS\$ = \alpha PC \tag{4.7}$$

where

$MIS\$$	=	life insurance reserves net of policy loans
P	=	the price index
C	=	consumption as defined in the FRB-MIT-Penn model
α	=	the desired ratio of life insurance to permanent income, a function of the rate of return on life insurance, rates of return on other assets, etc., specified below.

Given stable growth in C over time, and assuming constant P,

$$\Delta MIS\$ = \alpha \Delta CP = \alpha\rho C_{t-1}P \tag{4.8}$$

where ρ = the trend rate of growth of C, and $\Delta MIS\$$ is the current flow of life insurance reserves.

In the postwar period, the ratio $MIS\$/CP$ has shown a downward trend which accelerated after 1965. This behavior could be due to both changes in α and changes in P, with lags present in restoring equilibrium. Consequently, the current flow is restated in terms of two components. The first component reflects the accumulation attributable to permanent income, scaled by an average of prices over time. The second component reflects the flow necessary to rebalance the portfolio when α changes. A stock adjustment term is used for the latter.

$$\Delta MIS\$ = \rho\alpha C_{t-1}\bar{P} + g(\alpha C_{t-1}P_{t-1} - MIS\$_{t-1}) \tag{4.9}$$

This expression can be restated as follows:

$$\frac{\Delta MIS\$}{P_{t-1}C_{t-1}} = (\rho + g)\alpha - ga_{t-1} - b\,\frac{P_{t-1} - \bar{P}}{P_{t-1}} \tag{4.10}$$

where $a = MIS\$/PC$ and $b = \rho\alpha$, the latter assumed constant so long as α does not fluctuate widely.

Further, the price ratio term is expressed as a weighted sum of the rate of change of prices over the averaging period.

$$\frac{P_{t-1} - \bar{P}}{P_{t-1}} = \frac{1}{n}\sum_{1}^{n-1} \tau\dot{P}_{t-n+\tau} = \frac{n-1}{2}\;\frac{\Sigma\tau\dot{P}_{t-n+\tau}}{\Sigma\tau}\,.$$

It is assumed that α for life insurance reserves should include some measure of the spread between the return on life insurance accumulation (RI) and the return on other money-fixed claims (RO). There are no data available for RI directly, so a weighted average of past values of the mortgage rate, RM is used.[4] In addition, since RM is also collinear with RA and RCB, the current value of RM is used as a proxy for RO. That is, the term $b(RI - RO)$ is approximated by

$$b_1 RM_t + b_2 \sum_{\tau=1}^{m} w_\tau RM_{-\tau}$$

where $b_1 < 0$ (since it measures the effect of other rates) and $b_2 > 0$ (the effect of RI).

In both the short and the long run, policy loans affect life insurance reserves. These loans are assumed to be an increasing function of the spread $RO' - RIL$, where RIL is the rate charged on policy loans and RO' is a measure of the cost of borrowing elsewhere. Since RIL was basically constant over the period of observation, and assuming that RO' can again be proxied by RM, this spread was approximated by a linear function of RM, say $b_3 RM + b_4$, with $b_3 > 0$. Remembering that an increase in policy loans implies a fall in α, one arrives at the following hypothesis for α:

$$\alpha = c_0 + c_1 RM + c_2 \sum_{1}^{m} w_\tau RM_{-\tau}$$

where

$$c_1 = b_1 - b_3 < 0 \quad \text{and} \quad c_2 = b_2 > 0. \tag{4.11}$$

Other factors that might have affected life insurance reserve behavior in the postwar period include the expected rate of change of prices ($\dot{P}^e$), the growth of Social Security ($OASI\$$), and the growth of private pension funds. It is assumed that the first would not have a pronounced effect unless price changes were very large, while the second should have reduced the growth of life insurance reserves. The effects of pension growth are hard to specify on a priori grounds since life insurance companies manage some of these funds, increasing their reserves. On balance, it is assumed the effect has been negative, but since no variable is avail-

4. In the development of the time deposit equation, the notation RM was used to refer to the rate of return on demand deposits. Since that variable was subsequently dropped from explicit use, no confusion results.

able to use as a measure, this variable is ignored, except insofar as it is proxied by *OASI$*.

Including these factors, the complete relationship becomes:

$$\frac{\Delta MIS\$}{CON\$_{t-1}} = g\left(c_0' + c_1' RM + c_2' \sum_{\tau=1}^{m} w_\tau RM_{-\tau} + c_3' \dot{P}^e + c_4 \frac{OASI\$}{CON\$_{t-1}}\right) - g\frac{MIS\$_{t-1}}{CON\$_{t-1}} + c_5' \sum_{\tau=1}^{n} v_\tau \left(\frac{\Delta PCON}{PCON_{-1}}\right)_{-\tau} \quad (4.12)$$

where

CON$ = nominal consumption expenditures at current prices as defined in the FRB-MIT-Penn model

PCON = the price deflator for consumption expenditures.

This expression is simplified by deleting expected price changes since they would have to be estimated by a lag on past prices. Therefore, this coefficient is unidentifiably absorbed in the last term. Thus

$$\frac{\Delta MIS\$}{CON\$_{t-1}} = c_0 + c_1 RM + c_2 \sum_{\tau=1}^{m} w_\tau RM_{-\tau} + c_3 \sum_{\tau=0}^{h} v_\tau \left(\frac{\Delta PCON}{PCON_{-1}}\right)_{-\tau} + c_4 \frac{OASI\$}{CON\$_{t-1}} + c_5 \frac{MIS\$_{t-1}}{CON\$_{t-1}} \quad (4.13)$$

where $gc_0' = c_0$, etc. Here,

$$c_0, c_2 > 0; \quad c_1, c_3, c_4, c_5 < 0; \quad \text{and} \quad c_1 + c_2 < 0.$$

Onc final modification based upon considerations of dynamics is made to this formulation before estimation. An inspection of the data for policy loans indicates sharp, short swings which were felt to indicate credit availability and rationing effects in addition to relative cost factors. The Jaffee-Modigliani credit rationing hypothesis suggests that increases in rationing are accompanied by narrowing of the spread between the commercial loan rate (*RCL*) and short-term market rates such as the commercial paper rate (*RCP*).

Consequently, an attempt to capture a rationing effect was made by adding a rate spread variable when the spread narrowed below some threshold. That is, policy loans (*PL*) as a ratio of life insurance reserves can be written:

$$\frac{PL}{MIS\$} = k^* [(RCP - RCL) - TR] + k_0 \tag{4.14}$$

where

TR = the threshold spread

$$k^* \begin{cases} > 0 \text{ if } [(RCP - RCL) - TR] > 0 \\ = 0 \text{ otherwise} \end{cases}$$

k_0 = all other policy loan influences

Taking $MIS\$$ proportional to $CON\$_{t-1}$ gives

$$\frac{PL}{CON\$_{t-1}} = k_0 + k^*(RCP - RCL) - k^* TR. \tag{4.15}$$

Since $\Delta MIS\$$ is reduced by an increase in PL, the following terms are added to the $\Delta MIS\$$ equation:

$$c_6 J + c_7 [J(\overline{RCP - RCL})]$$

where J is a dummy equal to 1 when credit rationing exists and 0 otherwise. $(\overline{RCP - RCL})$ is the average spread (in the current and previous quarter), c_7 is a measure of $-k^*$, < 0, and $-c_6/c_7$ measures TR. It was tentatively concluded that $J = 1$ whenever the spread narrowed beyond -.7.

Supply Equations

The supply equations currently in the FRB-MIT-Penn model are a part of a far more complex version of the savings deposit relationships developed by E. Gramlich and D. Hulett.[5] For reasons indicated below, these equations must be reestimated for use in the model since they incorporate features inconsistent with the current demand equations.[6] Consequently, the discussion of the supply equations will be brief.

The supply equations for three of the assets discussed above – time deposits at commercial banks (less certificates of deposit) and savings deposits at

5. For the complete description, see Gramlich and Hulett in [3], ch. 2.

6. Since this summary was prepared, the supply equations have been revised by Myron Slovin and they are now consistent. The basic approach of the supply equations developed by Slovin remains similar to the discussion in this summary. There are, however, substantial differences in specification and estimation in the new version. See Slovin in [3], ch. 4. Time constraints prevented revision of this section of the summary.

savings and loan associations and mutual savings banks – take the form of rate setting functions for each intermediary. Since no series on rate of return is available for life insurance companies, it is assumed that the rate of return was constant over the sample period, and no equation is included.

For the explained rates, it is assumed that the intermediaries, in the absence of ceiling restrictions, would maximize expected utility, written as a function of expected returns, and variances of returns. The intermediaries are treated as price takers with respect to the acquisition of assets, setting deposit rates on the basis of these returns (and their estimates of the certainty of the returns), and on the basis of their evaluation of the demand conditions for their respective deposits. It is assumed that the greater the cross elasticity of demand for other savings deposits, the greater is the rate response by a given intermediary to changes in competing rates. Empirically, this is incorporated by imposing the demand elasticities estimated by Gramlich and Hulett as partial constraints on the rate response coefficients in the supply equations. Since these demand elasticities differ from those in the equations estimated by Modigliani, the supply equations are no longer consistent, and are currently being reestimated.

Intermediaries are viewed as holding mortgages, market securities, and liquid reserves in their asset portfolio. Uncertainty in the decision-making process concerning the composition of these assets is due to uncertainty in the rates of return, and uncertainty concerning deposit fluctuations which are controlled by the public.

Consequently, intermediary asset demands are assumed to depend upon relative rates of return, rate uncertainty, and exogenous deposits. The deposit rate, by which the intermediary controls deposits to some extent, then depends positively upon asset rates and rates on other liquid assets which are (partial) substitutes, and negatively upon other (unspecified) factors which increase deposits. That is:

$$R_{D1} = a_1 RM + a_2 R_B - a_3 (b_1 R_{D2} + b_2 R_{D3} + \ldots + b_n R_{Dn}) + a_4 u_1 \tag{4.16}$$

where

R_{D1}	=	one of the deposit rates
RM	=	the mortgage rate
R_B	=	market instrument rates (e.g., bonds or commercial loans)
$R_{D2}, \ldots, R_{Dn}$	=	deposit rates or market rates on competing liquid assets
$b_1, \ldots, b_n$	=	demand elasticities for the competing liquid assets, with all $b_i < 0$

u_1 = other factors affecting deposits, empirically the rate of change of total deposits less the rate of change of commercial loans.

These expressions are based upon the assumption that no ceiling rates are imposed upon the intermediaries. The existence of ceiling rates is incorporated in two ways in the determination of the actual rates observed. The only ceiling rate considered is that imposed upon passbook savings deposits at commercial banks. First, it is assumed that changes in ceiling rates may lead to the expectation that competing deposit rates will change shortly thereafter due to the existence of oligopolistic rate setting behavior among financial intermediaries. This effect is accounted for by including the ceiling rate and its rate of change directly in the desired rate equation for passbook savings deposits.

Second, a rather complex procedure is followed which allows the existence of a ceiling to depress the observed rate relative to the desired rate, the closer the latter is to the ceiling. It is assumed for convenience that the desired rates have a triangular distribution, given any set of arguments in the desired rate functions. If the ceiling rate lies above the range of this distribution, the desired rate equals the observed rate, at the mean of the distribution. If the ceiling rate lies within the range of the distribution, all of the frequencies to the right (above) the ceiling rate are shifted to the ceiling rate. This has the effect of shifting the mean of the distribution the left, and is a way of allowing the ceiling rate to affect the observed rate even if the mean unadjusted desired rate lies below the ceiling. The limiting case at the other extreme occurs when the distribution lies entirely above the ceiling rate, in which case the observed rate is the ceiling rate.

Operationally, this is carried out in the following manner. Given the ceiling and the observed rate, and assuming different parameters for the triangular distribution, several desired rate series were generated. These alternatives were then used as dependent variables in regressions on the arguments of the desired rate function. The series which was best explained statistically was chosen as the desired rate series, thus also defining the triangular distribution parameters.

The empirical equations for the saving and loan rate and the mutual saving bank rate follow the form indicated above, with the exception that the rate of change of prices enters the saving and loan equation reflecting possible substitution with real assets, and neither of these equations contains ceiling terms or deposit terms directly.

The Mortgage Market

The current version of the mortgage market in the FRB-MIT-Penn model was developed by Professor D. Jaffee.[7] Within the overall model, the mortgage

7. For the complete description, see Jaffee in [3], ch. 5. To simplify the exposition given the complexity of the mortgage sector, we have used the notation employed by Jaffee rather than the notation used in the FRB-MIT-Penn model.

sector serves as a link between private savings at financial intermediaries and investment in housing capital.

In terms of the supply of mortgages, the sector includes provision for the activities of the FHLBB and FNMA, and treats in considerable detail the dynamics of the mortgage market stemming from the use of advance commitments. The relationship between commitments and mortgage flows is specified, and these flows, in conjunction with household demand for mortgages, determine the mortgage rate.

Institutionally, the mortgage sector deals with the same intermediaries as those discussed above: commercial banks, savings and loan associations, mutual savings banks, and life insurance companies. The availability of appropriate data dictated differing treatment of these institutions.

The Supply of Mortgages

The supply of mortgages by the intermediaries is analyzed in terms of portfolio selection criteria. It is assumed that some degree of substitution exists between portfolio assets on the basis of yield and liquidity differentials. Lags in adjustment in the portfolio are assumed on the grounds of uncertainty, transactions costs, etc.

In a manner similar to the treatment of savings flows, desired mortgage stocks (M^*) are specified as some proportion of deposits (D) at the intermediaries. The proportion is determined by the spread between the mortgage rate (RM) and the corporate bond rate or other rates (RB). Empirically, only one competing rate is used to avoid multicollinearity problems. That is:

$$M^* = [a_0 + a_1(RM - RB)]D \tag{4.17}$$

The intended or desired change in the stock in any period ($\overline{\Delta M}$) is written in the form of a partial adjustment model with the addition of an impact term, changes in deposits (ΔD), which allows variations in the basic adjustment model.

$$\overline{\Delta M} = g_0(M^* - M_{-1}) + g_1 \, \Delta D. \tag{4.18}$$

Adding repayments (R) to both sides yields the expression for gross mortgage flows ($\overline{\Delta Mg}$).

The existence of advance commitments is then introduced because of their effect upon the dynamics of the market. Commitments are made on the basis of current information available to an intermediary, but these conditions may change prior to the take-down of the commitments made. As a consequence, mortgage volume in the current market may not reflect the desired volume since it is based upon commitments made earlier.

Assuming that desired gross changes in the mortgage stock are reflected in current commitments made, the supply of commitments (new or outstanding) is explained as a behavioral relationship. Mortgage flows are then expressed as a distributed lag on commitments.

Desired mortgage flows can be met in three ways: (i) direct mortgage acquisitions; (ii) conversion of outstanding commitments to mortgages; or, (iii) issuance of new commitments. Recognizing that it represents an oversimplification, it is assumed that direct placements are a constant proportion of gross mortgage flows, and similarly for the proportions of new and outstanding commitments not taken down. This results in the following desired gross mortgage flow identity:

$$\overline{\Delta Mg} = b\,\overline{\Delta Mg} + aNC + a'OC_{-1} \qquad (4.19)$$

where

NC = new commitments

OC = outstanding commitments

b,a,a' = the constant proportion of direct placements, the constant proportion of NC taken down, and the proportion of OC taken down, respectively.

By substitution, the following expression for NC can be written:

$$NC = \frac{(1-b)g_0}{a}\,[a_0 + a_1(RM - RB)\,D - M_{-1}] + \frac{(1-b)g_1}{a}\,\Delta D$$

$$+ \frac{1-b}{a}R - \frac{a'}{a}\,OC_{-1}. \qquad (4.20)$$

Current outstanding commitments are equal to last period's commitments plus new commitments, less cancellations and take-downs. Assuming that take-downs are a constant proportion (m), and cancellations are a constant proportion (c) of last period's outstanding commitments, we have:

$$OC = NC + (1 - c - m)OC_{-1} \qquad (4.21)$$

Substituting from (4.20) for NC, and rearranging terms yields the following expression for outstanding commitments:

$$OC = a_0 d_0 D + a_1 d_0 (RM - RB)\,D + g_1 d_0 \Delta D - d_0 M_{-1} + d_0 R$$

$$+ (1 - c - m - d_1)OC_{-1} \qquad (4.22)$$

where

$$d_0 = \frac{1 - b}{a} \quad \text{and} \quad d_1 = \frac{a'}{a} \, .$$

It was necessary to derive estimation equations for both new and outstanding commitments due to data problems. New commitments are available only for life insurance companies, and outstanding commitments are available for savings and loan associations and mutual savings banks. The absence of any commitment data for commercial banks forced Jaffee to estimate bank mortgage flows directly.

In order to be able to solve for the mortgage rate, mortgage flow equations are necessary. They are specified essentially as realizations of earlier commitments in the model.

For life insurance companies, the relationship is as follows:

$$\Delta Mg = \frac{1}{B}\left(\sum_{i=0}^{T} w_i NC_{-i}\right) \tag{4.23}$$

where

$$\sum_{i=0}^{T} w_i = 1.$$

Here, B refers to the percentage of mortgage flows attributable to commitments, discussed in more detail below. For savings and loan associations and mutual savings banks, the expression must be in terms of outstanding commitments. From (4.21), we have

$$\Delta Mg = \frac{1}{B}\left(\sum_{i=0}^{T} w_i [OC_{-i} - (1 - c - m)OC_{-i-1}]\right) \tag{4.24}$$

or, more simply,

$$\Delta MG = \frac{1}{B}\left(\sum_{i=0}^{T} v_i OC_{-i}\right) \tag{4.25}$$

with the weights properly redefined.

On the grounds that B may decline during periods of large deposit inflows in order to avoid lost earnings (and vice versa), Jaffee tried four possible additions to (4.23) and (4.25): (i) the deviation of actual deposit flows from a moving average deposit flow; (ii) current period commitments (as a measure of pressure to make direct placements); (iii) the determinants of current commitments; and, (iv) for savings and loans, the amount of FHLB advances as a measure of availability. These factors appear in varying combinations in the final equations included in the model.

For commercial banks, due to the lack of data, the mortgage flow equation was estimated directly. It is assumed that bank mortgage flows depend upon past deposits, interest rates, and the lagged mortgage stock. That is:

$$\Delta M^{CB} = c_0 \, \Delta DD + c_1 \sum_{i=0}^{T} v_i TD_{-i}^{CB} + c_2 \sum_{i=0}^{T} w_i TD_{-i}^{CB} \, (RM - RCL)_{-i}$$

$$- c_3 M_{-1}^{CB} \qquad (4.26)$$

Here, both time deposits (*TD*) and demand deposits (*DD*) are entered separately, with time deposits expected to be the dominant factor for mortgage flows. The competing loan rate used here is the commercial loan rate (*RCL*). [In the equations for life insurance companies and mutual savings banks, the competing rate is the corporate bond rate (*RCB*); and for savings and loan associations, the FHLBB advance rate (*RP*) is used.]

The Demand for Mortgages

Household demand for mortgage funds is viewed in terms of the theory of portfolio choice, with net worth as the fundamental determinant. Where borrowing is not possible, the household is assumed to allocate net worth such that the marginal utility of all assets is equal. With borrowing possible, it will occur whenever the marginal cost or disutility of borrowing is less than the marginal utility of assets acquired.

Institutionally, there are constraints which prevent borrowing except on the basis of certain specific collateral requirements associated with different types of borrowing. For this reason, Jaffee relates the demand for mortgages to the stock of houses rather than to net worth. He assumes that the desired ratio of mortgages (M^d) to the market value of housing stock (*H*) is dependent upon the relative cost of mortgage financing, measuring the alternative rate by the corporate bond rate (*RCB*). That is:

$$M^d = (e_0 + e_1 RCB - e_2 RM)H \qquad (4.27)$$

Equation (4.27) gives the long-run optimum ratio of mortgage debt to the stock of houses, both old and newly constructed. However, while this ratio directly determines the demand for mortgage funds to finance the increase in the stock of housing, ΔH, one should expect that the adjustment of the outstanding stock of debt on existing houses to the outstanding stock of such houses will occur very slowly. Indeed, except when old houses change hands, the readjustment of the stock of debt requires renegotiating mortgages currently in force, which is costly both financially and in terms of decision and arrangement time. Accordingly, Jaffee writes the short-run demand function for the current flow of mortgage funds as the sum of a component related to current additions to the stock of houses, and a component reflecting gradual adjustment of the initial stock of mortgages toward its equilibrium value. The first component is obtained from (4.27) by replacing H by the current gross additions ΔH. The second term takes the form of $\lambda_0(H^* - M_{-1})$, where H^* is given by the right side of (4.27) but with H replaced by H_{-1}, and λ_0 is the quarterly speed of adjustment, which one would expect to be quite small. Combining these two terms yields

$$\Delta M^d = (e_0 + e_1 RCB - e_2 RM)(\lambda_0 H_{-1} + \Delta H) - \lambda_0 M_{-1}. \qquad (4.28)$$

The Mortgage Rate

The equilibrium mortgage demand and supply relationships can be used to determine the equilibrium mortgage rate, RM^*. But, as indicated earlier, mortgage supply is unresponsive to the current mortgage rate in this model due to the existence of advance commitments. In the mortgage flow equations above, the mortgage rate enters only indirectly.

Consequently, Jaffee assumes that the short-run mortgage rate adjusts in order to equate current mortgage demand and a predetermined supply. This is accomplished in the model by setting the change in demand equal to the observed gross mortgage flows of the intermediaries, and solving for RM.

$$RM = \frac{e_0}{e_2} + \frac{e_1}{e_2} RCB - \frac{1}{e_2} \frac{\Delta M_g^T + \lambda_0 M_{-1}^T}{\Delta H + \lambda_0 H_{-1}} - \frac{1}{e_3} \frac{OC_{-1}^T}{\Delta H + \lambda_0 H_{-1}} \qquad (4.29)$$

where

ΔM_g^T = total observed gross mortgage flows of the intermediaries

M^T = total mortgage stocks of the intermediaries.

The last term, containing total lagged outstanding commitments (OC^T_{-1}), is included on the grounds that the expectation of additional mortgage flows resulting from outstanding commitments will depress *RM*.

Equation (4.29) is based upon the assumption that the mortgage market clears every quarter. On the grounds that institutional reasons and empirical evidence indicate that this is not the case, Jaffee puts this equation into a partial adjustment framework.

$$RM = \lambda_1 \frac{e_0}{e_2} + \lambda_1 \frac{e_1}{e_2} RCB - \frac{\lambda_1}{e_2} \frac{\Delta M^T_g + \lambda_0 M^T_{-1}}{\Delta H + \lambda_0 H_{-1}} - \frac{\lambda_1}{e_3} \frac{OC^T_{-1}}{\Delta H + \lambda_0 H_{-1}}$$

$$+ (1 - \lambda_1) RM_{-1} \qquad (4.30)$$

This specification allows for a disequilibrium mortgage rate, and implies that credit rationing exists in the mortgage market. Since all of the commitment equations were estimated using actual flows, the implied assumption of Jaffee's model is that the market was never in excess supply – i.e., excess demand existed in the mortgage market throughout the period of estimation (1955 through 1968).

One final consideration is necessary to complete the mortgage sector. The model contains equations for gross mortgage flows, and in order to specify the increment to stocks period-by-period, it is necessary to know something about mortgage repayments (*R*).

Jaffee found that the long-run trend in repayments was approximately a constant percentage of the stock, but that short-run variations exist. Given that normal repayments are contracted as part of the mortgage, and in the absence of evidence that prepayments vary much in the short run, the short-run variations are attributed to turnover of the existing stock.

It was assumed that trading volume is related to the availability of mortgage credit measured by the deviation of the mortgage rate from a twelve-quarter moving average ($RM - \overline{RM}$), and the lagged value of gross mortgage flows. Thus, the repayments equation for each intermediary is of the form:

$$R = [\alpha_0 + \alpha_1 (RM - \overline{RM})] M_{-1} + \alpha_2 \Delta M_{g-1} \qquad (4.31)$$

The Housing Sector

Since the housing sector in the FRB-MIT-Penn model is fairly complex, it is convenient to begin this section with a simplified description of the fundamental model.[8] The treatment is static, ignoring the distinction between single and multifamily housing markets, and it assumes that all markets clear in the period of analysis. Discussion of most adjustment lags, credit rationing, and a number of other complicating factors is deferred until later.

Reduced to simplest terms, the housing sector of the model can be summarized in the following manner. It is assumed that the housing stock is proportional to the supply of rental space, and that the implicit rental price for rental space clears that market. The determinants of demand for the housing stock, the housing cost of capital, and the existing supply of housing determine the asset price of the stock. This asset price, relative to construction costs, stimulates or depresses construction of new homes, thereby affecting current expenditures and income.

In turn, changes in the rate of construction (and depreciation or destruction) of houses alter the existing stock and affect construction costs. These changes affect the subsequent asset price of housing, the cost of capital, and the amount of subsequent construction undertaken. In equilibrium, the housing stock, the housing price, the cost of capital, and construction costs adjust to steady-state values which terminate the stimulus for further net investment.

Demand

Demand for the existing real stock of houses (K_H) is approached in terms of demand for the service flows derived from occupancy of rental space, assumed to be proportional to the housing stock. The determinants of per capita demand are assumed to be real per capita permanent income (Y^P/N) and the implicit rental price for the stock of houses relative to general consumer prices (P_r/P_C).

$$\frac{K_H}{N} = e^{\alpha_0}\left(\frac{Y^P}{N}\right)^{\alpha_1}\left(\frac{P_R}{P_C}\right)^{-\alpha_2} \qquad \alpha_1, \alpha_2 > 0 \qquad (4.32)$$

Or, written in terms of the unobservable implicit rental price for the service flows from the stock:

8. The housing sector of the FRB-MIT-Penn model represents the work of numerous contributors over a period of several years. During this period, the principal contributors have been Gordon Sparks, Franco Modigliani, Frank de Leeuw, Edward Gramlich, and Albert Ando. It is impossible to disentangle their individual contributions, and those of numerous others, at this point. Nor is it possible to indicate points of disagreement which any of the above might have concerning the current form of the sector. The present author, currently responsible for the housing sector, assumes full responsibility for any misinterpretations in this paper of the contributions of those named above. For the complete description, see Kalchbrenner in [3], ch. 6.

$$P_R = e^{\alpha_0/\alpha_2} \left(\frac{K_H}{N}\right)^{-1/\alpha_2} \left(\frac{Y^P}{N}\right)^{\alpha_1/\alpha_2} P_C \qquad (4.33)$$

In equilibrium, market clearing for homeowners requires that the cost of capital (R_H) be equal to the ratio of the implicit rental price to the equilibrium price of the housing stock (P_H).

$$R_H = \frac{P_R}{P_H} \qquad (4.34)$$

Expressing (4.34) in terms of P_H, and substituting for P_R from (4.33) yields the expression for the equilibrium price of houses.[9]

$$P_H = \left(\frac{P_C}{R_H}\right) e^{\alpha_0/\alpha_2} \left(\frac{K_H}{N}\right)^{-1/\alpha_2} \left(\frac{Y^P}{N}\right)^{\alpha_1/\alpha_2} \qquad (4.35)$$

Supply

In deriving the unobservable equilibrium price of the existing housing stock, the supply is treated as given in the short run. Three factors can alter the real stock: (i) depreciation, (ii) additions and alterations, and (iii) new construction. In terms of importance to current economic activity, the latter is the factor of principal interest.

For the present, specification of the determinants of these factors in the model remains rudimentary. The first two, depreciation and additions and alterations are assumed to be constant proportions of the existing stock through time.[10] Similarly, the explanation of new housing starts remains quite simple. Builders are assumed to respond to variations in the difference between the housing asset price and housing construction costs (including labor, materials, and construction financing), represented by P_{HC}. That is, builders are assumed to vary real per capita housing starts positively with housing prices and negatively with the various components of cost. Written in the functional form of the demand equations:

$$\frac{HS}{N \cdot P_{HC}} = e^{\beta_0} \left(\frac{P_H}{P_{HC}}\right)^{\beta_1} \qquad \beta_1 > 0 \qquad (4.36)$$

9. Equation (4.34) is based upon Jorgenson [4], pp. 45–46.

10. The means of obtaining an estimate of additions and alterations in the empirical equations involves a complex iterative estimation process described below.

Substituting for P_H from (4.35) yields the housing starts equation:

$$\frac{HS}{N \cdot P_{HC}} = e^{\gamma_0} \left(\frac{P_C}{R_H \cdot P_{HC}} \right)^{\gamma_1} \left(\frac{K_H}{N} \right)^{\gamma_2} \left(\frac{Y^P}{N} \right)^{\gamma_3} \tag{4.37}$$

where

$\gamma_1 = \beta_1 > 0$ the elasticity of housing starts with respect to the price ratio from (4.36), and the elasticity of housing starts with respect to the cost of capital

$\gamma_2 = -\dfrac{\beta_1}{\alpha_2} < 0$ where $-\alpha_2$ is the elasticity of demand for the housing stock with respect to the rental and consumer price indexes from (4.32)

$\gamma_3 = \dfrac{\beta_1 \alpha_1}{\alpha_2} > 0$ where α_1 is the elasticity of demand for the housing stock with respect to real per capita permanent income from (4.32).

Housing Expenditures

Although the housing starts equation is the core of the housing sector, it is necessary to relate housing starts to current expenditures for use in the overall model. The dollar expenditure relationship in the model is dependent upon two components. First, current expenditures will be generated by housing starts initiated in the current period. And, since it takes time to construct housing, there will also be some current expenditures associated with construction activity initiated in earlier quarters. Second, it is necessary to take into account additions and alterations to the current stock.

Denoting current dollar expenditures by E_H, the lagged current dollar value of the housing stock by $\$K_{H-1}$, the addition and alteration rate by a, and using the lag operator $\mathcal{L}$, the considerations above result in

$$E_H = \mathcal{L}HS + a\$K_{H-1} \tag{4.38}$$

The Relationship Between Housing Starts and the Stock of Houses

In order to close the sector, an expression for the relationship between housing starts and the housing stock is required. Conceptually, this is accomplished quite simply by writing the current real stock as the sum of the lagged stock less depreciation (δK_{H-1}, where δ is the depreciation rate), plus additions and alterations, and a lag on real housing starts reflecting the time required to carry starts to completion.

$$K_H = (1 - \delta + a)K_{H-1} + \pounds HS/P \quad (4.39)$$

Empirical Estimates of the Model

On the basis of the simplified model outlined above, we next turn to the empirical estimation of the housing sector. For estimation purposes, several matters not discussed above have been included in the final equations.

First, the housing sector is divided into single-family and multifamily housing unit relationships. This was done for several reasons: (i) Purchasers of multifamily units are more likely to be institutional investors rather than owner-occupants of the housing space; (ii) financing arrangements and supply sources differ somewhat between multifamily and single-family units; (iii) there may have been a recent shift in favor of multifamily units on the part of consumers; and (iv) the two types of units differ in the average length of time required for construction.

Second, in the current version of the model, quarterly mobile home retail sales have been added to single-family housing starts. This step has several disadvantages; but, hopefully, it represents an interim improvement over the previous means of treating mobile homes.

Finally, the empirical equations allow for the existence of lags in adjustment and the possibility of credit rationing in the markets most closely related to housing.

Single-family housing starts.

The treatment of mobile homes. In earlier versions of the FRB-MIT-Penn model, mobile homes expenditures were included as a part of consumption expenditures for durable goods since that is how they are treated in the National Income Accounts. The decision to move mobile homes to the housing sector in the model was made on the basis of the recent growth in this form of housing. Since the end of World War II, mobile home sales increased from an estimated annual rental sales volume of \$146 million in 1947 to almost \$2.5 billion in 1969, with rapid growth during the 1960s. A comparison of sales of new single-family homes and new mobile homes shipments for 1969 indicates that mobile homes account for almost the entire market under \$15,000, and 48 percent of the total, regardless of price (on a unit basis).[11] Consequently, mobile homes can no longer be ignored as a substantial component of the housing market.

There are problems involved in treating mobile homes in the same way as conventional single-family units, but lack of data necessary to estimate mobile homes separately resulted in the addition of mobile home retail sales to single-family housing starts. For example, this procedure ignores the fact that the purchase and financing terms for mobile homes differ considerably from those of conventional single-family dwellings. Until 1969, when saving and loan associations were authorized to finance mobile homes, and the Federal Housing Administration was authorized to issue mortgage guarantees for their purchase, mobile homes were typically financed by means of a conditional sales contract with a fairly short maturity, much like automobile financing. Sales finance companies typically purchased these contracts from mobile home dealers.

In addition to this difference, others might be cited. But, the more important consideration at this stage of the development of the model was whether or not the total of single-family and mobile home units could be explained adequately without further disaggregation. Although exploration of possible benefits of separation is desirable, it does not appear that ignoring substitution, financing differences, and other factors seriously affects our ability to explain this total.

In order to include mobile homes in the housing sector, a quarterly series on mobile homes expenditures was required. No such series existed, so an approximation was constructed based upon annual expenditure figures from the Mobile Home Manufacturers Association (MHMA) and the Quarterly Office of Business Economics figures for mobile homes and recreation trailers.[12]

The dependent variable. For estimation purposes, the dependent variable in the single-family starts relationship is defined to include single-family units, mobile homes, and two-unit structures. This last addition was dictated by data availability. Their sum, *HS1$*, which is measured in value terms, is deflated by: (i) *N1*, the adult population most likely to live in single family dwellings (i.e., the population between ages 25 and 65); (ii) *PHCA*, the price deflator for housing construction costs adjusted for productivity increases; and (iii) real per capita capacity in the housing industry.[13] In earlier versions of the housing model,

11. *Flash Facts on Mobile Homes,* Mobile Homes Manufacturers Association, June 1970.

12. The OBE figures were converted to quarterly rates and aggregated to obtain annual figures. The ratios of the MHMA and OBE annual figures were then used to obtain interpolated quarterly ratios. Finally, the quarterly ratios were applied to the quarterly OBE data at annual rates to get the estimated series actually used (i.e., a series excluding recreational vehicles).

13. *PHCA* is based upon the Boeckh index of construction costs. The original index is computed entirely on the basis of wage rates and the cost of construction materials, ignoring increases in the productivity of labor over time. Edward Gramlich adjusted this index to re-

several unsuccessful attempts were made to specify and estimate the growth in capacity of the housing industry. Rather than simply ignoring this factor, the dependent variable is deflated by a time trend which grows at the rate of 2 percent per year. This trend has the effect of allowing a larger response by construction firms to the relationship between housing prices and construction costs as the economy grows over time.

The independent variables. Several comments are necessary concerning the independent variables used in the starts equation.

In the first term of equation (4.37), the price series used are the NIA price deflator for personal consumption expenditures (*PCON*) in the numerator, and *PHCA*, described above, in the denominator. The other component, the cost of capital for single-family housing (*RCH1*), is constructed as follows:

$$RCH1 = -1.46 + (1 - t)(.7RM + .3RCB + tp) \qquad (4.40)$$

This expression, an adaptation of the user cost of capital expression derived by Jorgenson [4], is based upon the following considerations. The cost of capital for housing should be a weighted average of the land and housing stock components of depreciation and capital gains, appropriate interest rates, and tax rates. The constant term reflects assumptions about the relative effects of depreciation and capital gains, appropriately weighted. All attempts to estimate expected capital gains statistically by a distributed lag on past prices met with failure.[14]

The interest rates entered are the mortgage rate (*RM*) and the corporate bond rate (*RCB*), with the weights obtained from the average ratio of mortgages to house values. The corporate bond rate is a proxy for the rate on own financing; an opportunity cost measure. *tp* is the estimated effective property tax rate obtained from the ratio of annual state and local property tax receipts to the estimated current dollar value of the housing stock and land. These rates are multiplied by $(1 - t)$, where t is the personal tax rate, reflecting the tax law provisions relating to the treatment of interest and tax payments for income tax purposes.

The complete first term is entered in the empirical equation (estimated in

---

flect productivity increases by assuming growth in labor productivity of 3.2 per cent per year, and applying this growth to the estimated ratio of labor costs to total costs (.30) derived from NIA data. This reduces the rate of growth of the Boeckh index by .0025 per quarter. *PHCA* is used as the deflator for housing starts rather than the final housing expenditures price deflator used in the housing expenditure equation because the original value series for *HS1$* is appropriately stated in terms of construction costs rather than final prices.

14. Since expected prices, as measured elsewhere in the FRB-MIT-Penn model, do not appear in the housing sector, the model implies that housing responds to nominal rather than real interest rates. The only price-change effect comes through the capital gains term which may not reflect general price changes completely.

log form), using an Almon distributed lag reflecting expectations, inertia, and the time required to initiate housing construction in response to changes in the differential between prices and costs.

The second term in equation (4.37) is represented by the real stock of single-family houses (*KH1*) deflated by the adult population (*N1*), and lagged one quarter in order to use beginning-of-the-quarter values. The third term approximates the real per capita permanent income by real consumption expenditures (*CON*) deflated by total population (*N*). Here real consumption expenditures are in terms of the FRB-MIT-Penn consumption definition, a more inclusive measure than that used in the National Income Accounts. In the current version of the equation, the long-run elasticity of demand for the housing stock with respect to real per capita permanent income is constrained to unity on the basis of the results of other studies, and the fact that unconstrained estimation led to unsatisfactory results.

In addition to the variables included in equation (4.37), three other terms are added to the final estimated equation. These terms are related to the dynamics of financial intermediary behavior, the mortgage market, and the housing market. As indicated in an earlier summary of the FRB-MIT-Penn model by de Leeuw and Gramlich [1], and elaborated in the work of Modigliani and Jaffee summarized above, these sectors exhibit the characteristics that lead to the expectation of rationing (defined as nonprice market clearing in the short run). Financial intermediary lending and deposit rates change slowly; deposit flows at these institutions are volatile; and there is little control over asset composition, especially in the short run. In the mortgage market, the considerations related to the use of advance commitments and the high adjustment costs described by Jaffee make it unlikely that the mortgage market clears quarterly. Finally, adding the time required to initiate and complete new housing space, it appears unlikely that the housing market is in equilibrium quarterly.

As a consequence, from the mortgage sector of the model, the change in outstanding mortgage commitments of savings and loan associations ($MCOS\$/MCOS\$_{-1}$) is added to the single-family housing starts equation.[15] In earlier versions of the housing model, a measure of deposit flows at financial intermediaries was used in this capacity.

Finally, the use of commitments reflects the institutional requirement usually imposed upon construction firms that they possess commitments prior to acquiring construction loans. As indicated in the discussion of equation (4.36), it would be preferable to enter a construction loan cost measure as well, but no

15. The change in outstanding commitments is used rather than new commitments, the preferable variable, since the latter are not currently available, as indicated in the summary of the mortgage sector. Only savings and loan commitments are included even though other financial intermediaries are important in the single-family housing market. Attempts to include more than one set of commitments led to multicollinearity problems as anticipated, and savings and loan commitments appeared dominant.

suitable variable is available in the overall model for this purpose (the closest approximation would be the commercial loan rate).

The second additional variable in the housing starts equation reflects the increased importance of the Federal National Mortgage Association activities in the mortgage market. On the basis of a rationale similar to that given for the addition of new mortgage commitments of savings and loan associations, an approximation of FNMA new commitments is currently added to the equation. In the absence of commitment data for FNMA, it is assumed that the arithmetic change in the stock of mortgages held by FNMA (*DZMFN$*) approximates outstanding commitments. The variable is added to the outstanding commitments of savings and loan associatons for estimation purposes. The logarithmic change of the sum of the two outstanding commitments variables is intended to serve as a proxy variable for the combined new commitments of the two institutions.

The final additional variable in the single-family housing starts equation was suggested by J. Enzler. One possible nonprice measure of ability of prospective purchasers to meet downpayment requirements for home purchases is variations in the value of the financial component of household net worth. Consequently, a measure of the change in household net worth, less the sum of the value of the housing stock and the stock of consumer durables in the current period (W_t) was added to the equation.

All three of these variables were estimated with lags to reflect the slow adjustment to equilibrium anticipated in the housing sector.

The final single-family housing starts equation estimated is of the form:

$$\ln\left(\frac{HS1\$}{N1 \cdot PHCA}\right) - .005\ \text{time} =$$

$$c_0 + c_1\left[\ln\left(\frac{CON}{N}\right) - \ln\left(\frac{KH1}{N1}\right)_{-1}\right] + \Sigma\, w_i \ln\left(\frac{PCON}{PHCA \cdot RCH1}\right)_{-i}$$

$$+ \Sigma\, w_j' \ln\left[\frac{(MCOS\$ + DZMFN\$)}{(MCOS\$ + DZMFN\$)_{-1}}\right]_{-j} + \Sigma\, w_k'' \ln(W)_{-k} \qquad (4.41)$$

Multifamily housing starts. The multifamily housing starts equation is similar to the equation for single-family starts, but less complex. The dependent variable includes real per capita starts of three or more units deflated by the same time trend to reflect growth in capacity. In this case, the price deflator is the same (*PHCA*), but the population deflator includes the population aged 20–25, and 65 and over (*N3*).

The estimated term corresponding to the first term in (4.37) does not include a cost-of-capital component. It is measured by the ratio of the consumer price index to the adjusted Boeckh index (*PCON/PHCA*). There exists in the model an equation for the cost of capital for multiunit construction, but that equation is currently suspended because the cost of capital yielded the incorrect sign and was not significant in the estimation of the current equation. In form, the multifamily cost-of-capital equation is similar to that for single-family units, but with different weights on interest rates, and allowance for different tax treatment.[16]

The second and third terms of equation (4.37) are represented by the real stock of multifamily houses (*KH3*) deflated by *N3*, and the proxy variable for real per capita permanent income (*CON/N*). As in the single-family starts equation, the long-run permanent income elasticity of demand for the stock is constrained to equal unity in the estimates.

Two commitments-rationing variables are entered in the equation on the same grounds as discussed above. Both the change in outstanding commitments of mutual saving banks ($MCOM\$/MCOM\$_{-1}$), and new commitments of life insurance companies (*MCNI$*) are included in the equation.

The final addition to the multifamily housing starts equation is a dummy variable for the four quarters of 1966 which takes on the value .5 for the first and fourth quarters, and 1.0 for the second and third quarters of the year. The dummy variable was entered to reduce the impact of the 1966 "credit crunch" upon the estimated coefficients of the commitments variables due to the sharp divergence of the data from normal variability during that year.

The final multifamily housing starts equation estimated has the following form:

$$\ln\left(\frac{HS3\$}{N3 \cdot PHCA}\right) - .005\ \text{time} =$$

$$d_0 + d_1\left[\ln\left(\frac{CON}{N}\right) - \ln\left(\frac{KH3}{N3}\right)_{-1}\right] + \Sigma\, w_i \ln\left(\frac{PCON}{PHCA}\right)_{-i}$$

$$+ \Sigma\, w_j' \ln\left(\frac{MCOM\$}{MCOM\$_{-1}}\right)_{-j} + \Sigma\, w_k'' \ln MCNI\$_{-k} + d_2 D. \qquad (4.42)$$

Expenditures on housing. Determination of the current expenditures on housing is complicated only by the problem of specifying additions and alterations to the existing stock. As indicated by equation (4.38), housing expenditures

16. In earlier versions of the multifamily starts equation, the rental component of the consumer price index was used directly rather than substituting for the implicit rental price as is done in the single-family starts equation. However, during the 1969 reestimation of the model necessitated by the NIA data revisions, the rental price index was not significant, so the substitution process was adopted.

are the weighted sum of current and lagged combined housing starts, plus additions and alterations to the existing nominal stock.

Gramlich devised the method currently used to obtain an estimate of a, the additions and alterations rate, employing a three-step iterative procedure.[17] The procedure is based upon the following relationships:[18]

$$EH\$ = \sum_j w_j\ (HS1\$ + HS3\$)_{-j} + a(KH1\$ + KH3\$)_{-1} \tag{4.43}$$

$$(KH1 + KH3)_{-1} = (1 - \delta + a)(KH1 + KH3)_{-2}$$

$$+ (\Sigma w_j)(HS1_{-2} + \frac{2}{3}HS3_{-3} + \frac{1}{3}HS3_{-4}) \tag{4.44}$$

These two relationships are simply restatements of (4.38) and (4.39) respectively, in the specific notation of the model. As shown, the housing stock inventory updating relationship is in real terms in the model. In the last term of equation (4.44), Σw_j is constrained to be the same as in (4.43) for reasons indicated below. The specific lags and proportions imposed upon the housing starts variable were derived from census data which indicated that an average of one quarter is required to build a single-family unit and multifamily completions are distributed approximately between two and three quarters after construction begins.

It is not possible to estimate (4.43) directly to obtain an empirical estimate of the w_j and a, since the capital stock required in the last term is not available without an estimate of a, as shown in (4.44). An iterative scheme was chosen to obtain estimates of both the w_j and a.

Multiplying (4.44) by PEH, the appropriate price index, lagging the expression by one period and employing a back-substitution process, the expression can be rewritten as

$$PEH_{-1}(KH1 + KH3)_{-1} =$$

$$(\Sigma w_j)\left[\sum_{i=0}^{\infty} (1 - \delta + a)^i PEH_{-1-i}(HS1_{-2-i} + \frac{2}{3}HS3_{-3-i} + \frac{1}{3}HS3_{-4-i}\right]. \tag{4.45}$$

---

17. Conceptually, additions and alterations would be expected to vary with economic conditions rather than remaining a constant fraction of the stock. Lack of data and a desire to avoid the addition of further equations to the model led to the current method of treatment.

18. In the overall model, mobile homes expenditures are subtracted from the value of housing starts. These expenditures are added back into the model in the consumption sector to preserve consistency.

Substituting this expression for the nominal housing stock into (4.43) yields

$$EH\$ = \sum_j w_j (HS1\$ + HS3\$)_{-j}$$

$$+ a\left(\sum_j w_j\right)\left[\sum_{i=0}^{\infty} (1 - \delta + a)^i PEH_{-1-i}\left(HS1_{-2-i} + \frac{2}{3}HS3_{-3-i} + \frac{1}{3}HS3_{-4-i}\right)\right] \cdot \tag{4.46}$$

Lagging this expression by one quarter and multiplying by $(1 - \delta + a)$ yields

$$(1 - \delta + a)EH\$_{-1} = (1 - \delta + a)\left[\sum_j w_j (HS1\$ + HS3\$)_{-j}\right]_{-1}$$

$$+ a\left(\sum_j w_j\right)\left[\sum_{i=1}^{\infty} (1 - \delta + a)^i PEH_{-1-i}\left(HS1_{-2-i} + \frac{2}{3}HS3_{-3-i} + \frac{1}{3}HS3_{-4-i}\right)\right] \cdot \tag{4.47}$$

Rewritten in terms of the infinite sum, equation (4.47) yields an observable expression which is substituted into (4.46) to form

$$EH\$ - (1 - \delta + a)EH\$_{-1} =$$

$$\sum_j w_j \left[\left[(HS1\$ + HS3\$)_{-j} - (1 - \delta + a)(HS1\$ + HS3\$)_{-j-1}\right]\right]$$

$$+ a\left(\sum_j w_j\right)PEH_{-1}\left(HS1_{-2} + \frac{2}{3}HS3_{-3} + \frac{1}{3}HS3_{-4}\right) \tag{4.48}$$

In the last term of this expression, real housing starts are multiplied by the price deflator for the capital stock *PEH*. This poses no problems since *PEH* is the appropriate price deflator for housing completions (here represented by lagged starts) in the determination of final expenditures.

From these expressions, equation (4.43) is used to estimate the $\hat{w}_j$, ignoring the capital stock component in the first iteration. The second step involves assuming that $a = \delta$ in (4.48), and estimating $\hat{a}$, imposing the $\Sigma\hat{w}_j$ from the first iteration. The final iteration involves a reestimation of (4.48) in which $\hat{a}$ from the second step is imposed only in the term $(1 - \delta + a)$, using the estimate of δ from Goldsmith (.0065 per quarter). The final values that emerge from this process are

$\hat{w}_1 = .3202 \quad \hat{a} = .0035$

$\hat{w}_2 = .6081$

$\hat{w}_3 = .1298$

$\Sigma\hat{w} = 1.0581$

The Stock of Houses

The final relationships in the housing sector are the expressions for the real single-family and multifamily housing stocks. As indicated earlier, the expressions employed in the model are based directly upon equation (4.44), using the estimates of $(1 - \delta + a)$ and Σw_j from the iteration procedure, but separating the total stock by housing type.

Since the two housing stock components are expressed in 1958 dollars in (4.44), real completions of houses are required. Real completions are obtained from lagged nominal starts deflated by the final housing expenditures deflator, *PEH.* This differs from the deflator used in the starts equation, *PHCA,* since starts are measured in terms of construction costs while final sales include value added during construction. This difference, minor for the purpose at hand, plus elements of uncertainty concerning the comparability of the starts and stock data series used in the model, led to the estimation of the weights for housing starts in the expenditures equation and the imposition of the sum of these weights in the stock equation.

Appendix 4A
Alphabetical Listing of Variables Used in Final Equations

CG	Change in household net worth less personal saving (capital gains)
CON	Consumption: 1958 dollars
CON$	Nominal consumption: Current prices
D	Total deposits at financial institutions: Mortgage model notation
DD	Demand deposits at commercial banks: Mortgage model notation
EH	Expenditures for residential construction: 1958 dollars
EH$	Expenditures for residential construction: Current dollars
H	Housing stock: Mortgage model notation
HS1$	Housing starts, single- and two-family dwelling units: Current dollars
HS3$	Housing starts, multifamily dwelling units: Current dollars
KH1	Stock of single-family houses: 1958 dollars
KH3	Stock of multifamily houses: 1958 dollars
M	Mortgage stocks at financial intermediaries: Mortgage model notation
MCNI$	New mortgage commitments of life insurance companies
MCOM$	Outstanding mortgage commitments of mutual savings banks
MCOS$	Outstanding mortgage commitments of savings and loan associations
ΔMg	Gross mortgage flows: Mortgage model notation
MIS$	Life insurance reserves less policy loans
MMS$	Mutual savings bank deposits
MS$	Savings and loan shares and mutual savings bank deposits
MSL$	Savings and loan association shares
N	Total population
N1	Population between age 25 and age 65
N3	Population between ages 20 and 25, and over age 65
NC	New mortgage commitments: Mortgage model notation
OASI$	OASI benefits excluding Medicare: Current dollars
OC	Outstanding mortgage commitments: Mortgage model notation
PCON	Price deflator for consumption expenditures
PEH	Implicit price deflator for expenditures on housing
PHCA	Adjusted Boeckh construction cost index
R	Mortgage repayments: Mortgage model notation
RA	Weighted average of RMS and RSL
RCB	Corporate bond rate (Moody's Aaa)
RCH1	Cost of capital for single-family dwellings
RCH3	Cost of capital for multifamily dwellings
RCL	Commercial loan rate
RCP	Commercial paper rate

RM	Mortgage rate (weighted average of monthly FHA series for new and existing)
RMS	Effective rate on deposits at mutual savings banks
RP	Interest rate on advances from FHLBB: Mortgage model notation
RSL	Effective rate on savings and loan shares
RTB	Treasury bill rate
RTD	Effective rate on passbook savings deposits at commercial banks
SP	Personal saving: Disposable income less consumption
TD	Time deposits at commercial banks: Mortgage model notation
time	Quarterly time index beginning 1947:1
tp	Property tax rate
t	Effective rate of personal income tax
V	Net worth of households
Y	Disposable personal income
ZMFN$	Stock of mortgage holdings of FNMA

References

1. de Leeuw, Frank, and Gramlich, Edward. "The Channels of Monetary Policy." *Federal Reserve Bulletin* (June 1969).
2. Goldsmith, Raymond. *The National Wealth of the United States in the Post-war Period.* Princeton: Princeton University Press, 1962.
3. Gramlich, Edward and Jaffee, Dwight, eds. *Savings Deposits, Mortgages and Housing in the FRB-MIT-Penn Econometric Model.* Lexington, Mass.: Heath Lexington Books, 1972.
4. Jorgenson, Dale. "Anticipations and Investment Behavior." In *Brookings Quarterly Econometric Model of the United States,* J. Duesenberry, et al., eds. Chicago: Rand McNally, 1965.
5. Mobile Homes Manufacturing Association. *Flash Facts on Mobile Homes* (June 1970).

5 Econometric Models of the Residential Construction Sector: A Comparison*

Gary Fromm

Concern about the structure and operation of the residential construction sector of the U.S. economy has mounted in recent years as a result of marked cyclical swings in building activity and a growing discrepancy between privately and socially desired and actual housing stocks. This has led to increasing direct federal government intervention designed to stabilize and raise the rate of construction of housing units. Currently, federal efforts also are underway to restrain the inflation in building costs. In part, this is for other national economic purposes, but it also is being undertaken to enable a larger number of families to purchase or rent new and more adequate housing.

While these actions are likely to stimulate building activity and contribute to the achievement of social objectives, the extent of that stimulus is highly problematical. At best, existing models of the residential construction sector still are relatively unrefined and incomplete. Notwithstanding the use of some common explanatory factors, they conflict in form and substance and in their impact and long-run multipliers. On theoretical grounds, no model clearly is preferred; each has a unique rationale and advantages. On empirical grounds such as goodness of fit or ex post prediction accuracy, it is difficult to make an assessment. The models are estimated over different periods and comparable subsector simulations are not available.

A survey of the residential construction sectors of eight currently operable, major, complete-system U.S. econometric models and three housing sector models may be found in Appendix 5A. The approach taken in tabulating the information, which generally is the latest available at the time of this conference, follows that pioneered by Marc Nerlove [3].

Seven sets of characteristics are listed. The first notes the frequency and type of data, the period and number of observations for the principal equations estimated, and the method or methods of estimation employed.

The second set gives the number of equations (equal to the number of endogenous variables) and the number of exogenous variables. The total number of equations is the sum of the number of stochastic equations (those with coefficients estimated statistically), definitional equations (identities), and a priori

*An earlier version of this paper was presented at the Housing Model Conference, Federal Home Loan Bank Board, Washington, D.C., March 1971.

equations. A priori equations are defined as relationships or inequalities whose parameters are not estimated by any formal statistical procedure.

The classification of variables as endogenous or exogenous in part is given by each of the authors and is dictated by whether they are determined within each of the models as a whole. But, in order to focus on the residential construction sectors, it is advantageous to reclassify some variables which are endogenous to the complete system as exogenous to the residential construction sectors. All housing starts, values and stocks, construction expenditures, costs and prices, and rent or consumption of housing services deflators are treated as endogenous if they are determined within the models. Other prices, wage rates, outputs, income, financial flows, and interest rates which may or may not be endogenous in the complete models are classified as exogenous to the residential construction sector. Aside from achieving a better perspective for examining this sector, the justification for this procedure is that in almost all the models the degree of dependence of the latter variables on residential construction is very limited (except for effects from the total level of output) and feedback impacts to residential construction are weak.

Classification difficulties arose for several models because of failures to identify all equations or to indicate whether variables are exogenous. In these instances the system was closed by the addition of definitional identities and, if necessary, appropriate exogenous variables.

The next three sets of information for each model list, respectively, the main equations, endogenous variables, and exogenous variables. They reflect the classification adjustments cited above. The final two sets contain comments on dynamic features and nonlinearities and some noteworthy characteristics which are central to each model. In most instances the independent variables which enter the primary stochastic equations are delineated.

Rather than an equation-by-equation comparison, the remainder of this paper briefly explores a number of broader issues – the basic theories underlying the models, their realism in describing actual housing market conditions, and some special issues in estimation and specification.

Long-Run Considerations

The models surveyed here all are oriented toward the explanation of short-run (monthly, quarterly, or annual) phenomena in the residential construction sector. Therefore, to a certain extent, the authors can ignore long-run influences on housing if these do not change appreciably over the sample or forecast periods, or if they are taken into account by appropriate proxy variables, or if they are collinear with other included explanatory variables.

Two of these long-run influences appear to be population growth and household formation.[1] From 1890 to 1960 the population of the coterminus United States increased 184 percent (from 62.9 to 178.5 million) while occupied housing units increased 316 percent (from 12,690 to 52,814 thousand).[2] Thus, in 1890 there were 5.0 persons, and in 1960 3.4 persons, per occupied housing unit (the decline was monotonic decade by decade).[3] This decline is due primarily to increases in the percentage of married couples and individuals with their own households – that is reductions in doubling-up (for example, between 1950 and 1968 total married couples increased 21.2 percent while those with their own household rose 27.0 percent).[4] In turn, this probably in large measure is attributable to rising real disposable income per capita and per family (the rise per capita between 1890 and 1960 was approximately 290 percent).[5] However, it is worth noting that constant-dollar residential investment per capita has fluctuated within more narrow bounds (per capita private residential construction expenditures, in 1958 dollars, were \$107 in 1889-1891, \$133 in 1949-1951, and \$125 in 1959-1961).[6]

All the models include one or more of these influences (see Table 5-1 and Appendix 5A), although sometimes this is done with a time trend proxy.[7] Household formation enters the DRI model most explicitly in the form of a long distributed lag of marriages. Most of the models (the Brady and Fair formulations are exceptions) include the level or change in real disposable income as an explanatory variable. (In the case of the FRB and OBE models, consumption is taken as a proxy for permanent disposable income.) Of course, income is a short-run as well as a long-run factor, which is the perspective from which the models view the residential construction sector.

1. A household comprises all persons who occupy a housing unit, that is a house, an apartment, or other group of rooms which comprise separate living quarters.

2. These and the following population-per-household, married-couples, and housing-unit figures are from *Statistical Abstract of the United States: 1969,* pp. 5, 35, 701.

3. The population per household declined from 4.93 persons in 1890 to 3.38 and 3.23 persons in 1960 and 1968, respectively. (The difference between population per housing unit and population per household arises because population includes members of quasi-households.)

Recently, there also have been more households with second homes (which causes a decline in persons per housing unit). In 1967, these comprised 2.9 percent of all households. Ibid., p. 699.

4. Within the last decade, the average family size has been approximately constant at 3.7 persons; in 1950 there were 3.54 persons per family. Ibid., p. 35.

5. See Evans [1], p. 186.

6. Derived from Evans [1], p. 187. Public residential expenditures in the earlier period are not available but, presumably were negligible; in 1959-1961 they were \$4 (1958 dollars) per capita (derived from *National Income and Product Accounts of the United States, 1929-65,* U.S. Department of Commerce, 1966, p. 83). Also see Grebler and Maisel [2], p. 487.

7. The negative time trend in the Brady model single-family conventional starts function is an anomaly probably arising from misspecification of the equation.

Table 5–1
Variables in Primary Stochastic Starts or Expenditures Function

		Independent Variables			
			Credit Availability		
Model	*Dependent Variables*	*Interest Rates*	*Prices*	*Change in Flows*	*Rationing*
Brady	Starts	Conventional mtg FHA ceiling	Construction cost	FHLBB advances	Loan/value ratio
Brookings	Starts	Bill rate	Real value per start	Only through bill rate levels	
DHL III	Starts	(See credit)	None		Interest rate inequality
DRI	Starts	New corporate	None		Interest rate inequality
Fair	Starts	FHA new home	None	S&L, mutual savings banks, FHLBB advances	Change in FHA new home interest rate
FRB-MIT-Penn	Real value of starts per capita	Cost of capital	Housing services construction cost	S&L mtg. com., △FNMA acq., MSB mtg. com., life ins. new mtg. com.	Dummy for 1966
Huang	Real value of starts (supply); real expenditures (demand)	Commercial paper	Rent/house price Rent/CPI; house price	Free reserves	Loan/value ratio amortization period
Maisel	Starts	Conventional mtg. FHA 203 new	Rent/construction cost	FNMA acq., FHLBB advances, est. invest. in mtg. S&L and MSB life ins. net acq. mtg.	
OBE	Real value of starts per capita	Cost of capital	Housing services/ construction cost		Interest rate inequality
Wharton Annual	Starts	(See credit)	Housing services/ construction cost	Interest rate differential	
New Wharton Quarterly	Expenditures	(See credit)	Rent/construction cost	Interest rate differential	

Model	Independent Variables			
	Capital Stock and Inventory Factors	Income & Wealth	Demographic	Time Trend
Brady	None	None	None	Negative in single family starts Positive in multi-family starts
Brookings	Lagged starts vacancies	Real disposable income per household	Only in income	Positive
DHL III	Lagged starts	Real disposable income	None	None
DRI	Change in real stock; lagged starts	Real disposable income change	Marriages	None
Fair	Lagged starts as stock	None	None	Positive for demand Negative for supply
FRB-MIT-Penn	Real stock	Net worth change and real consumption per capita	None	Positive for supply
Huang	Value of excess supply; lagged demand & starts values	Real disposable income	None	None
Maisel	Lagged starts vacancies	Real disposable income per household	Only in income	None
OBE	Real stock	Real consumption per capita	None	Positive for supply
Wharton Annual	Real stock	Real disposable income change	None	None
New Wharton Quarterly	None	Real disposable income	None	None

Supply and Demand

In all cases, the equations can be characterized, and often are specified, as supply and demand relationships. However, with the exception of the FRB and OBE models (it might be noted that the latter is not an original formulation and simply borrows an earlier version of the former model) the specification of the supply and demand functions is almost entirely ad hoc. The procedure generally followed is to postulate the existence of these functions and then arbitrarily select a string of explanatory variables which may be causally related to housing prices or quantities. Then, with housing starts or expenditures as the dependent variable, supply may or may not be set equal to demand.

Most of the models make the initial assumption that supply equals demand and then attempt to allow for disequilibria in housing markets. This is done by including short-run variables as additional explanatory factors. Sometimes these are credit flows, sometimes housing inventory changes, or sometimes both. But, as in the basic specifications, their inclusion is ad hoc and not based on any theory of the disequilibrium adjustment process. (This is true, too, of the FRB and OBE models in which greater rigor is used in specifying supply and demand relationships.)

Utility and Profit Maximization

Is is surprising, given the availability of sophisticated theories of business investment and consumer behavior (which are utilized in some of the macro-models reviewed here), that the same techniques have not been applied to the residential construction sector. None of the models formulate a rigorous maximization hypothesis in which homeowners, renters, and builders seek to maximize expected utility or profits (or minimize disutility or costs). If maximization conditions were imposed, many of the same explanatory variables (for example, relative prices, the rental price of capital, expected income, and so forth) would appear in the equations in nearly the same form, but they would be estimated differently and would be augmented by additional information.

To cite only one example, in the FRB and OBE models, the rental price of capital is badly misspecified in both the single- and multiple-family housing starts (values) equations. An attempt is made to incorporate an opportunity cost of capital as approximated by a weighted average of mortgage interest and bond rates. However, the weights selected improperly reflect marginal tradeoffs between housing and alternative investments. No account is taken of downpayments or of the declining exponential pattern of interest payments under the usual mortgage contract. In the case of multifamily capital rental prices, taxes are disregarded and no account is taken of any of the depreciation provisions and laws that apply to residential construction.[8] Therefore, it is not surprising that in recent versions of the FRB model significant cost-of-capital effects have not been found, which is what one would hope, given the poor a priori specification of this variable.

It might also be noted that in neither the FRB nor the OBE cost of capital, nor elsewhere in these or the other models, is any account taken, except perhaps indirectly and very implicitly, of the housing subsidies provided by the federal government – for example the FHA 235 and 236 programs. Furthermore, the equity participation in building ownership of some of the suppliers of housing capital (principally insurance companies and pension funds) is ignored in all the models.

Another problem related to utility maximization besets the FRB, OBE, and new Wharton quarterly models. In each of these, the dependent variables of the primary stochastic equations are measured in dollar expenditure terms. In essence, therefore, it is assumed that the elasticity of substitution between the number of starts and the value per start is equal to unity, or that, in the aggregate, people are indifferent whether they have a greater quantity of housing units or more valuable housing units. Since there is a requirement for shelter irrespective of its value, this does not seem plausible.

Supply Consideration and Disequilibria

On the cost side, the specifications of the models appear extremely primitive. Most of the price equations used are almost wholly autoregressive. No account is taken of construction labor costs or materials costs. Sometimes, labor and materials cost effects are introduced from elsewhere in the models in terms of price indexes of selected output or of private wage rates. But if construction costs change at different rates than costs in other sectors of the economy, which has been happening recently, then using these other costs as explanatory variables gives misleading estimates of costs in the residential construction sector.

Irrespective of the costs and profitability of construction, builders may be prevented from initiating projects by the lack of availability of funds. To some extent, such shortages are reflected in interest rates, but not completely. The housing market has periodically been beset by credit shortages and rationing, which has limited the number of starts. Several of the models include measures

8. The importance of doing so is demonstrated in a study by Taubman and Rasche [4]. They find that 96 percent of the variance in annual multifamily starts can be explained by only two variables, the difference between the present discounted value of apartment buildings and construction costs in the current year and lagged one year. The Taubman-Rasche analysis, however, suffers from some of the same deficiencies of the studies reviewed here in ignoring other crucial demand and supply factors.

of savings flows at savings and loan institutions, mutual savings banks, and life insurance companies, and support for housing from FNMA and GNMA purchases of mortgages, as partial indicators of credit availability. They do not take account of housing funds provided by commercial bank mortgages (the FRB model does so indirectly). Perhaps this variable would not be significant in spite of the substantial share of total outstanding mortgages held by commercial banks, but this would be an important and surprising finding.[9]

Disequilibria may arise, too, from sudden shifts in demand or in anticipations of builders. Thus, at any point in time, the number of available units may depart radically from the effective demand for them, which then influences subsequent building and demolitions. Because of imperfections and gradual adjustments to such gaps, the imbalance may persist for a considerable period. With the exception of the Brookings, Huang, and Maisel models, housing inventory influences tend to be ignored, or taken into account only very crudely through real values of capital stocks or combinations of this variable and time trends.

In general, real values of capital stocks have very low correlations with the number of vacancies, which are (due to sticky prices) the best guide to excesses or deficiencies in supply. Vacancies, unlike capital stocks, reveal significant cyclical fluctuations. Generally, as any builder can verify, when vacancies are high relative to available units, they are a "drag" on the market and reduce housing starts. Therefore, vacancies probably should appear in housing models explicitly rather than in the proxy form of other variables.

Rents, rental prices, and construction costs do react to gaps between supply and demand. The ratio of rental prices to construction costs is included in several models. But, movements in this variable normally are very sticky. Rents and rental prices usually change slowly and construction costs exhibit ratchet effects. Consequently, price–cost ratios do not mirror cyclical movements in vacancies and housing demand and supply.

Aggregation and Estimation

Another principal issue is the degree of disaggregation required to analyze housing markets, and first of all, by type of unit. Some of the models still are specified with the dependent variable as total starts or expenditures. Most economists have recognized, for a number of years, that there are distinct markets for single- and multi-family units, notwithstanding some substitution effects. These markets should be analyzed separately. Also those starts that are subsidized by government programs should be viewed differently than those that are conventionally financed.

---

9. Financial costs and constraints are, of course, relevant from the demand side too. Another factor which might be considered explicitly is the impact of repayment and prepayment of mortgages, for which some data now are available from the Federal Home Loan Bank Board.

In addition, units that are constructed and maintained by governments should not be ignored, as they are in all the models.[10] Until recently, their numbers have not been of great significance in terms of total volume, but they must still somehow be accounted for. There are substitution possibilities between these and other housing units. Moreover, they inappropriately have been neglected (the Brookings and Maisel models are examples) in the identity which relates the number of households, vacancies, and available units.

The second prime problem in disaggregation of housing markets is separation in space. The availability of a housing unit in California is not the same thing as the availability of a housing unit in New York or Washington. There is no transferability of the services of housing units in California to housing services in New York. Thus, if there are disequilibria in housing markets and the adjustment process to random shocks takes time (say several quarters or years), national aggregates are misleading indicators of conditions of markets in locations around the country. National figures can mask serious imbalances such as large excesses of units in some regions and serious shortages in others. This is likely to occur when there are rapid and substantial shifts in migration patterns.

The final issue in housing disaggregation is whether monthly, quarterly, annual, or even lower periodicity data should be used. The models examined here employ monthly, quarterly, or annual information. The most appropriate time period for housing models is not evident and the present analyses shed little light on the issue. It bears further investigation. Since equilibria in housing markets may only be achieved over a period of several years (demand and supply normally shift gradually) a longer-run framework may be desirable for some purposes.

A problem related to that of aggregation is the choice of estimation methods. Almost all the models are estimated by ordinary least squares. This leads to biased parameter estimates, especially if starts or values are disaggregated by type of unit. There are substitution effects between single and multiple units and, also, the residual errors in these equations are likely to be correlated. Therefore, some type of simultaneous estimation technique should be utilized.

Even for aggregate starts or expenditures, simultaneous estimation probably is indicated because of financial factors. The supply and demand for funds of the residential construction sector must have some influence on interest rates; and interest rates, of course, appear in virtually all the equations. Thus, again the application of simultaneous estimation techniques is appropriate and desirable.

Conclusion

It is possible to cite further difficulties with each of these models or for them all as a whole. In their present state they are not very satisfactory and have

10. Mobile homes, an increasing force in the home-building industry, also have not been taken into account in most of the models.

proven unreliable, without exception, for forecasting purposes. Those that have used the models for forecasting have found it necessary to ignore the equation predictions (and make their projections wholly exogenous) or to adjust them on the basis of a priori expectations and other information.

This is not to say that considerable progress has not been made.[11] Both in terms of specification and prediction, improvements have been realized and inaccuracies reduced. With continued progress in formulation of hypotheses and better data, it is feasible to produce models that have greater predictive ability and can validly be used for structural analysis and policy simulation purposes.

---

11. The advances recently pioneered in the FRB and Huang models are particularly noteworthy.

Discussion

Mr. Ricks: On behalf of Gary Fromm, let me say that with the other people we have been very careful in getting work that was either completed or quite substantially completed. This was not communicated to Gary, and he said, "I would like to make a presentation comparing the various models."

He was willing to take on what I think is a very brave assignment, and the subject was so intriguing and so appropriate to this conference that we encouraged him to go ahead, and if he has bags under his eyes, it is because it is off the midnight press.

Mr. Fromm: Well, as Bruce has indicated, I took on a task that was self-imposed. I was very foolish to do it. It has been a real drag. (Laughter.)

Mr. Ricks: With that remark of enthusiasm!

Mr. Fromm: I was asked to speak about the Brookings model but decided that was rather uninteresting. Therefore, I decided to examine other models, and selected the eight operating macromodels and the two operating housing models. There probably are some others around. Professor Huang's model, which is very interesting, will be added to this survey.

Turning to my own paper, let me emphasize a comment made in the first few pages before [Appendix 5A], about the split between endogenous and exogenous variables. There is very little difficulty in terms of deciding on the endogenous variables for the residential construction sector. However, the selection of exogenous variables is somewhat arbitrary. I took some of the endogenous variables and said they are exogenous to the residential construction sector. That is not always appropriate, but I decided to do that in an attempt to make the descriptions more comparable, and also so I wouldn't get drawn into explaining the entire structure of all the models, especially the Federal Reserve MIT-Penn model.

There is a justification for it, however, in addition, even in the case of the Federal Reserve-MIT model, in that the interaction of the residential construction sector (except through total real output) with other parts of the models generally is very weak, and the feedbacks from those other sectors to the residential construction sector, then, are even weaker.

In the case of the Federal Reserve-MIT model, it is true that total residential construction expenditures in current dollars influence mortgage interest rates; but there is a long distributed lag on expenditures, and movements in mortgage rates are relatively sticky, so it is unnecessary to worry about feedbacks to any great extent.

. . .

Mr. Friend: Wouldn't you need information for the aggregate?

Mr. Fromm: I am getting to that. Even for aggregate starts or expenditures, simultaneous estimation is probably indicated, because of the impact of financial factors. The supply and demand for funds of the residential construction sector must have some influence on interest rates, and interest rates, of course, appear in virtually all of these equations. Consequently, again, one ought to use simultaneous estimation techniques to obtain the equation parameters.

Now, I could go on with further problems for each of these models, or for the group as a whole. In their present state they are not very satisfactory. I do not find it surprising that most of the people who are using models for forecasting have had to go the route that Dr. Fair doesn't like – basically, to throw out their equation projections and predict housing starts or values completely exogenously or make some adjustments to what the equations predict.

This doesn't necessarily have to be true in the long run. With somewhat better specifications we should be able to produce models that have greater predictive ability.

Mr. Ricks: Unless there are already tears welling in your eyes from what Gary has said, let me give you a sad example. How would it be if you were a dentist and had worked through four years of predental and three years of dental school and had received your DDS and had been in practice for several years, and some chemist came along and developed a plastic that could coat the teeth so that people wouldn't have cavities, and you were made functionally obsolete?

I think the optimistic thing that Gary is saying is that there is plenty of work remaining to be done for model building that can keep them busy for an epoch.

Appendix 5A
Survey of Private Residential Construction Sectors

Brady Model

Type of data; period covered or used in estimation; type of estimation

Quarterly data, seasonally adjusted annual rates; 1960:3 - 1970:2, 40 observations; ordinary least squares and two-stage least squares

Number of stochastic equations, a priori equations, and definitional equations = total; Number of exogenous variables

5 + 0 + 3 = 8
7 exogenous variables

Main institutional, technical, and behavioral equations

4 stochastic starts functions: conventional, single FHA and VA single, multifamily, and mobile homes
3 starts identities: total single, total excluding mobile homes, total
1 stochastic nonfarm residential construction function

Endogenous variables

7 starts variables: total, total excluding mobile homes, total single, conventional single, FHA and VA, multifamily, mobile homes
1 expenditure variable: real nonfarm residential construction

Main exogenous variables

2 interest rate variables: true interest rate on conventional mortgages, interest rate ceiling on FHA mortgages
2 availability of mortgage finance variables: FHLBB change in outstanding advances; FNMA net acquisitions of FHA and VA mortgages
1 mortgage characteristics variable: loan-to-value ratio of conventional mortgages
1 construction cost variable: Boeckh residential cost index
1 time trend

Dynamic features and significant nonlinearities

Equations estimated in linear and logarithmic form
No time lags

Other noteworthy features

Conventional unit starts are a linear or logarithmic function of the Boeckh residential construction cost index (with a positive sign), the true interest rate and loan-to-value ratio of conventional mortgages, the net quarterly change in FHLBB advances outstanding, and a time trend (with a negative sign). Emphasis is on distinction between FHA and VA conventional single-family starts; mobile homes are treated separately.

Brookings Model

Type of data; period covered or used in estimation; type of estimation

Quarterly data, seasonally adjusted annual rates; 1954–1965, 48 observations; ordinary least squares

Number of stochastic equations, a priori equations, and definitional equations = total; number of exogenous variables

8 + 2 + 8 = 18
8 exogenous variables

Main institutional, technical, and behavioral equations

3 stochastic starts functions; single-family nonfarm, two-family nonfarm, multiple nonfarm units

1 stochastic housing stock function (available units)

3 stochastic price functions: implicit deflator for nonfarm residential construction, real market price for single-dwelling units, real market price for two-or-more dwelling units

1 stochastic expenditures function: real additions and alterations

1 price identity: market price of dwelling units

3 housing unit identities: vacancies, total nonfarm starts, two-or-more unit nonfarm starts

6 expenditure relationships: real nonfarm expenditures on dwelling units (a priori), real nonfarm residential construction (two equations, one a priori), real total residential expenditures, nonfarm residential expenditures, total residential expenditures

Endogenous variables

5 starts variables: total nonfarm, single- and two-family nonfarm, single-family nonfarm, two-family nonfarm, multiunit nonfarm

2 housing stock variables: available units, vacancies

4 price variables: nonfarm residential construction implicit deflator, market prices of single, two-or-more units, all units

4 real expenditure variables: total residential, total nonfarm residential, nonfarm dwelling units, additions and alterations and nonhousekeeping units

2 expenditure variables: total residential, nonfarm residential

Main exogenous variables

1 interest rate variable: government-bill rate

1 demographic variable: nonfarm households

1 income variable: disposable income

1 time trend

2 price variables: nonmanufacturing sector final demand deflator, implicit deflator for personal consumption expenditures

1 cyclical variable: national unemployment rate

1 expenditure variable: real farm residential construction

1 translation dummy variable: ratio of estimated data to actual data for real nonfarm residential construction

Dynamic features and significant nonlinearities

Linear functions

Discrete and moving average lags up to 3 quarters

Koyck lags on prices

Other noteworthy features

Starts are split by type and are functions of interest rates; real value per start; real income per household; time; the inventory under construction; and, for multiple units, vacancies. Prices of units are split by type, with those for multiunits depending on vacancies. OBE expenditure-price-starts identity is used.

DHL III Model

Type of data; period covered or used in estimation; type of estimation

Quarterly data, seasonally adjusted quarterly rates; 1959:1–1967:2, 34 observations; ordinary least squares

Number of stochastic equations, a priori equations, and definitional equations = total; number of exogenous variables

3 + 1 + 0 = 4

5 exogenous variables

Main institutional, technical, and behavioral equations

1 stochastic starts function: total nonfarm units
1 stochastic expenditure function: nonfarm residential construction
1 stochastic price function: implicit deflator for residential construction
1 inequality: interest rate differential

Endogenous variables

See main institutional, technical, and behavioral equations, above.

Main exogenous variables

2 income variables: real disposable income, disposable income
1 wage rate: nonfarm private compensation rates per manhour
2 interest rates: Moodys corporate Aaa bond rate, commercial paper rate (4 to 6 month maturity)

Dynamic features and significant nonlinearities

Linear equations
Discrete lags up to 3 quarters
Linear inequality on long- minus short-term interest rate differential

Other noteworthy features

Starts are a function of starts lagged one and two quarters, change in real income, and credit-crunch indicator

DRI Model

Type of Data; period covered or used in estimation; type of estimation

Quarterly, seasonally adjusted annual rates; 1953:1–1970:2, 70 observations;[a] ordinary least squares

Number of stochastic equations, a priori equations, and definitional equations = total; number of exogenous variables

3 + 1 + 2 = 6
7 exogenous variables

Main institutional, technical, and behavioral equations

1 stochastic starts function: total units

[a]Shorter period used for some equations

1 stochastic expenditures function: real residential construction
1 stochastic price function: residential construction implicit deflator
1 expenditure identity: residential expenditures
1 housing stock identity: real value of residential stock
1 inequality: interest rate differential

Endogenous variables

See main institutional, technical, and behavioral equations above.

Main exogenous variables

2 interest rate variables: Moodys new corporate bond yields, government-bill rate
1 demographic variable: marriages
1 income variable: real disposable income
1 starts-mix variable: ratio of single family to total starts
1 wage rate: nonfarm private compensation rates per manhour
1 time trend

Dynamic features and significant nonlinearities

Linear equations
Discrete and moving average lags up to 4 quarters
Almon lag (third-degree polynomial up to twelve-quarter lag)
Nonlinear inequality on long- minus short-term interest rate differential as credit-crunch indicator
Rate of change formulation for price deflator function

Other noteworthy features

Starts are a function of changes in real disposable income interest rates and the lagged stock, a credit crunch inequality, and long Almon lags on past starts and marriages.

Price deflator for residential construction is seasonally adjusted because of apparent seasonality in published figures. (The rate of increase of this deflator is made dependent on time and on distributed-lag moving averages of rates of increase of past prices, nonfarm wage rates, unemployment rates, and housing starts.) Use of OBE starts-completions-expenditures identity. Also mix of single-family to total starts-mix variable.

Fair Model

Type of data; period covered or used in estimation; type of estimation

Monthly, not seasonally adjusted; June 1959 to December 1969, 127 observations; restricted two-stage least squares.[a]

Number of stochastic equations, a priori equations, and definitional equations = total; number of exogenous variables

3 + 0 + 0 = 3
18 exogenous variables

Main institutional, technical, and behavioral equations

2 stochastic starts functions: demand and supply of total nonfarm units
1 stochastic expenditure function: nonfarm residential construction

Endogenous variables

Nonfarm housing starts, not seasonally adjusted
Nonfarm residential construction expenditures

Main exogenous variables

11 monthly seasonal dummy variables
1 working-days-in-month variable
1 interest rate variable: yield on FHA new-home mortgages
3 availability-of-mortgage-financing variables: net savings inflows to savings and loan institutions and mutual savings banks, and FHLBB advances to S&L's
1 time trend
1 expenditure-income-price variable: GNP

Dynamic features and significant nonlinearities

Linear equations

Supply and demand functions dichotomized and estimated separately on basis of first difference in FHA mortgage rates (negative or zero changes identify demand function, positive or zero changes identify supply function). Coefficient on change in mortgage rates constrained to be equal in the two functions.

Discrete and moving average lags up to 6 months

Other noteworthy features

Expenditures function is a simple linear relationship (using quarterly data) of GNP and starts in the current and preceding two quarters. Estimated relative weights on starts are approximately those used by OBE to generate actual expenditures data.

---

[a]Quarterly data are used in expenditure functions.

Demand for starts is a function of seasonal dummy variables past, starts (a stock indicator), time, FHA mortgage rates lagged two months, and negative or zero first differences in FHA mortgage rates. Supply of starts is a function of seasonal dummy variables, time, a six-month average of the change in deposit inflows at savings and loan institutions and mutual savings banks, a three-month moving average (lagged two months) of changes in FHLBB advances to savings and loan institutions, FHA mortgage rates lagged one month, and positive first differences in FHA mortgage rates.

FRB-MIT-Penn Model

Type of data; period covered or used in estimation; type of estimation

Quarterly data, seasonally adjusted annual rates;[a] various dates, 56 to 59 observations;[b] ordinary least squares

Number stochastic equations, a priori equations, and definitional equations = total; number of exogenous variables

3 + 7 + 3 = 13
17 exogenous variables

Main institutional, technical, and behavioral equations

2 stochastic real-value per capita functions: real per person value of single- and two-family starts value (including mobile homes), real per person value of multifamily starts

1 stochastic expenditures function: total residential construction

3 expenditure identities: value of single- and two-family starts, value of multifamily starts, total real residential construction

3 price relationships: Boeckh residential construction cost index, adjusted Boeckh residential construction cost index, implicit deflator for residential construction

2 cost of capital relationships: single- and two-family units, multifamily units (latter is not used in present model)

2 capital stock relationships: real value of one- and two-family units (excluding mobile homes), multifamily units

Endogenous variables

2 starts value variables: real value per person (population 25-64) expected

[a]Starts values are at quarterly rates; expenditures are at annual rates.

[b]Value of single- and two-family starts 1956:2–1970:3, value of multifamily starts 1954:4–1969:3, total real residential expenditures 1954:2–1968:4.

to live in one- and two-family units and mobile homes, real value per person (population 20–24 and 65+) expected to live in multifamily units

4 expenditure variables: total and total real residential construction (including additions and alterations and nonhousekeeping units), value of one- and two-family starts (excluding mobile homes), value of multifamily starts

3 price variables: Boeckh residential construction cost (also adjusted), implicit deflator for residential construction

2 cost-of-capital variables: single- and two-family units, multifamily units

2 real capital stock variables: real value of single- and two-family and multifamily units (no allowance for addition and alterations)

Main exogenous variables

2 population variables: persons 25–64 and 20–24 and 65 and over[c]

1 time trend

2 interest rate variables: Moodys corporate Aaa rate, yield on FHA existing home mortgages

2 tax rate variables: average effective federal individual income tax rate, average effective state and local real property tax rate

2 price variables: deflator for consumption of nondurables and services and depreciation of durables, implicit deflator for gross product originating in nonfarm business and households

2 expenditures variables: consumption per capita, mobile home purchases

4 availability-of-mortgages financing variables: net change in mortgage commitments of savings and loan institutions and mutual savings banks, new commitments of life insurance companies, and change in net acquisitions of mortgages of FNMA plus GNMA

1 credit-crunch dummy: 1966 adjustments

1 financial wealth variable: increase in value of households' net worth except capital gains on housing stock and consumer durables

Dynamic features and significant nonlinearities

Logarithmic starts value functions

Almon lags, second-degree polynomial up to seven-quarter lags, far-end zero constraints

Autoregressive correction of serially correlated residuals of logarithmic functions

Other noteworthy features

Log of real value of single- and two-family starts and mobile homes per person 25–64 a logarithmic function of: an a priori time trend (as a capacity

[c]This is net result of identities relating total population, proportion of total under 20, and proportion 25–64 of those 20 and over.

indicator); real consumption per capita relative to real housing stock per person 25-64; and Almon lags of consumption prices relative to construction costs multiplied by the cost of capital of such units, the rate of change of the sum of net changes in mortgages commitments of savings and loan institutions and changes in net acquisitions of mortgages of FNMA and GNMA, and the rate of change of net worth except capital gains on housing stock and consumer durables: and an autoregressive correction. Treatment of multifamily starts is similar except population variable is persons 20-24 and 65+, the cost-of-capital term is deleted because of lack of significance; mortgage commitments are the rate of change of mutual savings banks' net commitments and the levels of new commitments of life insurance companies. Also, the net worth variable is deleted and a dummy variable for the 1966 credit crunch is added. Real consumption in both equations is said to be an indicator of permanent income. Expenditures on residential construction are made a four-quarter distributed lag of housing start value outlays using a partial set of a priori weights to reflect completions. A priori definitions are used to define housing stocks, cost of capital, and Boeckh residential construction cost index adjusted for productivity changes.

Huang Model

Type of data; period covered or used in estimation; type of estimation

Quarterly data, seasonally adjusted quarterly rates; 1953:2-1965:2, 51 observations; ordinary and two-stage least squares[a]

Number of stochastic equations; a priori equations, and definition equations = total, number of exogenous variables

6 + 4 + 4 = 14
10 exogenous variables[b]

Main institutional, technical, and behavioral equations[c]

2 stochastic real expenditure demand functions: single and multifamily units
2 stochastic real construction expenditure supply functions: single and multifamily units
2 stochastic price functions: first differences in price index of new houses and CPI rent index

---

[a]Demand equations are estimated by ordinary least squares. A three equation mortgage sector (demand, supply, and average yields) is endogenous in the complete Huang model. It is estimated by three-stage least squares.

[b]The GNP implicit deflator is counted as an exogenous variable.

[c]Unless otherwise specified, real values of variables are derived by deflating by the GNP implicit deflator.

1 income relationship: expected real disposable income
1 price relationship: expected rent to price of new houses ratio
2 price identities: levels of price index of new houses and CPI rent index
2 excess supply identities: real values of single- and multiple-family units
2 supply relationships: real values of completions of single- and multiple-family units

Endogenous variables[c]

See main institutional, technical, and behavioral equations, above

Main exogenous variables[b]

2 interest rate variables: commercial paper rate (4 to 6 month maturity), estimated average market yield of all home mortgages

2 mortgage characteristics variables: change in average loan-to-value ratio of all mortgage loans extended, average length of amortization of all mortgage loans

2 construction cost variables: Boeckh residential cost index; Boeckh apartment, hotels, and office buildings index

1 price variable: consumer price index

2 availability of mortgage finance variables: net free reserves of Federal Reserve member banks deflated by the GNP implicit deflator, net savings inflows to savings and loan institutions, mutual savings banks, and life insurance companies deflated by the CPI

Dynamic features and significant nonlinearities

Linear equations
Discrete and a priori distributed lags up to seven quarters

Other noteworthy features

Supply and demand are estimated separately. Supply is indicated by a priori relationships to estimate values of single- and miltiple-family completions. Demand is given by estimated values of new houses purchased and new multifamily units occupied. Demand values for single-family houses are a function of values lagged one quarter, expected change in ratio of rent to new-house price indexes, expected change in disposable income, change in loan-to-value ratio, and the average amortization period. Demand values for multifamily units are a function of values lagged two quarters, the level of expected disposable income,

[b]The GNP implicit deflator is counted as an exogenous variable.

[c]Unless otherwise specified, real values of variables are derived by deflating by the GNP implicit deflator.

and the ratio of the rent to CPI indexes. Values of single-family houses started are a function of excess supply (negative sign), the new-house price index, commercial paper rate (lagged one quarter), free reserves (lagged two quarters), and starts values (lagged one and two quarters). Values of multifamily starts are a function of excess supply (positive sign), the rent index, commercial paper rate (lagged one quarter), current net savings flows and starts values (lagged one, two, and four quarters). Changes in prices of new houses and rents are linear functions of excess supply (with negative and positive signs, respectively) and changes in construction costs (and mortgage rates for the rent index).

Maisel Model

Type of data; period covered or used in estimation; type of estimation

Quarterly data, seasonally adjusted annual rates; 1955:2–1970:2, 60 observations; ordinary least squares

Number of stochastic equations; a priori equations, and definition equations = total; number of exogenous equations

5 + 0 + 1 = 6[a]
8 exogenous variables[a]

Main institutional, technical, and behavioral equations

1 stochastic total starts function (5 alternative versions)
1 change in housing inventory function (completions)
1 change in vacancies function
1 removals function
1 household formation function
1 housing stock identity (available units)

Endogenous variables

See main institutional, technical, and behavioral equations, above.

Main exogenous variables

2 interest rate variables: yield on FHA section 203 new-home mortgages, contract rate on conventional first mortgages (FHLBB data)

4 availability-of-mortgage financing variables: net FNMA acquisitions of mortgages from private holders; net acquisitions of mortgages of life insurance companies; FHLBB advances, net savings inflow to savings and loan institutions

[a]Precise number is ambiguous since model is not completely specified or estimated.

and mutual savings banks, in each case adjusted for proportion historically invested in mortgages

1 profitability variable: ratio of CPI rent index to Boeckh residential construction cost index

1 income variable: real disposable income per household

Dynamic features and significant nonlinearities

Linear functions
Use of moving averages and discrete lags

Other noteworthy features

Starts are a function of inventory factors – available units fit for use, vacancies, units under construction, as well as exogenous variables shown above

OBE Model

Type of data; period covered or used in estimation; type of estimation

Quarterly data, seasonally adjusted annual rates; 1957:4–1968:4, 45 observations; ordinary least squares

Number of stochastic equations, a priori equations, and definitional equations = total; number of exogenous variables

6 + 6 + 2 = 14
14 exogenous variables

Main institutional, technical, and behavioral equations

2 stochastic real-value per capita functions: real per person value of single- and two-family starts, real per person value of multifamily starts

1 stochastic real expenditures function: real expenditures on dwelling units

1 inequality: interest rate differential

3 stochastic price equations: implicit deflator for consumption of housing services, implicit deflator for residential construction, Boeckh residential construction cost index

1 price relationship: adjusted Boeckh construction cost index

2 cost of capital relationships: single- and two-family units, multifamily units

2 capital stock relationships: real value of one- and two-family units, multifamily units

2 expenditure identities: real residential expenditures, residential expenditures

Endogenous variables

2 starts-value variables: real value per person (population 25-64) expected to live in one- and two-family units, real value per person (population 20-24 and 65+) expected to live in multifamily units

3 expenditure variables: total and total real residential construction, real expenditures on dwelling units

4 price variables: implicit deflator for consumption of housing services, implicit deflator for residential construction, Boeckh construction cost index, Boeckh construction cost index adjusted for productivity change

2 cost of capital variables: single- and two-family units, multifamily units

2 real capital stock variables: real values of single- plus two-family and multifamily units (both include a priori allowance for real additions and alteration expenditures)

1 credit-crunch variable

Main exogenous variables

2 population variables: persons 25-64, persons 20-24 and 65 and over[a]

1 time trend

3 interest rate variables: Moodys corporate Aaa bond rate, commercial paper rate (4 to 6 month maturity), secondary market yield on FHA home mortgages

2 tax rate variables: average effective federal individual income tax rate, average state and local real property tax rate

2 price variables: implicit deflator for personal consumption expenditures, implicit deflator for nonfarm business product

4 real expenditure variables: real fixed business investment, real nonfarm business product, real per capita consumption of nondurables and nonhousing services, real expenditures on additions and alterations and nonhousekeeping units

Dynamic features and significant nonlinearities

Logarithmic starts value and construction cost index functions

Almon lags, second-degree polynomial, up to eight-quarter lags; far-end zero constraints

Nonlinear inequality for long- minus short-term interest rate differential as credit crunch indicator

Autoregressive correction of serially correlated residuals of logarithmic and linear functions

---

[a]This is net result of identities relating total population, proportion of total under 20, and proportion 25-64 of those 20 and over.

Other noteworthy features

Log of real value of single- and two-family starts per person 25–64 a logarithmic function of: time (a capacity indicator; coefficient is a priori); Almon lags of consumption prices relative to construction costs, the cost of capital for such units, and a credit crunch indicator; and a two-quarter moving average of real consumption of nondurables and nonhousing services per capita relative to the real housing stock per person 25–64. The residuals are autoregressively corrected. A similar function is used for multifamily starts only the consumption variable is deleted. Real expenditures on dwelling units are partially based on the OBE expenditure-starts identity; a priori definition of cost of capital. Model is an earlier version employed in the FRB-MIT-Penn model.

Wharton Annual and Industry Forecasting Model

Type of data; period covered or used in estimation; type of estimation

Annual data, 1954–1969, 16 observations; ordinary least squares

Number of stochastic equations, a priori equations, and definition equations = total; number of exogenous variables

6 + 2 + 6 = 14
12 exogenous variables

Main institutional, technical, and behavioral equations

1 stochastic starts function: total nonfarm units

1 stochastic expenditures function: real additions and alterations and non-housekeeping units

4 stochastic price functions: implicit deflator for consumption of housing services (autoregressive correction function), implicit deflator for residential construction (initial estimating function and autoregressive correction function), and market price of nonfarm dwelling units

2 price equations: implicit deflator for housing services (a priori specification), implicit deflator for nonfarm residential construction (identity)

5 expenditure identities: real residential construction, residential construction, real nonfarm residential construction, nonfarm residential construction, farm residential construction

1 a priori stock definition: real nonfarm housing stock value

Endogenous variables

1 starts variable: total nonfarm units

4 real expenditures variables: total residential, total nonfarm residential, total farm residential, additions and alterations and nonhousekeeping units

3 expenditures variables: total residential, total nonfarm residential, total farm residential

4 price variables: implicit deflator for consumption of housing services, implicit deflator for residential construction, implicit deflator for nonfarm residential construction, market price of nonfarm dwelling units

1 stock variable: real value of nonfarm housing stock

Main exogenous variables

2 interest rate variables: time deposit yield, commercial paper rate (4 to 6 months)

1 income variable: real disposable income

7 price variables: output originating prices for agriculture, manufacturing and mining, transportation, communications, utilities, commercial, government

1 expenditures variable: real farm residential construction

1 time trend

Dynamic features and significant nonlinearities

Linear functions

Discrete and Almon Polynomial distributed lags up to six years duraton

Koyck lag on response of market price of nonfarm dwelling units to construction costs

Other noteworthy features

Starts are a function of real income, a six-year distributed lag of ratio of construction cost deflator to consumption of housing services deflator, a five-year (0 to 4) distributed lag of difference between time deposit yields and commercial paper rates, and the initial real housing stock.

Additions and alterations are a function of the initial stock and a three-year (0 to 2) distributed lag of the same interest rate differential as in the starts equation.

All starts are assumed to be completed within the year initiated.

Housing services and residential construction deflators are linear combinations of industry output-originating deflators.

New Wharton Quarterly Forecasting Model

Type of data; period covered or used in estimation; type of estimation

Quarterly data, seasonally adjusted annual rates; 1954–1969, 64 observations; ordinary least squares

Number of stochastic equations, a priori equations, and definition equations = total; number of exogenous variables

3 + 0 + 4 = 7
8 exogenous variables

Main institutional, technical, and behavioral equations

1 stochastic expenditures function: real nonfarm residential construction
2 stochastic price functions: CPI rent index, implicit deflator nonfarm residential construction
4 expenditure identities: total real residential, nonfarm residential, farm residential, total residential

Endogenous variables

See main institutional, technical, and behavioral equations, above.

Main exogenous variables

2 interest rate variables: Moodys domestic corporate yields, commercial paper rate (4 to 6 month maturity)
1 income variable: real disposable income
1 time trend
1 price variable: implicit deflator for output originating from regulated sector
1 wage rate variable: labor compensation per manhour in commercial sector
1 output variable: output originating in commercial sector
1 expenditure variable: real farm residential

Dynamic features and significant nonlinearities

Linear equations
Almon lag up to twenty quarters

Other noteworthy features

No starts equation – presumed to be included as reduced form in real expenditures function which includes weights of OBE expenditures-starts identity on relative price (construction cost to rent indexes) and long- minus short-term interest rate differential variables, as well as the level of real disposable income.

References

The Models in Alphabetical Order

Brady Model

Brady, Eugene A. "An Econometric Analysis of the U.S. Residential Housing Market." Working Paper #11, Office of Economic Research, Federal Home Loan Bank Board, November 1970.

Brookings Model

Fromm, Gary, and George R. Schink. *Brookings Condensed Model.* Unpublished materials distributed at Seminar on Comparison of Econometric Models, Conference on Econometrics and Mathematical Economics, Philadelphia, January 1971.

Fromm, Gary, and Paul Taubman. *Policy Simulations with an Econometric Model.* Washington: Brookings Institution, 1968.

DHL III Model

Hymans, Saul H., and Harold T. Shapiro. "The DHL III Quarterly Econometric Model of the U.S. Economy." Research Seminar in Quantitative Economics, University of Michigan, Ann Arbor, 1970.

DRI Model

The Data Resources Econometric Forecasting System: A Preliminary Account. Lexington, Mass.: Data Resources, Inc., November 1970.

Fair Model

Fair, Ray C. *A Short-Run Forecasting Model of the United States Economy.* Lexington, Mass.: Lexington Books, Heath, 1971.

FRB-MIT-Penn Model

Ando, Albert, and Robert Rasche. "Equations in the MIT-PENN-SSRC Econometric Model of the United States." Unpublished materials distributed at Seminar on Comparison of Econometric Models, Conference on Econometrics and Mathematical Economics, Philadelphia, January 1971.

Kalchbrenner, John H. "The FRB-MIT-Penn Model: A summary of the Housing Sector of the FMP Model." Materials distributed for Housing Model Conference, Federal Home Loan Bank Board, Washington, D.C., March 1971.

Huang Model

Huang, David S. "A Study of the Market for New Housing Units." *Proceedings, Business and Economic Statistics Section.* American Statistical Association, 1969.

Maisel Model

Burnham, James B. "Housing Starts in 1966 and 1969: A Comparison Using an Econometric Model." Materials distributed for Housing Model Conference, Federal Home Loan Bank Board, Washington, D.C., March 1971.

Maisel, Sherman J. "A Theory of Fluctuations in Residential Construction Starts." *American Economic Review* 53 (June 1963): 359–383.

——. "The Effects of Monetary Policy on Expenditures in Specific Sectors of the Economy." *Journal of Political Economy* 76 (July/Aug 1968): 796–814.

OBE Model

Liebenberg, Maurice, George Green, and Albert Hirsch. "The Office of Business Economics 1970 Quarterly Econometric Model." Unpublished materials, U.S. Department of Commerce, Washington, D.C., January 11, 1971.

Wharton Annual and Industry Forecasting Model

Preston, Ross S., and Lawrence R. Klein. "The Wharton Annual and Industry Forecasting Model: Statement of Equations and Identities." Philadelphia: Wharton EFA, July 1970.

New Wharton Quarterly Forecasting Model

McCarthy, Michael D. "The New Wharton Quarterly Forecasting Model." Unpublished memorandum. Philadelphia: Wharton EFA, Inc., November 10, 1970.

Other References

1. Evans, Michael K. *Macroeconomic Activity.* New York: Harper & Row, 1969.

2. Grebler, Leo, and Sherman J. Maisel. "Determinants of Residential Construction: A Review of Present Knowledge." In Commission on Money and Credit, *Impacts of Monetary Policy,* Englewood Cliffs: Prentice-Hall, 1963.
3. Nerlove, Marc. "A Tabular Survey of Macro-Econometric Models." *International Economic Review* 7 (1966): 127–175.
4. Taubman, Paul, and Robert Rasche. "Tax Laws and the Apartment Building Industry." Unpublished paper. Philadelphia: University of Pennsylvania, 1971.

6 General Discussion of Models and Related Problems

Policy Instruments in the Models

Bill Branson (Princeton): One thing that worried me in Jaffee's work a bit and is worrisome in the Brady paper was the question of the role of FNMA and FHLB advances. It seems to me that there might be some sort of illusory results. These operations are endogenous rather than exogenous, so that when starts fall off the activity picks up in that area. If you just run an equation with their stuff on the right-hand side and starts on the left-hand side, it appears they are not doing anything, and it is a sort of dangerous result. You can't get any policy implications out of that. You have to go a lot farther than that, and I did notice that the implication might be that they weren't having any net effect. It came out fairly strongly in the Brady paper. They might be having a big net effect, but you might have the effect they are endogenous, so you don't see that effect. The policy conclusions that came out of the Brady paper might be modified and some thought given to making them endogenous, using the simultaneous technique.

Lawrence Smith (University of Toronto): What could well be happening is that FNMA and FHLB go into the market and have significant effects on funds, either raising interest rates or the willingness of private institutions to advance more mortgage funds.

Ray Fair (Princeton): There may be a difference between FNMA and the Federal Home Loan Banks going into the capital market. My feeling is that savings and loan associations are more restricted in what they can do with their assets than most other financial institutions; and if this is true, then the FHLBB activity of taking capital from various groups and transferring this capital to SLA's is likely to be more effective in terms of increasing mortgages than is the activity of FNMA.

Bill Branson: Obviously you shouldn't argue that FNMA operations don't get offset at all, because they are pulling money through this other route that would have gone into housing anyway. But, on the other hand, you get bad estimates of what their effect is, I would think, if you just put them on the right-hand side of a housing-start equation and don't worry about the fact that they read endogenously. The truth is somewhere between 100 percent effectiveness and the kind you get out of Brady's estimates or Jaffee's estimates.

Bill Silber (Council of Economic Advisers, Staff): There is a tremendous problem here for all models, because the nature of government intervention in the mortgage flows has changed since 1967. If you take total private mortgages and then take total private mortgages plus government mortgage purchases, and you look at the standard deviation from 1952 through 1966, it appears the government intervention was pro-cyclical in that period, very definitely procyclical. Since then it has been contra-cyclical. Anybody who is using these government-originated mortgage flows in regressions is going to have to work around that problem, I think.

Jim Burnham (Federal Reserve Board): In the Maisel specification, in two of the equations, we use FNMA acquisitions, but we do it in a mirror sense, so it has a negative sign, which is the way we expected, instead of the positive sign for the private financial flows.

Bruce Ricks: In terms of effect on the housing market, it seems to me it is not FNMA purchases as much as FNMA commitments that initiate a housing start. A builder will get a FNMA commitment based upon the "funds availability-hedge," if you like to call a commitment that. Then the builder initiates the start and looks for better private financing so he can renege on the FNMA commitment. In fact, he is encouraged not to exercise the commitment.

Gary Fromm (Data Resources, Inc., and American University): The FNMA purchases, as Mr. Branson said, must be viewed as support for the mortgage market, because without FNMA taking those mortgages off the hands of the sellers, they would tend to reduce their own commitments for new mortgages even more. Presumably, those that sell mortgages to FNMA have a preferred position in mortgages in their portfolio. Given the rate structure and the other demands for loans, they then have a reduced demand for holding mortgages. It is only the FNMA purchases that enables them to take on new mortgages.

Bruce Ricks: You have FNMA dealing primarily with mortgage bankers who deal primarily with life insurance companies. In a period of stringency, you have the mortgage bankers using FNMA more on a commitment and subsequent purchase basis. The mortgage bankers also increase their selling to savings and loan associations because the life insurance mortgage acquisition dries up, particularly if they are having large policy loan cash drains. In addition to a reduction in net residential debt outstanding during 1969 (a reinvestment less than repayments), there was a dramatic shift from single-family to multifamily residential lending, which in that period took place primarily because of the availability of equity participation in multifamily lending and its non-availability in the single-family sector. How much of a cyclical phenomenon that is, I don't know. Whether the life insurance companies will get back into the single-family market, I don't know, but it is a significant problem in the analysis.

Another problem you have is with regard to the Federal Home Loan Bank advances. It is a timing question. An SLA cannot predict with much accuracy its ability to get deposits. It can predict with increased accuracy its ability to get repayments and prepayments, but that is still quite difficult. Under the previous Board policy it could predict its access to advances pretty well, because in essence the association had an open line to its District Bank. The present Board has reduced the free, open-line access to FHLB advances. It has substituted an emphasis on negotiated lines of credit commitments for fixed-rate and fixed-maturity advances with commitment fees and prepayment penalties. So an association can loan funds with the presumption that if the savings flow repayments and prepayments are inadequate, it can make up that difference with FHLB advances. So you have a real question of timing with regard to the leads and lags involved in quarterly analysis.

Bill Branson: So the FHLB advances are completely endogenous, too, and you should put them on the left-hand side, or if you further worry about it, there are biases in the estimates of both of those things.

Lawrence Smith: The comments that have been coming out now, together with some of the comments that Gary Fromm made, lead to something that maybe could be added to our discussion in terms of the role that the FHLBB could play in supplying institutional information to a lot of us as to how these markets actually operate and what are the dominant institutional considerations. One of the problems seems to be the number of good econometricians who get involved to some extent in housing. They come in and they go out, and they are working without perfect knowledge of the way institutions operate, so we turn out models that bear little resemblance to reality. On the other hand, there are a number of people who have a lot of institutional knowledge, but don't seem to be doing the statistical work.

Macromodels versus Micromodels

David Birch (Harvard Business School): I can think of lots of reasons why knowing the total housing starts in the United States would be useful to you. On the other hand, there are a lot of other things about the housing market that you would want to know. One of the things that hits me about all these models is they all focus in on one particular kind of thing – i.e., good housing-start predictions. Gene has broken it down a little. But if I were a District Bank, I wouldn't be very much interested in gross housing starts. If I were operating a savings and loan association, I wouldn't be much interested in gross housing starts. I'd probably not be very interested in deposits and the supply of credit going into the system, at the gross level. If I were a bank examiner approving branch applications I would be likely to focus on the census tract level. None of the work done here today provides information at that level.

Question number one: to what extent do you want to deal with the aggregate for the branch application-approval guy? Even to distribute that pot of money you have coming in in a couple of months from repayment of advances, the aggregate is not very useful. There is no feeling for what the differential effects are on the supply and demand for funds.

If your purpose is to address anything other than the gross total number of housing units in the system and you try to disaggregate, the methodology does not scale down. You are presently relying on what I disparagingly call "number crunching." You pour a whole lot of time series into a computer and determine some regression coefficients. When you start to go down into any kind of detail, that methodology doesn't work, because the data aren't there. You are lucky if you get a cross-section every ten years. There may be one or two samples in between. That means that the skills you need and the methodology you use are totally different.

You need great conceptual and theoretical skills to fill in the huge interstices between the limited data. Sophistication in terms of number crunching is much less important. Your need for sophistication in terms of really understanding the behavior of the elements in the system you are trying to model goes way up.

I spend much of my time talking to demographers and social psychologists and all sorts of other people. When you get down to the behavior of individual elements in the system, you can't rely on statistical finesse. Not only must your focus be more theoretical and less empirical, but also you must range over a much broader set of variables and disciplines than do any of the things that I have read today.

Bruce Ricks: Let me call on Larry Kimbell and then Karl Fox, and then let me ask David Birch to describe briefly what he is doing in New Haven.

Larry Kimbell (University of California, L.A.): The microsimulation approach tempts one to reach for too much intricacy and involvement. This has been true of the early work which has been done on demography. I am not saying this to be disparaging, but the temptation in going in one direction is to get a system that is so colossally large that it can hardly be handled. We presented our conceptualization of a simulation model of health care at the Econometric Society meetings, and perhaps the most devastating criticism we suffered was almost inadvertent when the discussant said that after two years of work he had run out of data storage on a CDC 6600 computer and would make his microsimulation model data available free of charge. No one held up his hand to take it. (Laughter) I think there could be useful effort made at the microlevel, but it would be very ambitious to encourage those people on the panel to disaggregate housing starts to the SMSA level, as well as by types of starts.

Karl Fox (Iowa State University): I think that you can have the luxury of theoretical conceptualization, which I like very much, and also retain whatever value there might be in number crunching and large numbers of equations, although for smaller geographic areas. I suggested in 1963 that it would be instructive to look at the Brookings econometric model and come down from it to the stabilization, employment, and other problems of an SMSA or a multicounty functional economic area (FEA). Some of the national monetary policy variables that appear in the Brookings national model would at least be exogenous when you looked at the problems of a particular FEA commuting field or housing market (which, I think, are coextensive). But some of the kinds of variables that have appeared in the national models here today would still belong in a model of the housing market for a multicounty area around, say, Indianapolis. You could decide this question and also let in some of your theoretical conceptualizations in an area small enough so you can see and talk with principal agents in the area. You could ask home buyers or home owners "how does this support your life style, living out here or buying this or that kind of house?"

It would be good if some person or persons could pioneer this kind of thing for simply one area, and you would have a quarterly area model to fit in with the other models that have been presented here. A development planning model for the same multicounty area would also be illuminating. Some very good people have worked on development planning models for "open economies" in the less-developed countries, and a multicounty FEA is simply another kind of "open economy." I think there is lots of room here for research and for a model that would work reasonably well to start discussion for one multicounty area. If it has good points, these would be replicated in models for many other population clusters of roughly the same population and area. There is a fine field for research here. You don't have to discard sociological theory or econometrics.

David Birch: I think that in our New Haven project we are doing more or less what you are proposing. We are moving our faculty and our research assistants into a one-county area. We are talking to a large sample of residents. We are working with their individual census questionnaire responses in a very well-guarded, protected way. We are looking in very great detail at twenty or thirty different kinds of housing in each of sixty or seventy different tracts – what kinds are there and what kinds are likely to be built. When you talk to builders in New Haven, they are absolutely indifferent as to interest rates and availability of credit – indifferent to most of the variables in the model. One thing they do look at is the vacancy rate. We are modeling *builders,* as distinct from *housing starts.* If all they look at is vacancy rates, that is all we let them look at. We have a replication of behavior instead of events.

We all know that it isn't just the vacancy rates. But the interest rates manifest themselves in the behavior of the people that initiate the housing start, not the builder. The builder doesn't look at the interest rates, but the demand for housing. The demand for housing, then, is manifested in the availability of credit to the buyer of the house as a separate phenomenon. There are different kinds of things at work, and the response of the buyer to the interest rate is totally different from the response of the builder to the interest rates, the latter being trivial, except in the case of a large, multiunit project. When you really get down to details, you find funny things happen that get lost in the aggregate, but we are able to predict this kind of detail with reasonable accuracy at this point over a twenty-year period of history, and we will run ten or fifteen years into the future.

Irwin Friend (University of Pennsylvania): I think it is highly desirable to have the same kind of disaggregation we were talking about, so long as we don't lose sight of the objectives. I mentioned earlier that I am all for continous cross-section data, which would include data, notably at the SMSA level, over time. But there can be two types of objectives for the gathering of this kind of data. The FHLBB has to have this in view of its clientele. Most of us here are much more interested in the use of such disaggregated data for national analysis, national economic policy.

It is far from clear that through such disaggregation you are necessarily going to improve your overall predictions. I notice, for example, I think in Kalchbrenner's paper he says if you have total expenditures and you break them up, you get better results if the two expenditures are substitutable.

My own reaction is opposite. If the two expenditures are perfect substitutes, unless you have what accounts for substitutability, then you get worse results. You can't predetermine, or you shouldn't, what you are going to get out of this disaggregation.

I have certain biases; others have others, but there is no necessary magic about improving your overall economic model through disaggregation.

Ray Fair: With respect to regional models, SMSA models of housing starts, it seems to me there is a very serious problem involved in this. Kindleberger used to tell us all the time that money is "fungible," moves around easily from one area to another. You may have a particilar area that has a rather large demand for housing. If you just looked at flows of deposits into the S&Ls in that area, you might conclude that the area is not going to have enough funds to finance the housing; but, indeed, if the general economy has a lot of funds around, it is likely that people within that SMSA will find money outside, somewhere. So it is not trivial to take models and disaggregate them. Indeed, theoretically there are times, I think, when you wouldn't want to do that.

Bruce Ricks: We are increasing the fungibility of funds in the SLA industry. What you are saying is, when the housing markets are supply-constrained, and the suppliers of funds have funds which are nonmobile, you get better statistical results. I think that is perfectly reasonable and consistent with the results we would expect to get, which would say you can't get good results all the time from the same type of framework.

In terms of fungibility we now have a secondary mortgage market, the Federal Home Loan Mortgage Corporation; and FNMA is increasing its activity. The Home Loan Bank advances mechanism is looked at in national models through the variable increases in total advances outstanding nationally. But there are tremendous differences from Bank District to Bank District and within local areas.

One of the most important uses of FHLB advances as a policy instrument is in the movement of funds interregionally. The location of funds probably has more effect on housing starts than has the absolute level outstanding. If it is in an area of savings surplus, it will go into liquidity unless instruments for interregional funds transfer are used.

Now, we do have some advantages of funds circulation. Associations buying FHLB obligations is one way of getting the money from areas of capital surplus to areas of capital deficit. The use by a District Bank of the time and demand deposits of some associations for advances to other associations is another way. Also, one District Bank can lend another one money through interbank transfer. We don't have to go through the capital markets to transfer the funds geographically. It is somewhat like a longer-term federal funds market.

Gary Fromm: In my opinion, Mr. Birch's approach has real limitations. It only works in a case where you are talking about small, independent units without any interconnections with the outside world and without interdependence with any of the surrounding SMSA's.

David Birch: We have tremendous interregional flows. We are looking very much at flows, not only into and out of the region, but where they come from and where they go to as well. So we have crude skeletal national models, region by region, going all the time to drive the particular region under study.

Larry Kimbell: I would like to encourage David Birch to continue his work on small areas and also studies of aggregation problems, but suppose you were to take eighty SMSA's and try to get gross flows of funds and populations to and from each of the eighty, quarterly for ten years. You would have 6400 different patterns of entry and exit, and you have this over forty different time periods.

Just to assemble that data, much less begin to analyze the flows for funds, people, etc., becomes a horrendous task.

It might be useful to promote work at three levels of detail and aggregation: (1) detailed studies of a single area; (2) crude models for all areas in terms of interregional flows; and (3) aggregate macromodels.

The main problem is not the mere existence of detailed data. It is trying to get a well-specified and theoretically plausible set of interrelationships for each of thousands of interdependent variables. It is a formidable task to get a structural equation for each of many interregional flows of population and funds. One has to be extremely judicious in the selection of aggregates, and not, therefore, so critical of the aggregate models.

If you disaggregate to the local region, you must throw out a lot of the other markets involved, whereas at the national level it is possible to treat sectors of the economy other than housing as endogenous.

Irwin Friend: There are a couple of things that worry me about some of these ideas. My thought at the beginning of this discussion was that a way to proceed with some of the data you are collecting is to start thinking in terms of doing cross-section analysis instead of time series. You can do that only if you put through the assumption that people in the different parts of the cross-section behave more or less the same way. It has seemed to me that, in a way, that is what economic analysis is all about – some notion about behavior; and you can assume that a certain sort of people behave a certain way in different places, so you might be able to do cross-section analysis.

If the people in New Haven act completely differently from the people some place else (*Bill Branson*). . . . If the people in New Haven behave yesterday as they do today (*Irwin Friend*). . . . If you had that kind of data, you wouldn't have that kind of problem (*David Huang*). . . . A continuous cross-section of panel data.

Gary Fromm: I think there has been an overemphasis on two polar extremes here. Clearly there is a need for both (1) macroeconomic analysis and economic models, and (2) regional models of differing scales for purposes of investment or portfolio planning of Federal Home Loan Banks and S&L's and for regional economic policy-making groups.

To fill that need, to build both kinds of models, we need time series, both on the macro-level and at the micro-level. It is extremely important that FHLBB keep on collecting this kind of information on a continuous basis.

It is clear that resources for building housing models or any kind of model are limited. Thus, with the resources available, we can build, say, a few macromodels and a few SMSA models, but certainly not 263 SMSA models.

I would encourage those looking for a research strategy, to attempt to get some resources in both areas and improve the macromodels that we have now, but also stimulate the construction of regional models.

Bill Branson: I think there is a bridge to what we were talking about. There was a talk this morning about most of the housing start models, and the problem they have of not getting very clearly specified the supply and demand functions of the various sectors in the area. And that point comes out clearly, I think, in some of the models presented. Variables seem to get mixed signs, and some of the variables from the equations with plus and minus signs indicate a mixture of supply and demand equations. You don't know quite what it is. It seems to me that direction for modeling which would be useful from the policy peoples' point of view and useful for understanding the housing market in a structural sense, would be the direction Ray Fair was suggesting.

First, you could get a better handle on what is moving housing in an aggregate sense if you had these supply and demand equations. You could know whether you are producing too many houses because people think them too expensive, or you are not producing the number of houses you expected because funds are not available.

Second, if, as I suspect, people act more or less the same across the country (builders act like builders and banks like banks, and housewives like housewives, etc.), once you get that accurate supply model specified and estimated, you might be able to carry that model to the different regional places and have a framework ready to apply regional data.

It seems to me that the direction of movement that ought to be supported is in the direction Ray was talking about – being more careful about supply and demand and what the constraints are, and getting those estimated on an aggregate basis, and getting the data available to do that.

In the Brady paper there is this price variable which has the wrong sign. It is positive. It ought to be negative. Then there is this trend term in the equation that seems to have the wrong sign. The coefficients of the two variables are almost always exactly the same size. Now you have to wonder when you see the equation what is going on. The term has a coefficient of minus 49. The point is, if you followed Ray's line of doing something about how to figure out when a supply regime is operating and when a demand regime is operating, you start sorting these things out as in the Fair-Jaffee paper. A good example is the mortgage rate. In Fair's work, in one equation it is positive and in the other it is negative, which is what you would expect on theory. I wouldn't want to have an equation where I threw in all demand and supply variables and the mortgage rate and wondered about the sign of that. That doesn't impress me as the way one should go about it.

David Huang: It does not measure short-run demand or supply directly.

That does not account for it completely, either. How do you start? From the demand point of view (the housing starts question aside), the number of housing units *bought and occupied* in any period is a full concept of demand. Supply is the number of housing units made available – *completed and occupied and vacant also.* In any time period this is a flow concept. These, I think we don't actually have as yet.

Ray Fair: The one equation I dropped was the construction side of the market. I didn't consider at all the third equation. It seems to me this is a very important area that should be looked into. It may be that builders are not only the constraint at times (which I am ignoring) but, as argued, perhaps the reverse at times. They may overbuild relative to the demand in the area. This problem relates very closely to the vacancy question. This whole area is quite interesting and something I haven't looked into.

Bruce Ricks: How would you think it would work better: substracted from the dependent variable, or added on the right-hand side?

Ray Fair: I have a vacancy variable in the demand equation to the extent that the stock of houses is important but this specification is very crude. With respect to how I would specify the construction equation and how it would relate to vacancies, I really don't know at this stage.

Larry Smith: One of the things that strikes me about some of these sign problems goes back to something Gary Fromm said this morning concerning the lack of formal models that the whole thing is built on. As a result, I have the feeling that in a number of these papers there are important variables that are being omitted for various reasons that perhaps theoretically shouldn't be left out. I also think there is a bit of distinction that is being omitted here, the difference between the demanders of housing services and the builders of services. That becomes more important if you think of the multiple-unit sector where you have a builder who is building and going to own, but he is building on a profit basis to obtain a profit by selling the housing services at a return that is going to leave him a proper return on investment. That kind of behavior is quite different from the kind of behavior you have in single-family homes, and within the single-family home market there is a difference between speculative builders and those who build on contract. Until all these different facts get sorted out, you often could have the independent variable with the wrong sign, because the other side of the picture is being omitted. Maybe construction costs should be there. They may mean one thing for a family homeowner but something else in the case of a person who is building for investment.

It really wouldn't matter if you had price or construction cost, but it makes a big difference, and that ratio could be important to people building on speculation and building multiple buildings.

On the mortgage side there is a big problem for some reason when you use either the bond rate or mortgage rate by themselves, as they always seem to work better together in equations. If you develop the supply of mortgage funds, it seems to me the variable should be based on a relative return basis. Yet it depends on how you specify your function.

If you take that view of financial institutions, it is a question of how the mortgage rate is related to the bond rate. Then it should be the differential that becomes important.

There is a lot of similarity between these two things. If you have a prior notion that the mortgage approvals will fall when bond rates go up, they should rise when mortgage rates go up. Sometimes you don't get both of those going, and then you just drop the one that does not fit the theory. If you have a positive sign on one interest rate, you put in whichever of the mortgage or bond rates you want. That causes problems, because the results don't match the basic theory, again. So while I think Ray's idea of disequilibrium models is worth pursuing, I also think that using vacancies and trying to get a more structured model approach is the way to proceed, paying particular attention to the different behavior of the participants.

Bill Branson: You should be developing structural models of the different factors in the whole housing sector, but if you think that the markets aren't always clearing, you should be estimating the way Ray Fair has it cooked up, or some better way.

Ray Fair: The vacancy question can be incorporated within the disequilibrium framework. In a demand equation you could put the vacancies as one of the variables determining the demand for houses. Likewise, the vacancy level should help determine the supply of housing from the construction side.

Al Hirsch (Office Business Economics): I think the inventory under construction would be a useful variable if it were augmented by the inventory of unsold speculative houses. I guess one could build up a series from the Census data on sales. I think that is a more meaningful aggregate than inventory of unbuilt houses.

Jack Kalchbrenner (Federal Reserve Board): Ed Gramlich experimented in 1967 or 1968 with both an inventory under construction and available, vacant, finished houses. He was unable to get them to do the formulation that we are using.

Irwin Friend: Has anybody recently tried a portfolio balance disequilibrium model for housing involving the initial stock of housing and other assets? I am talking about the demand side of the model. The idea is that people have a desired portfolio of different kinds of assets and liabilities, and take time to reach the desired portfolio. So you would need in your arguments, explaining the demand for new housing, not only relative interest rates but also the initial stock of the particular asset you are talking about, and the stock of all other assets. Tobin and Watts as well as others carried out such an analysis on a cross-section basis a number of years ago and obtained interesting results. But I have not seen much in this area lately.

Bruce Ricks: If you think of a vacant, existing, previously occupied unit, then the owner of that may well hold two houses. He is either occupying an apartment by preference, or occupying an apartment because of the fact that his funds are tied up in that first house, or holding two houses. Once that is the case, then the guy is converted from a home-owner-occupant getting nonprice benefits or imputed rents (which are very hard to measure of course), to one of deciding on what basis to withhold that inventory from the market. He has a reservation price. One can then look at the carrying costs (which would be his mortgage interest, plus property taxes and insurance and maintenance plus opportunity cost on capital tied up) versus the sales price. And I would think you would have the same type of model you would have in a securities portfolio model. You would have the methodology already and convert the example to housing.

Gary Fromm: Aren't most of the vacant units multi-family units? There are cases where a person has two houses or lives in an apartment or a house or has a house and is moving into an apartment. Those cases must be very few in number, and in most cases the vacancy decisions are made by owners of multiple units, and they have to decide whether to lower the rent.

Even the single-family vacancies of new homes are those owned by developers and not by individual homeowners; thus, there is a similar pricing and investment decision.

David Huang: It seems to me that in respect to equilibrium models, perhaps in the housing sector there are enough lags so that one can possibly think of specifying a purely recursive model. This is an alternative that I am suggesting. Perhaps it ought to be looked into.

With respect to supply of housing units during any time period it is the various considerations preceding that time period that determine the current supply. Such determining variables could be brought to bear in specifying the supply relation. As far as demand is concerned, perhaps demand is more affected by current price than by lagged prices. I am just thinking "off the cuff" as to whether this sort of consideration could be built into the model.

Ray Fair: In my work, the mortgage rate was lagged two months. This gave the best fit, but the fits using other lags were close.

Don Kaplan (Harvard Business School): I think you mentioned last night,

Bruce, that when we see a mortgage rate reported for January, it reflects earlier conditions in the market, because of the mechanism. I am not sure what the relative lags are, but I am concerned about this reporting lag.

Bruce Ricks: The FHLBB conventional mortgage rate series is on permanent loans *made,* and that lags commitments. Now, the lagging is different, depending on whether it is new or existing homes. A small percentage of *existing* housing is transacted with a previous mortgage commitment, taken out in the two separate steps of issuance of commitment, and then making of loan. On the new homes, that is not the case. Because of the construction period, the disbursal of permanent financing lags the commitment by the time it takes between the commitment and the start plus between the start and the completion plus between the completion and the occupancy. The lags are probably very unstable over time. They are partly a function of credit availability, but it does mess up things, since the lag fluctuates with interest rates. It seems to me good research could be done just measuring the lags involved here. Josie McElhone of FHLBB is beginning to do that. I think it will be very, very promising work.

Ray Fair: I don't know what that means. If the supply schedule is responding to a particular rate, I don't know what it means to say that is affected by credit availability. Flows into S&L's shift the supply curve around. Whether the flows affect its slope or not, I don't know.

Jack Kalchbrenner: I was talking about the length of the lags being affected. For instance, if credit is very tight a builder will build a smaller percentage of his homes speculatively, because the interest cost which he has to pay for carrying that unsold inventory is very high. In a period of more credit availability, you will tend to get more housing built speculatively. As vacancies rise, you would tend to get a smaller percentage of the housing built speculatively; so the lag between the decision and the advancement of funds and the mortgage rate that you are looking at have nonrandom fluctuations. They are a function of some of the variables you have on both sides of the equation. I would think that the level of housing starts in a given period would have some effect on the proportion of these units built speculatively.

If you tell the builders the forecast is for a high level of housing starts, builders will raise their plans. So some say give them a goal, not a forecast. This is one of the reasons I say you can get more starts if you are willing to tolerate vacancies.

With respect to the new commitment flow lag, in Jaffee's model the flow for the insurance companies for which he had new commitment data is distributed very evenly, beginning in the current quarter. The flow is .17, .17, .16, etc., distributed across seven periods. It is not a discrete lag.

Bruce Ricks: Has anybody thought of demolitions as a policy instrument?

Perhaps if one wants to get more starts, one should, as policy, remove some existing units.

James Burnham: The demolition data is certainly the worst of all elements of housing statistics. I think it is very fruitless, really, to try and worry about them, given the complete absence of any reliable numbers. We estimate removals by comparing the stock between the adjacent quarters and the completions, and then compare the two periods and then smooth that series out.

Gary Fromm: That is different than the demand and supply consideration that was suggested this morning of taking *net* starts as a decision variable; because, except in a few areas like Washington where land is very limited, most builders do not tear down a unit in order to build a unit. Removals and starts are independent. Most of the removals are due either to complete dilapidation, or they are due to replacement by office buildings and parking lots.

Bruce Ricks: But those are the units I want to tear down – not the good ones, obviously. I want to tear down the bad ones to free land space, reduce the price of land. I want to clear title, and I want to get more starts per dollars of expenditure, if the objective is starts. I want to tear down the unoccupied, *non-rehabilitable* units.

Jim Burnham: That is the most regressive policy of all. You put pressure on the price of slum housing, because a certain percentage of these dilapidated units are affecting the stock of slum housing.

Larry Smith: You get that because you knock down that kind of housing and put up highrises with one-bedroom and bachelor apartments suited for different people. You are shifting your composition of your housing stock at the same time. I don't think you should argue a priori that the switching from dilapidated housing to new housing will do that. It depends upon the nature of the house you substitute for what you knock down, and whether government subsidizes the price at the same time.

Bruce Ricks: Most of the removals, I understand, come from highway programs and government construction of a nonhousing variety. Why don't the modelers have in their models government expenditures which would tend to increase the number of demolitions.

Isn't that variable very, very random? (*David Huang*). . . . I don't know. I haven't analyzed it (*Bruce Ricks*). . . . They knock down houses all over the country. I would think the average quarterly rate shouldn't fluctuate (*Bill Branson*). . . . We look at a residual removal series, so sometimes it is not clear, really. Maybe we are measuring removals; maybe not. It is not random. There are definite cycles involved (*Jim Burnham*).

Ray Fair: I guess Gary's point is that people who make decisions on whether to build houses are not the ones who make decisions on tearing down houses; so it is not clear that you want to look at a net variable.

Gary Fromm: In terms of introducing removals as a policy consideration, I would back you one hundred percent. As a matter of fact, it does appear in the Maisel model, because it enters into the vacancy rate and available units, and actually indirectly must also enter into household formation.

Bruce Ricks: I don't think the Maisel model uses vacant sites; I think it is vacant units. A demolition would create a plot of land as distinguished from a unit, and it would probably drop out of the vacancy statistics.

Charles Field (HUD): The kinds of units that may be demolished have locational characteristics incompatible with the construction. You might have to split your models to give this kind of reflex. That goes back to the sort of thing that Dave Birch is working on, with those two things tied together.

John Heinberg (The Urban Institute): I think it also begins to get into the question raised earlier about whether starts are the objective. If you begin thinking about removals or demolitions as a policy objective, you also have to raise the prior issue of whether or not it might not be more cost effective or efficient to slow down the rate of abandonments which led to removals and demolitions as a way of keeping housing going to serve the poor. This is particularly true if you are concerned with the distributional effects of housing policy.

On Government-Academic Interface for Improved Housing Modeling

Bruce Ricks: Many of us express frustration that things are not better – more coordinated and more cooperative than they are. I submit that as a challenge of discussion to you to figure out with us how the agencies and departments can be more helpful to you academicians and researchers – how you people can apply your increasingly sophisticated methodology to better and better data to make better and better approximations and simulations and sensitivity analyses so that policy can be better.

Harry Finger (HUD): It is very important to focus on the patterns of growth. We face substantial mobility of population and overall growth in population. My concern, then, is how we assure that the housing needs of that population will be satisfied most effectively. That is, location, numbers of units, quality of units, the services that are indeed provided for you. All of those factors are of real concern to us and they tie in with the overall issues of national growth and trying to satisfy it in our population. That really is my very broad interest and I see this as a very significant part of that concern.

Charles Field: We have started programs dealing with housing allowances and abandoned housing, and from those efforts we will seek policy solutions or suggested directions for policy solutions. I am terribly concerned that perhaps we do not have the kind of methodology and perhaps understanding of how the housing market operates.

Harry Havens (OMB): We are interested in housing in the Office of Management and Budget because housing costs resources. It costs economic resources, as Mr. Friend has pointed out, and, therefore, is an element in economic policy.

It also costs budget resources, as Harry Finger can indicate. It will cost about $1.3 billion of budget resources of HUD alone in fiscal 1972.

Therefore, we have a very great concern as to how we go about getting the housing that we need from a fiscal policy standpoint, and how we go about matching the housing that we produce with the people that need to have the housing. And last but not least, what is the federal role in producing the housing and making sure that it gets to the people that need it, what should we be doing, how should we be going about doing it in the way that makes some sense from an economic policy standpoint and from a budget policy standpoint.

Our data and our methods of arriving at policy judgments at the presidential level have not been very good up to now. Our past results have not been, shall we say, wholly satisfactory. Anything that you other gentlemen here can tell us about how to go about making policy decisions in the housing area will help us in arriving at the decisions that are going to have to be made on a national level over the next year, five years, ten years, twenty-five years. And if we don't improve the methodology of those decisions we are not going to improve the output.

Jack Kalchbrenner: The Federal Reserve Board has remained concerned with housing recently via the internal Federal Reserve study of the degree to which monetary policy affects housing cyclically. The question is whether restrictive monetary policy does affect housing disproportionately in some sense. If so, what means are available, if any, to alleviate the problem without causing other problems. Such a study obviously involves subjective judgments or criteria, and requires fairly precise knowledge of the effects upon other sectors of the economy (and upon monetary control) of insulating housing partially from restrictive monetary policy.

Bill Silber: There is one particular question which the Council of Economic Advisers has been interested in, and that is the extent to which the activities of the various federal agencies concerned with housing actually succeed in increasing housing starts or increasing mortgage flows.

We all know that for a billion-dollar increase in Fannie Mae operations, or a billion-dollar increase in FHLB advances, you don't necessarily get a billion-dollar increase in mortgage flows, or any lasting effect. You may not get any lasting effect on housing starts.

So we really have to look into the question as to what extent the behavior of private financial institutions offsets the behavior of the FHLB and Fannie Mae.

Franco Modigliani (MIT): I got interested in housing because when you build a model there is unfortunately no area that you can keep away from. You have to become involved in everything. I have been particularly intrigued in the case of housing by some fairly basic theoretical considerations. We do have, for instance, in our model, basically four distinct kinds of investment stocks and flows – consumer durables on the one hand, housing, plant, equipment. And in each case we have sort of somewhat different structural approaches to them, and it is quite an interesting question why, for instance, the way we specify the investment in equipment is very, very different from the way we specify the housing sector. It's quite an intriguing question why.

Of course, this is then connected with why monetary policy has very different impacts. From what I can see at this point, it always has different impacts. I don't know that we really should erase the difference. There may be some other considerations, but I think this is in the nature of it.

Larry Kimbell: I have a feeling that many of the agencies now are cooperating and getting the data in very fine shape, and such organizations as Data Resources are making it readily accessible, so we have a capability of handling data, inputting data, retrieving data, that may almost overwhelm us unless we look at some of the other problems.

One of the problems is that after people estimate econometric models, they afford others the data itself at times, and also the estimated equations; but these are almost meaningless if not supplemented by simulation results. Mere inspection of 200 individual equations, or even 15 or 20 equations, gives one almost no sense of how the model is going to behave as a unit. So it's very difficult to know what the model means afterwards. You can inspect individual equations and try to trace relationships among them, but you have little sense of how the model will perform under simulation. The authors will occasionally run a few simulations, which are purely illustrative, but for real testing and understanding of the model one must have hands-on operation.

There might be very considerable economies of scale in providing access to large-scale models. Instead of having each university and each agency trying to debug and develop a simulation model, it might be better to provide access to a central computer installation.

One achievement might be to have Data Resources or some such organization afford users simulation experimentation capability. It would have to be very selective in the model that would be employed.

Then other users might be able to simultate the models and have a much more thorough understanding of their weaknesses as well as their strengths.

The strategy of not providing simulation versions until the models are finished is weak. I have the feeling that some models are never finished. These models are always in a state of evolution. If the model is very large there is virtually no meaning to a listing of individual equations. The models are dynamic and nonlinear, so no analytic reduced form can be found and presented compactly. You can look at it under simulation. You can simulate alternative policies and then begin to evaluate the plausibility of the reactions of the endogenous variables. That is presumably one of the reasons it was developed originally. It may well be that no model is running that deserves any confidence. If so, a wider audience will appreciate the weaknesses if more researchers can experiment with them.

Irwin Friend: I still think one of the most useful exercises is to look at the Federal Reserve Bulletin for January 1968, where they have the policy multipliers for four different models. And I think there is a pretty strong suggestion that they are all still in the methodological state – very useful methodology. I am suggesting that you look at them and take them with a considerable grain of salt.

Bruce Ricks: We should use them for policy purposes but adjust them with judgment?

Irwin Friend: No. You should use them for policy purposes only if the different tenable models give similar answers.

Harry Havens: I want to reinforce it. I happen to agree largely with Dr. Friend. The policy makers that we have to deal with, the people who are going to make the policy decisions, are only very rarely econometricians. My point is slightly different from Dr. Friend's. We happen to have several pretty good econometricians at OMB right now, and we have had on several occasions in the past. But these are not the only policy makers we are talking about. We are also talking about politically sensitive department heads and politically sensitive congressmen who are not econometricians. We as economists have a very serious problem when we advise an official who is not an econometrician. When you present him with an equation that says he ought to do thus and so if he wants to produce this result, he doens't understand the equation. He doesn't understand why this particular input brings a given output.

One of the biggest problems we have right now in economic policy, it seems to me – and this applies to housing as well as other sectors – is getting across to the policy maker the impact of the econometric model, telling him why this model is right, or why we have to take it with a grain of salt.

This is something that is a problem not only to the policy makers. It is also a problem to the econometrician, because you can sit back and build all the beautiful models that you like, but if you don't come out with a convincing policy recommendation – if you can't influence policy with those models or with the economic principles that underlie the models – then you have done an exercise in futility.

I would suggest that one of the challenges of economics right now is moving perhaps slightly in the other direction from that in which we have been moving over the past twenty years or longer. We should be moving in the direction of translating the economic theory that we have, and the principles that underlie that economic theory, into terms that are understandable to the people who have to make the decision, so that they don't have to say, "Okay, he's a good economist, therefore I trust his judgment, and if he tells me to do this, I'll do it" – because they are not going to make decisions that way. They are going to insist on understanding what it is that you are telling them to do. If all the economist can do is to present the official with an equation or a series of equations – a series of 200, 400, or 1000 equations – he is not going to operate on trust, because there will be other economists, with other equations, telling him to do something different.

It has got to go beyond just equations if we are going to make economics, and particularly housing economics right now, into an effective tool for dealing with public policy questions.

Irwin Friend: I don't want to leave the subject on this negative note. I think it is extremely important to do this work in models. It is also extremely important not to be mesmerized into thinking you have something you don't have. The point is, this is the only way we are going to make scientific progress in the long run. It is the only way we are going to eventually quantify our theories. But in the long run I think you do no one a service by thinking that you have something that you don't have, something that you are terribly confident of.

Gary Fromm: May I speak to that point? I would agree with you, Irwin, that anyone who points to a forecast and says *this is it*, is a dammed fool, especially for applications for policy purposes. Our models are not that good, and actual forecasting is still probably 50 percent art and 50 percent science. On the other hand, I would not want to go to the extreme suggested by Mr. Havens, to say that any simple explanation that a policy maker can understand is a good one, and as long as he can understand it, he can make sensible policies.

The models do have something to say. They can be used for policy implications. But they should not be applied without the ingredient of judgment. And the models, as Professor Friend has indicated, will improve in time and they should get better and give us more valuable policy advice.

On the other hand, to simply state that a complicated model, because it has many equations, does not have anything to say and we can't get anything out of it is not enough. Some models are utterly inaccurate and shouldn't be used in the first place. It is just that there are different theories about how the economy functions and there are different theories underlying the models.

Bruce Ricks: I wish we could go on, but I see we have run out of time. So, on behalf of the twelve Federal Home Loan Banks that have sponsored this conference and on behalf of those who have attended, let me express my appreciation to those who have prepared papers and delivered them, and to all of you who have participated so actively and with such helpful comments in the discussion sessions. I look forward to a series of future meetings on this and related subjects, and I hope that you have found the views and information presented in this conference to be of use in your own work. I hope the distribution of the prepared papers, the oral presentations, and the discussion will assist researchers and students of the housing markets.

About the Contributors

R. Bruce Ricks was born in Oakland, California, in 1934. His early and advance studies were in economics and business administration specializing in real estate and housing problems at the University of California, Berkeley. Here he received the degrees of B.S. in 1956, M.B.A. in 1957, and Ph. D. in 1963. He was Chief Economist and Director, Office of Economic Research, Federal Home Loan Bank Board, Washington, D.C., 1972. He is now president of R. Bruce Ricks, Inc., a real estate finance and investment consulting firm. His principal publications are "Imputed Equity Returns on Real Estate Financed with Life Insurance Company Loans," *Journal of Finance* 24 (December 1969): 921-937; *Real Estate Investment: The Investment Process, Investment Performance, and Tax Policy*, Washington, D.C.: U.S. Treasury (for selected distribution), 1968; *Portfolio Management: An Investment Game*, Prentice-Hall, 1965; *Recent Trends in Institutional Real Estate Investment*, Berkeley, California: Center for Real Estate and Urban Economics, 1964. In 1964 Dr. Ricks received the Arthur A. May Award of the American Institute of Real Estate Appraisers for the best technical literature in real estate for that year (national). In 1968 he performed research under a U.S. Treasury contract to the University of California, entitled "Analysis of the Impact of U.S. Treasury Policy Variables on Real Estate Investment." Current research interests embrace primarily subjects related to asset and liability diversification of savings and loan associations; innovative techniques of housing finance; modeling of housing and savings markets as aids to policy and decision making in government; large-scale land development processes; and real estate investment techniques.

Eugene A. Brady was born in Chicago in 1930. He received both his B.A. and M.A. degrees at the University of Washington. Continuing his graduate studies at the University of California at Berkeley, he received his Ph.D. in 1961 for research in mortgage credit and monetary policy. He has been Professor of Economics at Iowa State University, and is presently Professor and Chairman, Department of Business Economics and Public Policy, Indiana University. His principal housing publications are "Regional Cycles of Residential Housing Construction and the Interregional Mortgage Market: 1954–1959," *Land Economics,* February 1963; "A sectoral Econometric Study of the Postwar Residential Housing Market," *Journal of Political Economy,* 75 No. 2 (April 1967) and 78 No. 2 (April 1970); "Predicting U. S. Residential Housing Starts – Methodology and Forecast," *Business Economics,* September 1971. In 1959-1960, he held the Earhart Foundation Fellowship, and in 1960 was awarded the Cipolla Prize in Economic History at the University of California. His current research interests are primarily housing forecasting, housing policy, and macro-economic theory.

James B. Burnham was born in 1939 in New York City. He received his A.B. degree at Princeton and later pursued advance studies in economics at Washington

University where he received his M.A. degree in 1968 and his Ph.D. in 1970. After a tour of duty with the Federal Reserve Board in Washington, D.C., he became Senior Economist, Mellon National Bank and Trust Company, Pittsburgh, which is his present position. His principal publications include "The Demand for Housing: A Comment" (with S. J. Maisel and J. Austin), *Review of Economics and Statistics,* November 1971; and "Private Financial Institutions and the Residential Mortgage Cycle, With Particular Reference to the Savings and Loan Industry," a paper prepared for the Federal Reserve Board's Housing Study (forthcoming).

Ray C. Fair was born in 1942 in Fresno, California. He was an economics major at Fresno State College where he received his B.A. degree in 1964. He received his Ph.D. at the Massachusetts Institute of Technology in 1968 with a dissertation on the short-run demand for employment. He is at present Assistant Professor of Economics at Princeton University. His principal publications are *The Short-Run Demand for Workers and Hours,* North-Holland Publishing Company, 1969, 225 pp.; "The Estimation of Simultaneous Equation Models with Lagged Endogenous Variables and First Order Serially Correlated Errors," *Econometrica* 36 (May 1970): 507-516; *A Short-Run Forecasting Model of the U.S. Economy,* Heath-Lexington Books, 1971, 264 pp.; "The Optimal Distribution of Income," *Quarterly Journal of Economics* 85 (November 1971). His research interests lie primarily in econometrics, macroeconomics, and income distribution.

John H. Kalchbrenner was born in Chicago in 1937. He received his B. A. and M.A. degrees at the University of Iowa in 1958 and 1960 respectively. After military service, he pursued graduate studies in economics at the University of Wisconsin, where he received his second M.A. degree in 1967, and his Ph.D. in 1970. In 1968, he became a staff economist with the Board of Governors of the Federal Reserve System in Washington, and in 1972 transferred to the Federal Reserve Bank of Chicago. His principal publications are "monetary and Fiscal Actions: A Test of Their Relative Importance in Economic Stabilization – Comment" (with Frank de Leeuw), Federal Reserve Bank of St Louis *Review,* April 1969 (reprinted in S. Mittra, *Dimensions of Macroeconomics: A Book of Readings,* Random House, 1971); "A Model of the Housing Sector," in E. Gramlich and D. Jaffee, *Savings Deposits, Mortgages, and Housing in the FRB-Mit-Penn Econometric Model,* Heath-Lexington Books, 1972; "A Constrained Estimation Approach to the Demand for Liquid Assets" (with E. Gramlich), Special Studies Paper No. 3, Federal Reserve Board, January 1970.

Gary Fromm attended Cornell University, where he received a B.M.E. degree in mechanical engineering in 1956. He undertook advance studies in industrial management and received his M.S. degree at the Massachusetts Institute of Technology in 1958 and a Ph.D. in economics at Harvard in 1960. At present he is Professor of Economics at American University, Washington, D.C., and a consultant to Data Resources, Inc., which partially supported the research for his paper in this volume. His principal publications include: *Economic Criteria for Federal Aviation Administration Expenditures*, 1962; *The Brookings Econometric Model of the U.S.*, 1965; *Transport Investment and Economic Development*, 1965; *Policy Simulations with an Econometric Model*, 1968; *The Brookings Model: Some Further Results*, 1969; *Tax Incentives and Capital Spending*, 1971; and *Public Economic Theory and Policy*, 1973.

Index

Abandoned houses, rate of, 171-172
Accumulation of liquidity, 91
Additions and alterations, problems of, 112, 119, 144
Age, factor of, 65
AFEDF, 40
Aggregation problems, 136, 163-164
Allowances, housing, 172
Almon lag, 97, 116, 141, 144-145, 149-152
Amortization periods, 2, 4, 146
Ando, Albert, cited, 153
Assets: acquisition of, 102; income yielding, 30; liquid, 91, 93, 102; physical, 95-96; portfolio of, 3, 14, 102; short-term, 95
Automobile financing, pattern of, 114

Barter terms of trade, 37
Behavioral equations, 137-152
Birch, David, cited, 159-161, 163, 171
Birnbaum, John, cited, 42
Boeckh residential cost index, 11, 25, 32-33, 118, 137-138, 143-149
Bond rate, corporate, (RCB), 90, 96-97, 99, 102, 104, 107, 115, 130, 167
Borrowing: cost of, 86; flow of, 14, 74, 107
Brady, Eugene A., and Model of, 1-47, 58, 60, 128, 153, 157-158, 165, 177
Branson, Bill, cited, 64, 157-159, 164-165, 167, 170
Brookings Institute, and Model of, 61, 128, 132-133, 135, 138-139, 153, 161
Budget resources, 172
Builders, home, 61, 70-72, 75, 87, 89, 111, 130-132, 162, 169
Building costs, inflation in, 67, 85-86, 125
Burnham, James B., cited, 49-67, 154, 158, 170, 177
Business Economics, Office of, and Model of, (OBE), 65, 114, 127-128, 130-131, 139, 142, 148-150, 154, 167
Business investments, 130, 149
"Buy now," effect of, 11

CD run-off, 50, 63-64
California, 64, 133
Cancellations, 105
Capital: cost of, 110, 115, 117-118, 130, 150; gains and losses, 94-95, 97, 115, 131, 145; stocks, 119, 120, 132
Census, Bureau of, 58
Census data, 64, 161, 167
Ceiling: rates, 3-4, 22, 103, 137-138; restrictions, 43, 102
Central Bank efforts, 14
Certificates of deposit, 95, 101
Classification adjustments, 16, 126
Cochrane-Orcutt technique, 81
Collateral requirements, 107
Commerce, Department of, 73
Commercial Banks, 49-50, 63, 71, 82, 85, 93-96, 101-107, 132
Commercial loans (RCL), 100-103, 107
Commercial paper rate, 100-101, 140, 151-152
Commitments; 107, 158, 169; advance, 104-106; data on, 116-117; mortgage, 145; outstanding (OC), 109, 118
Communications, 151
Congress, enactments of, 22, 43
Construction costs, 2-4, 25, 32-33, 59, 110-111, 114-115, 121, 128, 132, 145, 147-150; loans, 116; residential, 1, 11, 72, 125-126, 130-131, 135-137, 141, 144, 148-150
Consumer behavior, 130
Consumer durables, 117, 145, 173
Consumer price index (CPI), 67, 112, 118, 145-148, 152
Consumption expenditures (CON), 97-100, 113, 115-116
Contracts, conditional sales, 114; on interest rates, 36-37
Cost index, 143
Credit: availability of, 100, 128, 132, 169; crunch, 118, 144; long-term, 71; rationing, 101, 113; reckoning, 110, 159; short-term, 70, 86; shortages, 131; supply of, 160
Cyclical fluctuations, 51, 60, 125, 132

DHF, 74
DHL, 128, 139-140, 153
DSF, 74
Dallas, Texas, 91
Data Resources Inc., Model of, 3, 42, 127-128, 140-141, 153, 158, 173-174
Decision-making process, 102
Definitional equations, 125-126, 137-146
Demand and supply equations, 71, 74-77, 83, 86-89, 93-95, 108-111, 170
Demography, influence of, 2, 65, 129, 139, 141, 160
Demolitions: housing, 4, 62, 132, 169-170; right-of-way freeways, 1-2
Depository institutions, 49, 51
Deposits: demand, 95, 97; flow of, 71, 81-82, 88, 106-107, 116; 162; private, 74;

rates of, 102–103, 116; savings, 3, 95–96, 101, 102; supply of, 93; time, 49
Depreciation provisions, 110, 113, 115, 130, 144
Destruction, housing, 110
Developers, housing, 60, 62
Diamond, Arnold, cited, 91
Dilapidation, housing, 1
Disaggregation, degree of, 62, 132–133
Disequilibrium markets, 88, 91, 109, 132–133, 167
Disposable income, 2–4, 96, 127, 129, 139, 146, 148, 151–152
Distribution, 103
Dollar value expenditures, 59, 131
Dummy variables, 9–10, 59, 73, 81, 96, 118, 139
Durable goods, 113

Econometric models and work, 1, 3, 58, 89, 125, 159, 161, 173–175
Econometric Society, meeting of, 160
Econometrica, 88
Economic Advisers, Council of, 158, 172
Economic Research, Office of, 44
Economy, The, effect of, 1–2, 9, 14, 65, 97, 111, 115, 125, 161, 164
Empirical applications and equations, 95–97, 113, 115, 119
Employment, 161
Endogenous variables, 31, 125–126, 135, 140–143, 146–152, 157–159, 164
Enzler, J., cited, 117
Equilibrium: long-run, 94; models, 168; mortgage rates (RM), 104, 108
Error term in equations, 83–86
Evans, Michael K., cited, 154
Exogenous variables, 102, 125–126, 135–142, 146–152, 157, 161
Expenditures, housing, 118, 121, 133, 136

Fair, Ray C., and Model of, 61, 63, 69–92, 128, 136, 141–143, 153, 157, 162, 165–171, 178
Fannie Mae operation, 43–44, 173
Federal Home Loan Banks, 3–4, 10–11, 14–15, 33, 35–44, 50, 63, 74, 82, 88, 93, 104, 107, 142–143, 147, 157, 159, 162, 164, 173, 176
Federal Home Loan Mortgage Corporation, (FHLMC), 91, 163
Federal Housing Administration (FHA), 4–5, 11, 19, 24, 29, 32, 38, 41, 43, 49, 67, 114, 131, 137–138, 142–144, 149
Federal National Mortgage Association (FNMA), 3–4, 14, 22, 50–51, 63, 82, 104, 117, 132, 145, 157–158, 163
Federal National Mortgage Association (FNMA) and GNMA, role of, 10–11, 14–15, 24, 32, 37–41
Federal Reserve Board (FRB), 42, 127, 130–131, 146, 158, 167, 172
Federal Reserve Board: FRB-MIT-PENN Model, 93, 98, 100, 103, 109, 113, 116, 128, 132, 135, 145, 150, 153–154
Federal Reserve Bulletin, 5, 174
Federal Reserve System, 58
Federally underwritten mortgages, 29, 37–40, 43
Feedbacks, impact of, 126, 135
Field, Charles, cited, 171–172
Figures and tables, 7–9, 12–13, 17–21, 26–30, 33–34, 36, 52–57, 128
Finance companies, 114
Finances: automobile, 114; flow variables of, 50, 61; markets, 49; terms of, 11, 114. *See also* Mortgages
Financial intermediaries, 71–72, 86–87, 93, 102–104, 108, 116
Finger, Harry, cited, 171–172
Fires and floods, effects of, 1
Forecasting and estimation, housing, 32, 89, 133–134
Fox, Karl, cited, 62, 65, 160–161
Friedman, cited, 61, 89
Friend, Irwin, cited, 66, 135, 162, 164, 167, 172, 174–176
Fromm, Gary, cited, 89, 125–155, 158–159, 163–164, 168, 170–171, 175, 178
Functional economic area (FEA), 161
Funds: availability of, 60, 131, 157–158; flow of, 49, 51, 164

Geography, influence of, 1, 96
Gibson, Bill, cited, 44
Ginny-Mae operation, 43–44
Glossary of chapter terms, 45, 122–123
Goldsmith, cited, 120
Government National Mortgages Association (GNMA), 3, 132, 145; and Federal National Mortgage Association (FNMA), 10–11, 14–15, 24, 32, 37–41
Graham, Dr., cited, 65–66
Gramlich, Ed., cited, 101–102, 116, 119, 16 167
Grebler, Leo, cited, 155
Gross National Product, (GNP), 69, 91, 142, 146
Growth, rate of, 96–97

HC, 16, 22, 26–27, 31, 34–35, 38, 40
HFHA, 16, 22, 24
HTTT, 6, 13, 16–17, 32, 34
HTUS, 15, 34

HVA, 16, 20, 22, 24
Harvard Business School, 159, 168
Havens, Harry, cited, 43, 172, 174–175
Heinberg, John, cited, 171
Highway programs, 170
Hirsch, Al, cited, 167
Home Loan Bank System, 44, 58
Home Loan Banks, 44, 64, 91, 163
Home owners, problems of, 111, 130, 161
Households: formation of, 2, 4, 64, 127, 171;income of, 49, 61, 67, 133
Housing: boom in, 22; costs, 25, 86, 118, 121, 132; industry, 114–115; inventory, 132, 147; market, 5–6, 10, 60, 116, 126, 163; private, 3, 5, 49; starts, 6, 9, 12–18, 25–27, 49–50, 59, 69–73, 81, 85, 89–90, 111–112, 120, 126, 130, 145, 160, 162, 166, 169; stock, 107–108, 110–112, 117, 119–121, 125
Housing Urban Development (HUD), 91, 171–172
Houston, Texas, 91
Huang, David, and Model of, 128, 132, 135, 145–147, 154, 164–165, 168, 170
Hulett, D., cited, 101–102
Hymans, Saul H., 153

IC, 35
Income: anticipated, 70, 130; disposable, 2–4, 127; national, 30, 97; permanent, 97–98, 110, 112, 116, 118; personal, 67; trends in, 72, 81, 86; and wealth, 128
Income tax, 144, 149
Insurance and insurance companies, 131, 168–169
Interest: and mortgages, 23–24, 49–50, 130, 135–136, 168; rates of, 1–2, 6, 11, 15, 32–33, 35, 43, 61–62, 71, 107, 115, 118, 126, 128, 146–149, 152, 162, 169
Interregional mobility, 2, 9, 43, 163–164
Inventory, factors of, 49–50, 60–61, 64, 67, 119, 128, 132, 147, 167
Investments and investors, 1, 14, 30, 113

Jaffee, Dwight, cited, 14, 69, 76, 88, 100, 103, 106–109, 116, 157–158, 165, 169
Jorgenson, cited, 115

Kalchbrenner, John H., cited, 93–124, 154, 162, 167, 169, 172, 178
Kaplan, Don, cited, 168
Kimbell, Larry, cited, 44, 64, 160, 163, 173
Kindleberger, cited, 162
Klein, Lawrence R., cited, 154
Koyck lag, the, 151

Labor force, 1, 65, 70, 111, 131
Land, price of, 115, 170–171
Laws, housing, 130
Liabilities, classes of, 11, 14
Life Insurance Companies, 82, 85, 102, 104, 106–107, 118, 132, 145–147, 158–159; reserves of, 63, 93, 97–101
Life styles, 161
Liquid reserves, housing, 91, 93, 102
Loan-to-value ratios, 2–4, 11, 15, 33–37, 43, 137–138, 146
Loans. *See* specific type of loan
Long-run housing policies, 1, 59, 71, 94, 109
Los Angeles, Calif., 44, 91
LVC, 10, 35

Macromodels versus micromodels, 159–171
Maintenance, housing, 168
Maisel, Sherman, and model of, 42, 49, 58–61, 64, 128, 132–133, 147–148, 154–155, 158, 171
Management and Budget, Office of (OMB), 172, 174
Manufacturing, 151
Marginal tradeoffs, 130
Market instruments, secondary, 11, 14, 38–41, 67, 97, 102
Marriages, rate of, 127, 141
Martin, Preston, cited, 43
Materials and supplies, cost and use of, 70, 111, 131
McCarthy, Michael D., cited, 154
McElhone, Josie, cited, 169
Meltzer index of stringency, 6, 32–33
Migration, patterns of, 1–2, 43, 64–65, 133
Mining, 151
Mobile Home Manufacturers Association (MHMA), 114
Mobile Homes, 1, 5, 15–16, 21–25, 28, 30, 61, 113–114, 137, 143–144
Mobility, interregional, 2, 9
Modigliani, Franco, cited, 93, 100, 102, 116, 173
Monetary policies, impact of, 1, 4, 6, 32–33, 50, 60–61, 161, 172
Money, supply of, 1, 14
Moody's corporate Aaa bond rate, 140–141, 144, 149, 152
Mortgages: conventional, 23, 30–37, 49, 67, 137–138, 169; debts, 108; demand for, 107–108; equilibrium and disequilibrium of, 104, 108–109; federally underwritten, 11, 24, 29, 37–40, 43, 149; flow equations of, 107, 109, 173; funds for, 67, 70, 72, 87, 157; instruments of, 2, 14, 60, 64, 132, 145; interest rates on, 24, 50, 71, 74–77, 81–82, 86, 88, 90, 99, 102, 107–108, 115, 130, 135–

136, 163, 167–168; limitations on, 3; market, 15, 22, 32, 37, 43, 69, 85, 93, 103–104, 116–117, 158; private, 63, 157–158; supply of, 104–107
MSBS, 74, 82
MSS, 97
Multi-collinearity problems, 94, 96, 104
Multi-family dwelling units, 1, 5, 16, 22, 25, 30, 32, 43, 59, 61, 110, 113, 117–121, 130, 132, 137, 143–149, 158, 166, 168
Mutual Savings Banks, 74, 85, 88–89, 93, 96–97, 102–106, 118, 128, 132, 145–148

National Housing Inventory in 1960, 42
National Income Accounts (NIA), 113, 115–116
Nerlove, Marc, cited, 125, 155
Net worth, changes in, 94
New Haven, Conn., 160–161, 164
New York, 133
New Wharton Quarterly Forecasting Model, 151–152, 154
Non-durables, housing, 144
Non-farm residential units, 5–6, 138–139, 142, 144, 149–150
Non-mortgage assets, 14
"Number crunching," phrase of, 160–161

Occupancy, rates of, 60–61
Occupation, industry of, 65
Office buildings, 170
Old age security programs, 65
Ordinary least squares (OLS), 3, 6, 10, 23–24, 30–31
Owners and ownership, 113

Parking lots, 170
Passbook savings, 93, 103
Pension funds, private, 99, 131
Per capita incomes, 2–4, 127
Personal savings, 94–95
Physical assets, 95–96
PHCA, 114–115, 117
Plant and equipment, 173
Policy loans, 93, 98–101
Policy making and makers, 58–59, 61, 164, 172, 175
Population, 70, 127, 144, 163; adult, 116; deflators, 117; growth of, 60, 72, 81, 86, 126; mobility of, 171
Portfolio: assets, 3, 14, 102; behavior, 94, 96, 102, 167–168; holdings, 95, 107; planning, 67, 98, 158, 164; restrictions, 37; selections, 104
Postwar housing period, 3, 6, 9, 94, 98, 113
Preston, Ross S., cited, 154
Price: behavior, 76; deflators, 120, 141; equations, 131; index, 74, 86, 98, 119, 131, 145–147; ratios, 98
Priori theories and reasoning, 2–3, 6, 15, 126
Private savings, 104
Profit maximization, 130–131
Property tax rate, 115, 144, 168
Psychology, social, 160–161
Purchase power in housing, 38–39, 71, 74, 87, 96

Rasche, Robert, cited, 153, 155
Rate settings, housing, 4, 96–97, 99, 102–103, 115
Rates of return on equities, 94, 96, 102
Rationing, amount and effect of, 62, 76–77, 81, 100, 116, 128, 131
RA, 96, 99
RM, 97, 99, 102, 115
Recession, periods of, 14
Regression, forms of, 3, 6, 9–10, 15–16, 23–25, 30–31, 34, 38–39, 42, 103, 158, 170
Removals, housing, 72–73, 170–171
Rental prices, 110–111, 113, 125–126, 128, 130, 132; index on, 145–146, 148, 152
Repayments, 109
Residential housing, demand for, 1, 60
Ricks, R. Bruce, cited, 42, 44, 58, 62–66, 85, 91, 135–136, 158, 160, 163, 166–171, 174, 176–177

Sales, final, 121, 168
San Diego, Calif., 44, 91
Savings, private, 93–95, 103–104, 163
Savings and Loan Associations, 14, 49, 51, 63, 74, 82, 85, 88–89, 93, 96–97, 102–107, 114–117, 128, 132, 142, 145–147, 157–164, 169
Schink, George R., cited, 153
Seasonal factors, 72–73, 75
Securities, 14, 102
Shapiro, Harold T., cited, 153
Short-run and short term policies, 1, 59, 70–71, 86, 95, 108, 111, 126
Silber, Bill, cited, 44, 158, 172
Single family dwelling units, 5, 10, 16, 23, 25, 30, 32, 34, 39, 59, 113–117, 121, 132, 138, 141, 146–148, 158–159, 166, 168
Slum housing, 170
SMSA, 60, 64, 66, 161–162
Smith, Lawrence, cited, 62, 90, 157, 159, 166, 170
Social objectives, 125
Social Security (OASIS), 65, 99–100

Stochastic equations, 125, 131, 137–150
Stringency, monetary index of, 1, 4, 6, 32–33
Substitution, elasticity of, 119, 131
Sumichrast, Mike, cited, 43
Supply and demand variables, 85, 90, 130, 132–133, 146, 165
Supply equations, 63, 72, 75, 81, 101–103, 169
Swan, Craig, cited, 61

Taubman, Paul, cited, 153, 155
Taxation, forms of, 115, 118, 130, 144, 168
Time deposits and periods, 63, 95–97, 101, 151, 163
Time Trend (TT), 35, 37, 72, 74, 81, 88, 115, 127, 129, 133, 137–139, 142, 144, 151
Tobin, cited, 168
Tornadoes, effect on housing, 1
Tradeoffs, marginal, 130
Trading, volume of, 109
Transportation, 151
Treasury Rate Bill, 96
Two-Stage Least Squares (TSLS), 3, 30–31

Unemployment, rate of, 141
Urban Institute, The, 171

Vacancy rates, housing, 50, 59, 64, 89, 133, 138, 147, 166, 171
Veterans Administration (VA), effects on housing, 4–5, 11, 22, 24, 38, 41, 137–138

Wage rates, 66, 126, 141
Wallace, Henry, cited, 62
Washington, 133, 170
Watts, cited, 168
Wealth and income, 128
Weather, effect on housing, 73
Wharton Annual and Industry Forecasting Model, 128, 131, 150–151, 154
Working day variables, 73, 81